PSYCHIATRY IN BRITAIN

MEANING AND POLICY

SHULAMIT RAMON

CROOM HELM
London • Sydney • Dover, New Hampshire

©1985 Shulamit Ramon
Croom Helm Ltd, Provident House, Burrell Row,
Beckenham, Kent BR3 1AT
Croom Helm Australia Pty Ltd, First Floor,
139 King Street, Sydney, NSW 2001, Australia

British Library Cataloguing in Publication Data

Ramon, Shulamit
    Psychiatry in Britain: meaning and policy.
    1. Psychiatry—Great Britain
    I. Title
    616.89'00941   RC450.G7
    ISBN 0-7099-2279-5

Croom Helm, 51 Washington Street, Dover,
New Hampshire 03820, USA

Library of Congress Cataloging in Publication Data

Ramon, Shulamit.
    Psychiatry in Britain.

    Includes bibliographies and index.
    1. Psychiatry—Great Britain—History—20th century.
2. Mental health services—Great Britain—History—20th
century. 3. Mental health policy—Great Britain—History
—20th century. I. Title. (DNLM: 1. Mental health
services—History—Great Britain. 2. Politics—History—
Great Britain. 3. Psychiatry—History—Great Britain.
WM 11 FA1 R1P)
RC450.G7R34   1985   362.2'0941   85-4170
ISBN 0-7099-2279-5

Printed and bound in Great Britain by
Biddles Ltd, Guildford and King's Lynn

Contents

TO THE MEMORY OF MY MOTHER,
HANNA, AN UNSUNG HEROINE

Because we are in the world, we are condemned to meanings, and we cannot do or say anything without its acquiring a name in history.
Merleau-Ponty(1)

..It is a fact that psychiatry is the Cinderella of the health services.
Dr. Broughton(2)

1.Merleau-Ponty, M. (1967) The Origins of Perception, p.xix.
2.Hansard, vol. 578, p.81, 1957.

Preface

This book is concerned with the interaction of meanings, policies and practice of British psychiatry in this century.

We have witnessed a considerable expansion of the psychiatric system since the First World War. The expansion has been expressed not only in the number of users, units and professionals. It has also been reflected in the tendency by the professionals and the lay culture towards an increasing inclusiveness of categories of our experience within the parameters of psychiatry. Thus the current status of psychiatry expresses the growing social legitimation given to psychiatric meanings and policies as well as their use for social and personal purposes. We should therefore be asking what attracts us as a culture in the variety of meanings which are given to some very uncomfortable aspects of our life.

Moreover, despite the diversity of available professional and non-professional practices, the prevalence of employing physical means of intervention surpasses overwhelmingly the use of all other methods. As a society, have we therefore opted for the view of mental distress as a physical illness? Or have we simply opted to leave it in the hands of "the experts"?

A considerable part of the book is devoted to the meanings, policies and practices in psychiatry during the 20s and the 50s in Britain. Two broad groups have been selected for the investigation of the evolution of meanings and policies, the professionals and the politicians. They have been chosen because of being in a prime position from which to shape and reflect definitions and practices. The inter-relationships between these two groupings in the field of psychiatry will

1

occupy us too, as they have implications for the type of psychiatric system we have.

Methodologically the study is based on content analysis of parliamentary debates, legislation, official papers and professional literature in the periods under investigation. The professional camp - or the psy complex - includes psychiatrists, nurses, psychologists and social workers. The criteria for analysis are set out in chapter 1.

The British psychiatric system can be accredited with both success and failure, depending on what is seen as the objectives of such a system.

Both politicians and professionals have been stating since the 20s their wish to have a psychiatric system based on community care principles. With the introduction of the 1959 Mental Health Act we have been told that the era of psychiatric community care has arrived.

Yet in the quarter of a century which has elapsed since 1959, not even one psychiatric hospital has closed down fully in the UK(1). Even this single fact should make us examine the state of community care in Britain.

In the chapters on professionals' and politicians' stands (chapters 3,6,4,7) the manifest and latent meanings of community care are explored together with their implications for resource allocation.

The need to reconsider alternative psychiatric systems has become acute with the pressure from the current central government towards cuts in the NHS hospital sector and the realistic possibility of unemployment and redeployment of professionals in psychiatry. The manifest failure of the present system to prevent the process of chronicity for a considerable component of its clientele provides a more positive motive for rethinking.

The list of groups unlikely to favour the approach taken in this project, its findings and conclusions, is rather long. The book will displease those who beleive in the disease model, those who would prefer to ignore the subjective and intersubjective levels of mental distress and its roots in our social structure.

The future of the psychiatric service is seen here as rightly belonging within a public sponsored welfare system. The availability of economic resources for psychiatric care is not taken as a given from above but as a product of a socially negotiable process.

The last chapter looks at the implications of the historical analysis for today's issues.

I believe that alternatives to our current psychiatric system do exist. I hope that the book will be sufficiently provocative to lead to a public and professional debate on alternatives, theories, policies and practices in psychiatry.

References
1.South West Thames Regional Health Authority (1983) The Future Pattern of Services for the Mentally Ill, p.8.

Acknowledgements

My thanks are due to the Nuffield Foundation for a research grant during 1978-79 which enabled me to start the research project on which this book is based, and to the London School of Economics for a sabbatical term in 1983 in which the writing up was completed.

I would like to thank Mr. K. Robinson, Minister of Health in 1966-70, for being the only politician ready to be interviewed and for providing me with useful information on the 50s debate. Mike Bury, Jean Comaroff, Judith Harwin, Jane Lewis and Robert Pinker have taken the trouble to comment on different sections, at different stages of the manuscript. The responsibility for the views expressed in the book remains mine only.

During the four years which have elasped between the beginning and the completion of this book I have been encouraged and discouraged by many people. More often than not the dismissal of the issues the study raises as unimportant convinced me of their crucial significance to the underlying problems of our psychiatric system.

Teodor and Aelita Shanin had to live with me as an irritable, workoholic person throughout this period. Both have consistently supported me in their own different ways; for which I am grateful.

List of Abbreviations

1.BASW - British Association of Social Workers.
2.BMA - British Medical Association.
3.BMJ - British Medical Journal.
4.CC - Community Care.
5.CMH - Community Mental Health.
6.COS - Charity Organization Society.
7.H. - References from Hansard appear in the following form: H. volume number, page number. If followed by another volume the sign ; will appear after the first set of volume and page number.
8.MWO - Mental Welfare Officer.
9.NHS - National Health Service.
10.NM - Nursing Mirror.
11.PSW - Psychiatric Social Workers.

1 Introduction

The introduction will outline the framework and dimensions of the study. It will also spell out what this project does not attempt to do.
The book is concerned with the interface of meanings given to psychiatric phenomena and their translation into policy decisions.
It is written from the perspective of a social scientist interested in the theory and practice of psychiatry and their relationships to the social context in which they develop.
Throughout the book "psychiatry" or the "psy complex" are used in the wider sense, i.e. to cover not only psychiatrists but also allied professionals and all mental distress experiences. When a particular profession or mental distress category is focused on, it will be specified.
In the following exposition of approaches to the subject matter of psychiatry and throughout the book no attempt will be made to assess the truthfulness of any school of thought. Approaches are treated here as social products, which are a given in a particular moment in time but which have been and will continue to be modified by processes of cultural construction. Consequently, no attempt will be made here to present the evidence for and against an approach because the study is concerned primarily with meaning and policy.
The term "scientific" will be used only to denote the type of science employed within a specific approach or when a claim to scientific status is made by its protagonists.
Instead, a set of criteria by which to evaluate the contribution of each model will be

outlined, based on what the author considers to be the essence of mental distress and its social significance.

Mental distress is perceived as a phenomenon which incorporates elements of our social and natural worlds. By virtue of being a human condition it is likely to be affected by and to have an effect on our minds and bodies.

Our understanding of reality is mediated by the social context in global and specific ways. Our attempt to change this reality is even more sharply dominated by that context. Therefore the presentation of approaches to psychiatric phenomena is divided into two sections, paradigms of understanding and paradigms of intervention. The second set is derived directly from the first but is also always mediated by the dimension of social policy on psychiatry, or the translation into directives of social action.

The presentation of approaches to understanding and intervention is a necessary background on which to delineate the particular direction taken up in the book. Of necessity the description of a perspective will be brief. It will focus on the differences among the three models rather than within each of them.

1.a.The State of the Art of Understanding Mental Distress from Three Perspectives: The Somatic, the Psychological and the Social.

The description of psychiatric phenomena expands over a range of human expression so wide that often a justification is called for including it all under the same heading. The justification is provided via the approaches to understanding such experiences.

The phenomenon of mental distress usually hits the outsider and often the involved person too by its apparent unintelligibility, by being self-defeating and hence seen as irrational and motiveless. A lower level of functioning, especially at the psychosocial facet, is frequently noticeable. Thus a high degree of inter and intra cultural interpretation in rendering this experience intelligible is called for.

The main other feature to impress observers and those involved is the extent of suffering that accompanies it. Suffering is an uncomfortable concept for any model to account for; it is highly subjective, changeable and not easily given to generalization or quantification.

Criteria for judging the value of a theoretical approach to understanding mental distress should therefore include:
a.Definitions and descriptions of deviation from the ordinary which are viewed by the lay culture and the professionals as mental distress and disturbances. The parameters of the definitions and the dimensions for the descriptions have to be spelled out to allow an evaluation of the degree of comprehensiveness and systematization of an approach.
b.Rendering intelligible the unexpected behaviour and experience, including suffering and the lower level of functioning. Factors at work, or reasons, or causes, should follow as the next stage with an explanation of the links between them and the description.

The literature on approaches to mental distress is divided between those who ascribe causes and those who refrain from doing so. For an overview of the issues involved in each stand see Ingleby(1).

The following issues interact implicitly with the broad areas just outlined.
a.View about human nature.
b.Definition of and the relationships between rational and irrational behaviour and the experience of individuals and groups.
c.Relationships between individuals; their primary groups and society, in their impact on psychiatric issues.
d.The place of professional and non-professional activity in the field under discussion.

The disagreement among the three broad perspectives to be discussed below starts with the concepts of disease, distress and illness. The decision to use or not to use each one of these terms as a central concept denotes the inclination of the user towards a particular perspective.

Disease(2).
The existence of a disease implies a somatic cause for an apparent inability to function ordinarily, mainly at the psychosocial level. For it to be a disease it has to manifest a cluster of extraordinary behaviour (syndrome), follow a specific pattern of development, lead to a predicted level of deterioration or arrested

9

functioning if left without suitable intervention and have a specific cause. It clearly takes the view of psychiatric phenomena as a branch of physical disability.

Mental distress(3).
This concept focuses on the subjective experience of being considerably discontent with oneself and the world. It may or may not be accompanied by behavioural expressions and inability to function as before. Invariably, it will be reflected in an inability to take a definite course of action to change the state of discontent and with a continuous feeling of being such, at times without knowing why.

Mental illness(4).
The concept of illness stands in between disease and distress, containing features of both: illness comes to mean the experience of ill at ease, of discomfort with or without a specified cause. It is usually accompanied by change from ordinary to extraordinary behaviour, though such a change is likely to be limited to specific dimensions of one's life.
    In contrast to the notion of disease, both distress and illness do not carry with them a firm convinction as to the causes of the difficulties. They are also less prescriptive in regard to course and outcome. Distress and illness will be the terms used in this text. In all three concepts the actor is not ascribed conscious responsibility for having psychiatric symptoms.

The somatic perspective(5).
Historically this approach was located firmly within medicine. It applies knowledge of physical illness, accumulated practice wisdom and natural science methodology to the subject matter of psychiatry. Neurology, physiology and biochemistry have been the main background disciplines to be utilized.
    The disease concept became its core concept, directing the understanding of psychiatrists towards biological causes and their assumed manifestations. Most of the methodological effort went into observation, classification and interpretations of behaviour. The adherents of this approach see psychiatric illness as a variation of physical diseases. Therefore they claim for it a universal existence, free of normative biases. As

10

the behavioural and experiential components are seen as the manifestation of an underlying biological disturbance they are given only secondary importance at the conceptual level. Instead prime place is given to the method of classification. Proper diagnosis is believed to be the key to correct intervention and a lead to the underlying cause.

The fact that no specific biological factors have been identified for most psychiatric phenomena is put down to the short duration of the scientific pursuit of psychiatry. Likewise the indication of a minimal change in biological functioning - compared to greater changes in psychosocial functioning - is dismissed as due either to a narrow view of body-mind interaction or as the task of future research.

In some versions of this perspective psychological factors are perceived as indistinguishable from the biological dimension because an interaction between these factors is assumed(6). The mistaken notion of reducing an interaction back to the one-sided impact of a factor does not cause concern to the protagonists of this way of thinking.

Within this approach the social context is viewed either as irrelevant or as secondary to the impact of the biological dimension. Deterioration in functioning is firstly due to biological reasons, but may be made worse or improved by societal reactions.

It is clear from this brief exposition that the somatic approach opts for a narrow, economical definition and explanation of mental distress. It omits giving equal place to the subjective and intersubjective experience and has no conceptual place for the notion of suffering. It excludes the psychological and social dimensions from being primary factors.

One offshoot of the somatic perspective merits attention in this study because of the insight it offers into the twin concepts of cause and explanation(7). The current biochemical strand of the somatic perspective is very fashionable among natural scientists, doctors and the media. Thus it constitutes the latest cultural construction, though it is an approach that has been with us for some time.

Its innovative contribution is in locating the cause where the effect of chemical intervention seems to be. It argues that if drug A has influenced a particular structure/process of our body, then the fault/cause for mental disturbance must lie there. A unilinear, highly specific relationship is thus postulated between the synthetic drug and the totality of the person. The somatic approach has an undisputable social attraction in locating the causes for mental distress outside the range of personal and social responsibility. It makes it possible to view psychiatric phenomena as an issue unrelated to value preferences but which is instead wholly dependent on objectively verified knowledge of our biological make up. As such it appeals to both rulers and ruled, professionals and lay people, sufferers and the uninvolved alike in offering a clear-cut view which has a seemingly clear direction for research and intervention. It also gives a monopoly on interpretation to medically qualified people.

The psychological perspective(8).
The emphasis in this approach is on the psychological processes of the individual who is identified as mentally distressed. These processes (in particular learning, problem-solving and identity formation) are viewed as influenced by relationships with significant others. Therefore most models are also interested in the psychological processess of relevant interpersonal interaction.

In the majority of psychological approaches it is assumed that mental distress is the outcome of an internal, unresolved conflict between contradictory tendencies. Often the clash is between socially desirable and undesirable activity. The person is aware of the likely price of opting for either one of these two possibilities, though the awareness is not necessarily at the level of consciousness. Given that the clash is experienced as unresolved the next assumption is that "being stuck" is a sensation which individuals cannot tolerate for long and therefore will resort to action. The activity selected at the end of such a process would not necessarily be either one of the two options which were at the core of the conflict. Instead a third course might be taken up which will allow relief from the tension created by the conflict and which may also lead to interpersonal rewards (e.g. special attention, opting out of previously held responsibilities). Psychiatric

12

symptoms fall into this category.

A third assumption, shared by all theorists, is that such a choice is unlikely to be made at the level of fully rational and conscious thought. Some schools are relatively clear as to the level at which the decision is taken while others are not. However the location of the decision and the motivation for it away from the the rational facet has implications for the interpretation of the conflict by the actor as well as by others.

The psychological approach does not offer a straight-forward answer to the question why a particular behavioural or experiential manifestation appears or why one person reacts to a conflict with a psychiatric symptom, when another person - in a seemingly similar situation - reacts by choosing one of the available normative options or by questioning the validity of the norms. The enormous variations of individual differences in interpretation and ability to take action make the likelihood of finding a definitive answer remote. However attempts to indicate general factors which then have to be applied to given individual circumstances have been outlined.

Some psychological approaches take account of the biological component of our existence but do not go beyond postulating general principles which on the whole do not add much to our understanding(9). To state that a genetic predisposition to neurosis exists remains a fairly meaningless statement when it is not followed by an explanatory framework on the development and distribution of such predispositions and their interaction with the psychological dimension. More often physical features of mental distress are viewed as reflections of predominantly psychological states, since a body-mind interaction is taken for granted in every psychological approach.

Some psychological schools consider the possibility of a social dimension. On the whole this angle would be seen as a background feature which directs us to cultural-specific conflicts and their manifestation in mental distress.

Psychological orientations would view psychiatric phenomena as either illness or distress but not as a disease, depending on the degree of acceptance of a clinical perspective.

Within psychology today we find a range of methodologies and theoretical models which moves from the natural sciences to the social sciences.

The majority of the psychological approaches to psychiatry tend to utilize more the social sciences at their positivist end.

By definition psychology is out to capture subjective and intersubjective meanings, but the extent of keeping close to the authentic meaning or moving away from it depends on the type of interpretation employed. The more elaborate an interpretative scheme is the more removed it becomes from its original meaning. The sources for psychological interpretation vary considerably, being inspired by art and literature, assumptions about lay culture, anthropological work, physiological knowledge, studies of children and adults with and without mental distress.

The psychological model is attractive because it corresponds directly to the level at which all of us experience mental distress. Secondly it indicates a relatively clear perspective for intervention via individual and group psychotherapy. Thirdly it diminshes the attraction of the two main alternatives which are less accessible to commonsense understanding.

The social perspective(10).
This perspective focuses on the contribution of the social dimension to the phenomenon of mental distress. In some approaches this contribution is viewed as primary and causal. When this is the case the explanation will be located at the level of social structure factors. The manifestation of psychiatric symptoms and the cultural modes of tackling them are perceived as an exercise in balancing social control in the twilight area between the rational and the irrational, the social and the a-social. For example, experiences of persistent social deprivation and/or social conflict may lead to a breakdown in ordinary behaviour expressed as a mental distress by individual members of a society.

Labelling theorists(11) have proposed that the manifestation of mental distress is a necessary but insufficient condition for attributing a psychiatric disturbance to a person. Only when the first is accompanied by processes of social classification into the category of deviant, psychiatric type, does the second come into being. Thus a distinction is drawn between the manifestation of mental distress and the likely personal and social consequences.

There is a broad agreement among sociologists

14

as to the social consequences of being categorized
as mentally ill, including those who disagree with
the basic assumptions of the labelling approach and
the degree of irreversibility of such a
categorization. The label "mentally ill" is
associated with stigma and negative attitudes by
others. The inherent threat to the fragile balance
between the rational and the irrational in every
society and the fact that taken for granted rules
of conduct have been infringed lead to these
attitudes. A further depreciation of self-esteem of
the involved person and those closely associated
with him may follow, especially if social
segregation takes place.
    At the core of most social approaches there
is a component of a social psychology model
concerning processes of self-identity and
membership in a society. Often a parallel is drawn
between social and personal states of anomie(12).
By definition the focus of a social approach is on
the intersubjective and its significance for the
subjective perspective.
    Social approaches rarely mention biological
models and none of them offers a framework which
accommodates explicitly such a perspective. Some
orientations do account for the psychological
perspective, especially those interested in the
experiential component and in small group
processes. The social perspective relies on the
social sciences and the humanities, employing
sociology, history, anthropology, psychology and
economics. Methodologically and conceptually it is
divided into those more close to a positivist
approach vs. those more akin to a hermeneutic
paradigm(13).
    A sociological approach may attract those who
view mental distress as a socially constituted
phenomenon and those who wish that society owned up
to its obligations towards vulnerable members. It
attracts also those who see mental distress as
moving beyond a pure individualistic level, i.e. to
include the intersubjective and the social
structure dimension side by side with the
suejective.
    A social model cannot answer the question why
a particular individual has reacted with a
manifestation of mental distress in any given
situation. At most it can locate a group more
likely to express and sort out its social dilemmas
via psychiatric symptoms.
    Despite the often expressed lip service to an

integrative theoretical model which will include all three perspectives as equal components, we do not posses such a theory. At this stage, we do not even have the conceptual and linguistic tools with which to construct it.

Models of intervention.

The three perspectives of understanding the subject matter of psychiatry have implications for intervention(14). The biological model directs us to physiological and neurological means. The psychological perspective points to different types of psychotherapy and other forms of problem-solving interactions. The social perspective focuses on social networks, social skills, at-risk groups and structural factors.

There is one dimension which cross-cuts all intervention in psychiatry, namely the range between the clinical and communal perspectives.

The clinical appraoch is most manifest in the biological perspective because of its links to the disease model and medicine. Foucault's "clinical gaze"(15) is an apt description of accounting for the process by which a person is transformed into an objectivized entity, with a focus on a specific part of his totality. Professional neutrality, distance and the view of the professional as a natural scientist typify the approach. Emphasis on formal professionalism and clear-cut role division are additional features of this orientation(16). At the practice level we find that despite the firm belief in biological determinants, the clinicians spend most of their time on classification and symptom removal, perhaps because of the emphasis on outcome which is discussed later in this chapter.

The clinical model is equally prominent in some psychological forms of intervention, notably behaviour modification and psychoanalysis. We have had much less experience with interventions coming indirectly out of the social perspective. They lend themselves less comfortably to the clinical approach, but it is quite possible to envisage a policy maker approaching decisions from this angle.

At the other end of the range stands the communal approach to intervention. The term "communal" is used here for lack of a more precise concept to denote the opposite of the clinical model. Within the communal mode the emphasis is on social functioning rather than on the removal of symptoms. In addition the reintegration of the person to his/her social network and a greater

16

measure of control over his/her life are the main goals of intervention(17). Diagnosis, symptom reduction, the use of physical, psychological and social means of intervention are means to these ends. The intersubjective meaning is at the centre of attention, with the professonal providing just another version of reality. The professional is not aiming at being a scientist but more at being a facilitator with skills of working with distressed people and their environments.

Such an approach, or a variety of it, is more likely to be taken in conjunction with the social and psychological perspectives rather than with the somatic angle. The latter's commitment to the disease model and the natural sciences would make it considerably more difficult, if not impossible, to follow the communal approach to intervention.

At the practice level we are unlikely to come across pure cases of either ends of this dimension. Nevertheless it is possible and useful to differentiate the direction of an intervention.

The two poles of intervention have implications not only for the type of intervention selected but also for the type of power relationships between carer and helpee among the carers themselves. It is assumed here that carer-receiver power relationships are never equal. Yet within the inherent inequality there are forms of relationships which either increase or decrease the inequality. The clinical form of intervention would tend to accentuate inequality; the communal mode to minimize it.

The clinical and the communal reflect also on the positions taken on the general issues mentioned above, namely perspectives on human nature, the rational and the irrational, individual group and society relationships and the place of professional activity.

1.b.Mental Distress as a Social Problem and a Social Policy Issue.

All forms of intervention are mediated by cultural decisions. Social policies, including legislation, present one formulation of such decisions.

For mental distress to qualify as a subject matter of social policy it has to be recognized socially as a social problem and not only as a personal ill.

The following statistics should enable us to appreciate the magnitude of mental distress in present day Britain(18).

The daily average number of in-patients in psychiatric hospitals and psychiatric units in general hospitals was 75,000 in 1980, plus 10,000 day patients for England and Wales. When the Scottish figures are added, the total in-patient population becomes 90,000. This figure represents a decrease from the 135,000 in-patient population of 1959.

Yet the number of admissions was 169,310 in 1979 (tables 9 and 4, 1982), of which 49,237 were first admissions and 120,073 were readmissions (ibid,9.2,9.3). The decrease in overall admission number was very small and was wholly incurred by fall in first admissions (ibid). Instead an increase in readmissions took place, from 109,451 in 1970 to 120,073 in 1979. The combined effect of first admissions and readmissions is best exemplified by the lack of change in the rates of admission calculated per 100,000 during the seventies (table Al.1, 1980).

Pertaining to diagnostic categories no change is demonstrated. Schizophrenia and depressive psychoses continue to head the tables.

Concerning sex and age, considerably more females continue to be hospitalized than males (101,202 and 68,108 respectively in 1979 (1982,9.2)). This difference varies with age and is noticeable in the age group above 45 years, where it may also be related to longevity. Men tend to stay longer inside the hospital than women (9.5). This finding probably relates to the greater availability of socially acceptable marginal roles for women outside the hospital than for men and the lack of fear of violence from most female patients.

The duration of stay was fairly consistent from 1975 to 1979 (1982,9.6), with about 55% of the in-patients staying for less than a month, 28.5% for 1 month, 10% for 3 months and 2.5% for more than five years. These figures do not tell us how many of the in-patients come under more than one period of stay - i.e. how many times those who stay for a given period come back and for how long.

It is fashionable today to speak about the "new long stay", or those who stay for longer than two years and who are not part of the pre-60s generation of in-patients(19). Chronicity is a recurring feature of the life of many in-patients and may take place with repeated admissions of short duration as much as with the longer periods of hospitalization.

The duration of stay, combined with the high rate of readmissions and the sex/age distributions mentioned above raises the issue of the purpose that such a stay serves. It seems that it provides a temporary refuge from the pressure of life outside the hospital for the majority of the clientele. We should be therefore asking whether the present structure of the mental hospital is the best way of meeting the need for refuge in a crisis and of building up the confidence to face anew the world outside.

The fact that there are every day about 10,000 unused beds (tables 4,3, 1982) should alert us to the issue of what could/should be done about this state of affairs and the continuing investment of the bulk of the budjet into the hospital sector.

The figures concerning day attendance show a pattern of increase, and stood at 44,6000 clients in 1980, compared with 20,000 in 1969 (1982,9.1). Out-patient clinics attendance shows a consistent increase, reaching 1,691,400 in 1980.

On the whole this set of figures demonstrates the successes and failures of our current psychiatric policies and services.

These statistics do not include the data on people who seek their GP's advice on the manifestation of some psychiatric symptoms or on those who do not seek such advice but who suffer from mental distress. A recent survey of the first category estimated a prevalence of 230 per 1,000 people with psychiatric difficulties, i.e. a considerably higher number than those known to the psychiatric services(20). It would be important to know how those who opt out of primary care and the psychiatric services sort out their problems.

Regardless of specific lessons to be learned from these statistics, they reinforce the recognition of mental distress as a social problem, following the indicators of: 1.The number of people involved. 2.Their suffering. 3.The personal and social loss of potential and production. 4.The culturally growing interest in mental distress exhibited in the media, the arts and by the general public. 5.Mental distress poses a threat to the delicate balance of agreed upon standards of rationality and irrationality. This threat leads to the social requirement to contain mental distress in a way which will make it possible to keep the balance. 6.The investment of personal and social resources in the attempt to intervene.

An understanding of the significance of a social problem to a particular society necessitates an outline of its place in the given social context. Without this process of contextualization, the location of a social problem remains meaningless and artificially unatached to other social issues which influence it perception and handling.

The process of contextualizing calls also for the inclusion of the historical dimension. Without this perspective it is impossible to understand shifts in emphasis and radical changes of direction in the way a social problem is tackled. To unearth a pattern of relating to a social problem requires a comparison between at least two periods in the history of a society.

While mental distress has been accepted for a long time in Britain as a social problem it hardly ever became an issue of a wide ranging public debate, despite its relevance to the life of every one of us. One of the questions to be asked in this study is why mental ditress failed to raise public passion.

As a social policy issue policies on psychiatry are influenced by the ever present, yet changing, order of priorities of allocation of financial resources. The place in the hierarchy of priorities reflects the importance attached by a society and its rulers to a particular area of our lives. Traditionally welfare measures have a relatively low priority over economic matters (and at times over defence items) in parliamentary democracies, because they are concerned with the unproductive and unprofitable sector. At periods of an acute social crisis welfare issues are likely to resurge on the list of priorities, partly as a measure of social cohesion and partly because more people come into the category of the deserving yet unproductive. Within the wide range of welfare needs, physical health is usually more favoured than mental health, overtly on grounds of larger numbers and covertly perhaps on grounds of being less deserving since mental distress echoes of pathology and irresponsibility. For details on the uneveness of the distribution and the inferior position of the psychiatric sector see ref. 21.

The high social status of general medicine compared to the status of psychiatry is an additional contributing factor to this social preference.

20

A further division within the health sector pertains to the hospital vs. community based services, with the first being consistently favoured in the allocation of resources in the British NHS.

However, I shall be arguing that the failures and successes of our psychiatric system since the introduction of the NHS have not depended so much on the amount of money allocated to it but on the direction in which the money has been spent. Of course, this claim is valid only above a minimal standard of services and not below it. In the current situation where daily 10,000 beds are financed but left unused while community-based services are starved out of resources, it would seem that the thorny issue is more one of internal choice rather than externally imposed allocation of resources.

The internal distribution of available resources depends on power relations and attitudes of politicians, professionals and administrators. This state of affairs is one of the main reasons why this study does not focus on the financial and organizational aspects of our psychiatric system but on the attitude and power relations components, while not denying the importance of the first two aspects.

The psychiatric service is part of the NHS, itself a major element in our welfare system. The impact of the introduction of the NHS on the psychiatric system will be outlined in chapter 5 and referred to in chapters 6 and 7.

Bashing the welfare state from the right and the left has become a fashionable pastime. The author adheres to the view expressed succinctly by I. Gough(22) who sees the welfare state as a tool of capitalist social control and as the achievement of the British working class. The current psychiatric system will be treated as such a mixture.

Traditionally, the three main partners to a policy decision on mental distress have been the government, MPs and the professionals. It is a cultural decision not to seek the opinions of those themselves diagnosed as mentally distressed or of their relatives.

Each of these socially acceptable partners brings in an emphasis on certain interests and views which it hopes to see implemented in the policy. Apart from in exceptional circumstances, governments are usually interested in maintaining the existing social order and are the more conservative of the three groups in terms of reluctance to change existing systems. MPs can afford to be the most daring, because of being less tied down to organizational structures.

Professionals occupy the middle position between the government and MPs in regard to initiating change. They are in a position to promote ideas of change but are also bound by the vested interests of their group.

Moreover each component may in turn interpret and execute a policy in the light of particularistic interests rather than in the light of supposedly shared views.

Hall et al.(23) have outlined the processes of policy change. Their model assumes a mixture of consensus and conflict in regard to policy issues. They stress the need to look at the specificity of each case in terms of the degree of legitimation, feasibility and support given to a proposed policy change. This framework will be utilized in looking at changes in psychiatric policies (see chapter 7). The three components are unequal in terms of the type of authority and power invested in them.

The analysis of the relationships among the three partners in the two periods investigated should therefore enable us to distinguish the contribution of each from that of the two others.

Local councils and health authorities play an important role in the implementation and interpretation of psychiatric policies. This study does not investigate this role because of the considerable variations at this level. However, references to the implications of specific policy decisions on the local level will be made when relevant.

1.c.Requirements by and of the Psy Complex.

This section will focus on the mixture of theoretical knowledge and practice wisdom in the field of psychiatry. These components are influenced by the degree of professionalism and mode of organization of each group which will be referred to when relevant.

1.c.i.Outcome and control.
It is argued here that the main concern of a professional group is with the outcomes it can

produce, a concern required to justify both social and professional objectives. This preoccupation with outcomes can be found in the publications of the four groups discussed here(24). What is defined as a desirable outcome moves on a range from intervention at the practice level to giving meaning and naming behaviour which has been seen before as meaningless.

The requirement to provide effective social control and care over an aspect of life deemed as deviant provides a primary motive for the focus on outcome. The emphasis on effectiveness would imply different goals within different social contexts. In our social context it means that the ordinary course of life should not be disturbed while allowing a temporary postponement of ordinary functioning to those who suffer from mental distress. Disruptive behaviour should however be brought to as speedy an end as possible or else be removed from the visibility of the majority.

Thus effectiveness implies a quick recovery, as little public spending as possible and putting patients' and ex-patients' abilities to maximum economic and personal use. When such a use is in conflict with the visibility of mental disturbance the latter is judged as of greater social importance than the first. Professionals, especially psychiatrists, are asked to sort out such conflicts time and again. The specific resolution adopted would depend in part on the preferred model of social life of a society and its professionals. Not infrequently professional groups adhere to views which conflict with those of the ruling groups. The move to transform the Poor Law asylums into hospitals in the 20s or the recent BMA report on the effects of nuclear war on health are two examples of such a conflict(25). (For further discussion of this issue see the section on the role of the intermediary.)

The parameter of social control is hardly ever mentioned explicitly in professional writings on psychiatry and its existence is often denied in confrontation with social scientists. This omission is due to the explicit focus on the caring function which is the source of social legitimation for each of the helping professions. In addition it is perceived as an anathema to professional autonomy and the notion of unbiased scientists. The coercive and passive connotations attached to being agents of social control make the issue into a thorny one for professionals in psychiatry. Therefore not to

discuss it is likely to be an agreeable way out.
Social control is treated here as an inherent part of social life. Inequality in the helping relationships has been already assumed. Therefore the question asked here concerns not how to get rid of social control but the need to understand the types and degree of social control exercised in psychiatry; the types and areas relatively less controlled.

It has been argued convincingly that the spread of psychiatry as an integral part of our culture and welfare system denotes a greater use of psychiatry as a soft, subtle mode of social control(26). This control is achieved by imputing personal or biological meanings to potentially political issues which reflect on existing social contradictions. This type of control contrasts with the traditional and more openly coercive pattern of control associated with detaining the mentally ill.

While agreeing with the expansion of psychiatry as a soft control device, it seems to me that to conclude from this assertion that psychiatry is just a social control device is plainly misleading. Psychiatry is also about a genuine offer of help to those who suffer from mental distress, as well as a mode of providing meaning to issues which everyone of us has to sort out as part of coping with our human existence. The choice of psychiatric explanations as interpretations of social contradictions is a collective choice, which is not taken by the psy complex on its own. If it were not a cultural choice it would not carry with it the legitimation which it needs in order to become an effective measure of social control. Therefore the underlying issue is why and when do psychiatric explanations and interventions appeal as a social control measure; an issue which will be raised throughout this study.

1.c.ii.Restoration and reordering.
The wish for restoration, and for provding codes for reordering disrupted social relations is the second dimension required by and of the psy complex(27). The metaphors of restoration and reordering come from a framework of giving meaning to the experience and the processes involved. Such imagery comes to the psy complex via the beliefs on human nature and from its organized knowledge component.

The images that go together with restoration

24

have to be related to the acceptance of a degree of
vulnerability of the whole which is to be
reintegrated. The restorer must have a clear
picture of the ideal form of the object on which
he/she is going to lavish care and attention.
Restorers come as second to the gods and mothers -
i.e. eternal and universal life-givers, in being
endowed with the right to bestow a new life to a
nearly lifeless entity, or to create it anew.
    Although on the surface the care aspect is
more prominent in the restoration perspective it
equally follows ideals of social control. The
specific imagery on the ideally recovered
ex-mentally ill person employed in professional
literature will reveal the specific meaning of
restoration within a professional approach.
    However, for the majority of professionals
the interest in the ideal is likely to be limited
to the degree such aspirations can be translated
into the level of practice. Inevitably tension is a
permanent feature in balancing the ideal of
restoration with the maintenance of social control
and the means available to a professional group.

1.c.iii.Professional autonomy and knowledge.
Within the historical development of
professionalism in our society a positive value has
been attached to professional autonomy which should
include autonomy from other social institutions and
other types of social relations. To meet openly
social control functions is to admit to a
non-autonomous position, while to care and attend
the sick and the weak is seen as providing a
service to individuals and the collective. Autonomy
was perceived as the best protection for clients
and providers alike, precisely because it was
supposd to enable a free-from-pressure position to
the carers(28). Given the social mandate of any
professional group in our society it is naive to
assume a case of full autonomy with or without a
state welfare system. Instead degrees of autonomy
and corresponding functioing as social control
agents need to be investigated. However, a high
level of autonomy would not necessarily imply a low
level of meeting social control requirements, as
current analysis of the medical profession
demonstrates(29).
    The issue of professional knowledge is
closely related to the claims for autonomy,
monopoly and usefulness made by profeesional
groups. Their knowledge base tends to be collected

from more than one discipline, in part as the result of the pressure for outcomes. Thus an interesting situation arises in regard to the strength of the claim for professional uniqueness. The knowledge components are not unique to the group of professionals but the particular blend is and the skills which follow from it are declared to be unique too. For example, social workers admit openly that their knowledge foundation is based on psychology, sociology, psychiatry and social administration. Yet they argue that their contribution to the understanding of the mentally distressed differs in principle from that of other disciplines(30).

In addition pragmatic knowledge(31) forms an important component of the knowledge base of an applied discipline. In the analysis of professioanl literature we will look at what is blended together, what is omitted that could have been an integral part of the mixture, who claims more to be unique, in which direction and for which purposes.

The preoccupation with outcomes puts a premium on knowledge leading to predictions rather than to further understanding. Predictability offers the promise of a greater measure of certainty and of controlling reality. In principle predictions should point to parameters to be employed in order to achieve a specific outcome. The ability to predict outcome and effectiveness of an intervention is made complex in psychiatry by the multiple sources of definitions and intervening variables (e.g. social norms affect the perception of mental distress as a disturbance as well as the self-image of the person designated as mentally ill). The concern with results leads also to the need to act and at least to be seen as acting; the temptation of following a particular course of action "because it works" usually evokes sympathy in fellow-professionals and the general public. The risks of overlooking side-effects and misapplication and of curtailing opportunities for further knowledge due to the lack of understanding are brushed aside. The risks are overshadowed by the exhilarating feeling of having something tangible to offer to clients, society and the profession. The pressure of everyday professional practice to act means that individuals are doing so within a wide margin of uncertainty. The uncertainty is not easily visible to outsiders. The division of labour and the multidisciplinary language often reflect on in-built mechanisms for mutual support in facing uncertainty. Areas of specific types of uncertainty can be delineated among the four professional groups; the high degree of uncertainty is shared by all of them.

The hostility towards researchers, academics and the reported minimal use of research findings by practitioners(32) contribute too to the tendency not to enter into conceptual deliberations as much as they are the result of this reluctance. Practitioners complain - often justifiably - that theorists are unaware of obstacles in the practice situation and that theories are unhelpful tools because of the imprecise way in which they are phrased. Such a view omits the fact that theoretical models are by definition not more than a distilled reflection of reality and therefore a straight-forward correlation between theory and practice cannot be aimed at. At the same time these complaints point to the lack of mutual awareness of the requirements of each side.

The inevitable tension between theory and practice is at times recognized by professional groups. However its creative potential is more often than not ignored while its discomforting angle is stressed. The four professional groups difer in the degree of conceputalization they strive towards and use in their practice. It will be important to locate these differences, their origins and impact on the theoretical and practical work.

l.c.iv.The professionals in the role of the intermediary.

Part of the brief of professionals in our society is to act as intermediaries between the receivers of a service and those in control over resources(33). In psychiatry the consumers are in an inferior power position because of the stigma attached to being mentally ill and because of being the sufferers. Thus we find that social workers' status is usually lower than that of psychiatrists because their clientele is judged as being both mentally ill and poor.

What is entailed in the role of the intermediary? Philp's stimulating contribution concerning social work(34) can be extended to other professions too. The role includes care and control; advocacy and restraint; talking on behalf of each side to the other. The intermediary is part of the global social system, and depends on the establishment directly for its mandate and resources and less directly on the clients for the continuation of truce and/or trust. By definition this role is contradictory. The balance may be tilted to one side at a given period and more to the other side at another period but its apparent stability is quite fragile.

For example the creation of the NHS provides us with an illustration of the coexistence of mutual and conflicting interests between the government of the time and the medical profession. The doctors had to accept the introduction of a national health service and its bureaucratic organization. Yet the government accepted the clinical model of medical practice with all its ramifications for community based services.

The dependency is further complicated by the tendency of professional groups not just to provide the ruling groups with the solutions for a social problmes: such solutions are offered on the profession's own terms, which often include an active redefinition of the social problems in terms which are not necessarily those preferred by the state(35). In part the proliferation of the links between the state - the most obvious system of social control - and the professionals is related to the employment of the latter in the position of policy making and its implementation.

The degree of awareness to the intermediary role and the ways in which it is resolved at the periods under study by the different groups will be one of the dimensions to be investigated in the analysis of professional literature.

1.d.The Significance and Limitations of Studying Attitudes.

As already suggested the subject matter of psychiatry is viewed here as a cultural production in terms of the personal and social significance attached to it. Therefore the rules of analysis of such a construction apply to the meanings given to mental distress and social policies about it.

The ground rule of studying a field where meaning and method of handling depend so much on interpretation is to know the content of and to understand the structure of dominant interpretations. Without this component our understanding of both theories and practices will be inadequate. A good knowledge of the practice is

28

necessary too because interpretations are implemented and modified at this facet.

There are several primary participants in a mental distress situation. This study does not focus on the principal actor, i.e. the person identified as suffering from mental distress. Instead it centres on two other groups of participants, arguing that socially they are of primary importance to the construction of mental distress and to policy decisions.

The impact of the attitudes of politicians and professionals on their society's mode of understanding and reacting to mental distress is crucial, because they are given the social mandate to reach and implement interpretations and policies.

In the process of reaching the decisions an implicit consensus on the interpretaion of mental distres is negotiated. At times such a consensus is taken for granted by both sides and is not openly discussed. One of the questions raised in this study concerns the roots of interpretation, which may differ between politicians and professionals and within each group.

Politicians are expected to represent the general public, though by virture of being selected they are likely to differ from its majority. To the extent that politicians represent the public and its interests they equally participate in forming the public's views. In the tension between reflecting and shaping public opinion we may be struck by either a gap or a lag betwen the two processes, whereby at any given moment one of these two roles overshadows the other. Therefore only an historical perspective can ensure that both processes are taken into account.

As part of these processes politicians too are open to influence from other parties, notably the professions, the civil service, the media and pressure groups. Only one of these four groups has been investigated in depth here, the professionals. By analysing the Ministry's position we learn indirectly about the civil service's stand on psychiatry. References to the media are made when the latter's reaction surfaces via the politicians' comments. In the ideal study clients' perspectives, and those of civil servants, the media and pressure groups should be investigated in depth too.

The professionals were selected as the group which has the overt social mandate for both interpreting and intervening in the field of psychiatry. The prominence of the experts in our civilization has become part of its cultural ethos. Their views are officially requested by the Ministry and the politicians. The dependence of lay poeple on the judgement , advice, support and control exercised by professionals has grown accordingly. This centrality led to the choice of the professionals as one of the two groups to be investigated.

Attitudes are at the core of any act of interpretation and relating to people. They are formed on the basis of available yet selective information as well as being shaped by value preferences(36). Yet attitudes neither reflect directly the factors which led to their formation nor are they reflected frequently in a direct manner at the level of action. Both attitudes and action are mediated by additional factors which lead to variations in outcomes. These factors include situational features, organizational structures, the particular actors involved, previously cherished attitudes and the research methods employed.

Thus the study of attitudes cannot predict for us with a high degree of probability the next course of action. However, it can give us insight into the general direction of intervention and into the intrepretative process. Hence the crucial place of attitudes in the study of both meanings and social policy.

1.e.Methodological Framework.

This study will look at attitudes of politicians, theories and value preferences of professionals in psychiatry in Britain during the twenties and the fifties of this century.

1.e.i.Contextualizing mental distress.
The attitudes, theories and value preferences of both politicians and professionals will follow the presentation of the mental illness scene in the social context of the two periods. This presentation will include references to key issues of each period and how these issues were related to directions and developments in psychiatry. The comparison between the general context and the psychiatric system in the two periods will enable us to indicate the direction of change and

30

continuity in psychiatry.

1.e.ii.Content to be investigated. In order to investigate attitudes and theories the following material will be studied:
The politicians' perspective:
1.Parliamentary debates on psychiatry, especially during 1927, 1929-30, 1954, 1957 and 1959. The discussions in these years were of particular relevance in the reconsideration of the state of psychiatry, recommending policies and legislating in this field. Legislation is viewed here as providing a formal approval to policies. While at times legislation approves of already implemented policies, yet on other occasions it endorses recommendations for the future.
2.Official documents, such as green and white papers, statistics, committees' reports and the laws pertaining to psychiatry will be included.

It was attempted to interview MPs who were prominent in the 1959 debate and the then Minister of health. Only one of those approached agreed to discuss the debate and the Act, Mr. K. Robinson. The information provided by him was useful and is referred to in chapter 7. Those who refused to be interviewed claimed either that they are no longer experts on the subject (e.g. the MPs who were also psychiatrists), or that all of what they had to say on the issue has appeared in official documents.
The professional perspective:
Four professional groups are to be looked at: nurses, psychiatrists, psychologists and social workers.
The following journals will be analysed:

1.The British Medical Journal (BMJ).
2.The Lancet.
3.The Journal of Mental Science, which became the British Journal of Psychiatry in 1963.
4.The British Journal of Medical Psychology.
5.The British Journal of Psychiatric Social Work, which became the British Journal of Social Work in 1970.
6.Nursing Mirror (NM).

The content of the journals has been systematically investigated during the following years; 1920, 1921, 1924, 1930, 1951, 1954, 1957, 1959-62. These years were selected in conjunction with major relevant parliamentary debates on developments in psychiatry.

Relevant items were analysed in terms of the areas they cover, direction of emphasis, scope of coverage and the criteria set out in section e.iii. No attempt was made to evaluate the quality of the contribution.

It is arguable whether written papers in professional journals reflect realistically on the practice situation. It could be maintained that such contributions express the views of the elite of the profession and/or the ideal rather than the real. Evidence from statistical reports, research projects, clients' and staff's impressions can in part corroborate or disprove claims for a realistic description of existing practice. Letters to the editor are another measure which links closely practice to the theoretical message in journals. At the same time it is likely that the theoreticians express trends which either have not been previously presented or are not acceptable to the practising majority. To the best of our knowledge the majority of the contributors to the journals analysed below were practitioners at the time.

Major psychiatric textbooks of each period were included as an eye opener to a comprehensive exposition of conceptual positions and value preference systems. While contributions to journals are fragmentary in nature, a textbook should give the flavour of the totality of the field at a given time. The following textbooks were looked at:

1.Craig, M., and Beaton, T. (1926) Psychological Medicine.
2.Henderson,D.K., and Gillespie,R.D. (1927 and 1956) A Textbook of Psychiatry.
3.Mayer-Gross,W., Slater, W., and Roth, M. (1954) Clinical Psychiatry.

1.e.iii.Criteria for content analysis.
The criteria for analysis are based on several assumptions concerning the study and meaning of social policy. In addition the selection of dimensions for analysis has been linked to assumptions on the subject matter of psychiatry, the social role of the psychiatric system, its modes of practice and theory.

Each assumption and choice are the end product of extensive conceptual and methodological debates which cannot be reproduced here due to space limitations. The reader interested in these issues is directed to the references list for this section.

For the author, psychiatry, and especially

the study of its meaning and social policy, calls primarily for a non-positivist social sciences approach. Such an approach should be interested in the subjective and intersubjective interpretations and their translation into social decisions, professional activities and theories.

It would be difficult to deny that in the course of what is usually defined as mental illness a person's self-perception changes, as well as those of others and the non-human world(37). Given these changes and the component of suffering, the theoretical treatment of subjectivity, objectivity and intersubjectivity is a necessity. These related concepts cross-cut the issues of definition of mental distress, understanding and reacting to it, as well as the relationships among individuals, their primary groups and society.

Methodologically it is of equal importance to adhere to a consistent treatment of these concepts, for such a choice preselects the questions to be pursued.

It has been assumed above that mental distress is a phenomenon which incorporates both the social and the natural worlds. Hence both the social sciences and the natural sciences have a valid contribution to make towards the study of mental distress.

Schutz has summarized the main differences between the two types of sciences as follows:(38)

1.Observation has a different meaning and range in the two sciences.
2.The social sciences study primarily the intersubjective world; natural scientists investigate an objective world.
3.Natural scientists take the social world for granted; social scientists aim at researching it.
4.The place of the meaning attached to a phenomenon differs in the two sciences. Meaning is central within the social sciences.

Schutz's list omits the specific contribution added by Marxism to the study of the social world. Marxism emphasizes the importance of the economic system and of power relations to interpersonal relationships and consciousness. More specifically living in a given mode of production has implications for the definitions and reactions to mental ilness, including the place of professional activity(39).

Foucault's notion of power as positive and creative provides further insight into the use of power by politicians and professionals which should be incorporated into the analysis(40). This focus is simply absent in natural sciences methodology.

It would seem that the degree of interpretation and types of inferences called for in the process of understanding the social world are much greater than that of primarily observing it. The likelihood of direct manipulation of components of the social world for research purposes is both less realistic and less acceptable on ethical grounds. Thus a considerable reduction of the social world would be necessary for the sake of following closely natural science methodology.

Pertaining to psychiatry it should be remembered that the phenomenon under study is universal while it is being defined and treated differently in different cultures. Therefore while it is unlikely that mental distress will disappear, the ways in which it is conceptualized and dealt with socially and professioanlly have changed in the past and are likely to change in the future. This crucial qualification directs us more towards using social science understanding and tools than those of natural sciences in order to grasp the signficiance of the universality, variability and changeability of the phenomena. In addition, the existence of components such as the dependence of the meaning given to subjectivity and intersubjectivity on interpretation, the centrality of social reactions to personal and social attitudes towards the mentally ill warrant the use of an hermeneutic social science approach (see ref.13). This approach calls for an attempt of empathic understanding of the subject within its specific social context.

This conclusion does not negate the need for complementary natural science methodology concerning variables which are more a part of the natural world. For example physiological processes should be studied by this type of methodology, though the overall significance has to be looked at in conjunction with the other layers of mental distress.

While politics is openly based on value judgement, many professionals in the psy complex argue for value-free theories and practice, claiming that such freedom is both desirable and realistically attainable(41). However, the evidence for the existence of value preferences in the practice and theory of psychiatry cannot be refuted. Studies on cross-cultural comparisons show time and again how the same phenomenon is ascribed different meaning, ranging from the divine to the sick and bad(42). Studies within similar Western societies such as the US and the UK show systematic differences and similarities in regard to classification among psychiatrists themselves(43). Research such as that conducted by Rosenhan(44) in which psycholgy students passed themselves as insane and were accepted as such by all professioanls but not by the other patients, points to the extreme possibilities of biased perceptions. To claim as Clare does(45) that the findings in Rosenhan's study are simply an example of bad practice is to deny the significance of the issue.

The variety of views which are held currently within the psy complex is in part the outcome of applying different world views to the understanding of mental distress. The differences in the assumptions reflect adherence to different belief systems about human nature, rationality and irrationality, and the relations between individuals and their society.

Thus the existence of a belief component in any conceptual framework concerned with psychiatry is warranted. Accepting this existence in every theory does not invalidate in itself the contribution of the theory. Theories still retain the value of systematic, consistent and coherent distillation of reality into rules of thinking and observation which direct us to the practice. However within the parameters of this book theories in which the value base is acknowledged are perceived as more productive theories than those in which the relevance of this component is negated.

Following this analysis, the following will be adopted as methodological rules:

1.Making as explicit as possible my own views and those of others.
2.Checking whether claims made by politicians and professionals are in fact supported by their actions and other contributions.
3.Using the hermeneutic approach while extending it to locating what is taken for granted and by whom.
4.Employing the dialectical method in terms of looking for contradictions; comparing different versions on the same issue within and between groups; searching for missing issues.

The following content dimensions will be investigated:

1.Content areas of psychiatry covered by politicians and professionals at different points in time; those left uncovered.
2.The coverage of and the approach to issues of subjectivity, intersubjectivity and objectivity.
3.The portrait of the patient/client and the relationships between clients and professionals.
4.Ideals of care and restoration and the methods suggested for their attainment.
5.Attitudes and modes of coping with social control functions.
6.Prevailing conceptual systems and their value preference components.
7.Approaches towards professionalism, including the consideration given to the role of the intermediary, professional autonomy, expression of uncertainty.
8.The reflection of legitimation and motivation crisis(46).

A list such as the above is hardly ever exhaustive of the possiblities for analysis. Some of the issues mentioned in the section but not directly in the list appear in it indirectly. For example power relations are linked to the portrait of the patients; relations between clients and professionals; social control function, approaches towards professionalism.
It is hoped that the reader has not found the introduction too daunting. The complexity of the area of study necessitated a clear as possible delineation of the issues at stake.

References
1.Ingleby, D. (1981) Understanding Mental Illness. In: Ingleby, D. (ed) Critical Psychiatry, Penguin, Harmondsworth, pp.23-71.
2.Wing, J. K. (1978) Reasoning about Madness, Oxford University Press, London.
3.Szasz, T. (1961) The Myth of Mental Illness, Harper and Row, New York.
4.See ref.1 and; Sedgwick, P. (1973) Mental Illness is Illness, Salmagundi, 20, pp.196-224.
5.Hunter, R., Macalpine, I. (ed) (1963) Three Hundred Years of Psychiatry, Oxford University Press, London.
Lewis, A. J. (1963) Medicine and the Affections of

the Mind, British Medical Journal, 2, pp.1549-1557.
Siegler, M. Osmond, H. (1974) Models of Madness,
Models of Medicine, Macmillan, New York.
6.See ref.2.
7.Bignami, G. (1982) Disease Models and
Reductionist Thinking in the Biomedical Sciences.
In: Rose, S. (ed) Against Biological Determinism,
Allison and Busby, London, pp.94-110.
8.Freud, S. (1930) Collected Papers, Hogarth Press,
London.
Eysenck, H. J. (1957) The Dynamics of Anxiety and
Hysteria, Routledge and Kegan Paul, London.
Laing, R. D. (1960) The Divided Self, Tavistock,
London.
Manoni, M. (1973) The Child, his Illness and the
Family, Tavistock, London.
9.See ref.8.
10.Hollingshead, A., Redlich, F. (1958) Social
Class and Mental Illness, Chapman and Hall, New
York.
Cummings, J., Cummings, E. (1962) Closing the
Ranks, Columbia University Press, New York.
Brown, G., Harris, T. (1978) The Social Origins of
Depression, Tavistock, London.
11.Goffman, I. (1963) Stigma, Penguin,
Harmondsworth.
Scheff, T. (ed) (1975) Labelling Mental Illness,
Prentice Hall, Englewood-Cliffs, New Jersey.
12. Dunham, W. H. (1964) Anomie and Mental
Disorders. In: Clinard, M. (ed) Anomie and Deviant
Behaviour, The Free Press, New York, pp.128-54.
13.Connerton, P. (1978) Critical Sociology,
Penguin, Harmondsworth. Parts Two and Three.
Habermas, J. (1972) Knowledge and Human Interest,
Heinemann, London.
Habermas, J. (1976) Legitimation Crisis, Heinemann,
London.
Dorener, K. (1979) Madman and the Bourgeoisie,
Blackwell, Oxford.
14.Sargant, W. Salter, E. (1972) An Introduction to
Physical Methods of Treatment in Psychiatry,
Churchill Livingstone, Edinburgh.
Winnicott, D. W. (1978) The Piggle, Penguin,
Harmondsworth.
Jones, M. (1952) Social Psychiatry, Tavistock,
London.
15.Foucault, M. (1970) The Birth of the Clinic,
Tavistock, London.
16.Mishler, E. (1981) Viewpoint: Critical
Perspectives on the Biomedical Model. In: Mishler,
E. (ed) Social Contexts of Health, Illness and

Patient Care, Cambridge University Press, pp.1-23.
17.See ref. 10.
Ramon, S. (1983) Psichiatria Democratica: A Case
Study of an Italian Community Mental Health
Service, International Journal of Health Services,
13, 2, pp.307-324.
18.DHSS, Personal and Health Statistics, 1982,
HMSO, London.
DHSS, Inpatients Statistics from the Mental Health
Inquiry for England, 1980. HMSO, London.
Scottish Abstracts of Statistics, the Scottish
Office, 12/1983, table 3.5., p.20. HMSO, Edinburgh.
19.Wing, J. K. et al. (1972) Evaluating a Community
Psychiatric Service, Oxford University Press,
London.
20.Goldberg, D., Huxley, P. (1980) Mental Illness
in the Community, Tavistock, London, p.11.
21.Jones, K. (1972) The History of the Mental
Health Services, Routledge and Kegan Paul, London.
DHSS: Priorities for Health and Personal Social
Services, 1976, annex 2, tables 1 and 2, HMSO,
London.
22.Gough, I. (1979) The Political Economy of the
Welfare State, Macmillan, London.
23.Hall, P. Land, H. Parker, R. Webb, A. (1975)
Change, Choice and Conflict in Social Policy,
Heinemann, London.
24.Howe, D. (1980) Inflated States and Empty
Theories in Social Work, British Journal of Social
Work, 10, pp.317-341.
25.British Medical Journal (1930), 1, p.613.
British Medical Association, Board of Science and
Education (1983) Inquiry into the Effects of
Nuclear War, London.
26.Castel, R., Castel, F., Lovell, A. (1982) The
Psychiatric Society, Columbia University Press, New
York.
27.Comaroff, J. (1978) Medicine and Culture,
Medicine, Culture and Psychiatry, 5, pp.76-94.
28.Parry, N., Parry, J. (1976) The Rise of the
Medical Profession, Croom Helm, London.
29.Friedson, E. (1970) Professional Dominance,
Atherton, New York.
Johnson, T. (1973) Professions and Power,
Macmillan, London.
30.Butrym, Z. (1976) The Nature of Social Work,
Macmillan, London.
31.Baldamus, W. (1966) The Category of Pragmatic
Knowledge in Sociological Analysis, University of
Birmingham, Department of Sociology, Discussion
Papers on Social Science Methodology, series E,

no.1.
32.Carew, R. (1979) The Place of Knowledge in Social Work Activity, British Journal of Social Work, 9, pp.349-364.
33.Etzioni, A. (1969) The Semi-Professions and their Organization, Prentice Hall, Englewood Cliffs, New Jersey.
34.Philp, M. (1979) Notes on the Form of Knowledge in Social Work, Sociological Review, 27, pp.56-78.
35.Ingleby, D. (1983) Mental Health and Social Order. In: Scull, A., Cohen, S. (ed) Social Control and the Modern State, Robertson, London.
36.Jahoda, G. (1966) Attitudes, Penguin, Harmondsworth.
37.Barnes, M., Berke, J. (1976) Mary Barnes, Penguin, Harmondsworth.
38.Schutz, A. (1967) The Problem of Social Reality, Collected Papers, vol. 1, Martinus Nijhoff, the Hague.
39.Lukacs, G. (1971) History and Class Consciousness, Merlin Press, London.
Gramsci, A. (1971) Prison Notebooks, International Publications, New York.
Brenner, H. (1973) Mental Illness and Economic Depression, Columbia University Press, New York.
Scull, A 91975) Decarceration, Prentice Hall, Englewood Cliffs, New jersey.
40.Foucault, M. (1977) Discipline and Punishment, Allen Lane, London.
41.Clare, A. (1978) Psychiatry in Dissent, Tavistock, London.
42.Kiev, A. (ed) (1972) Transcultural Psychiatry, Penguin, Harmondsworth.
43.Kendell, R. F. (1975) The Role of Diagnosis in Psychiatry, Blackwell, Oxford.
44.Rosenhan, D. L. (1973) On Being Sane in Insane Places, Science, 179.
45.See ref. 41.
46.Habermas, J. (1976) Legitimation Crisis, Heinemann, London. In this book Habermas develops a typology of crisis characteristic of Western industrialized societies. Two of these, the motivation and legitimation crisis are particularly relevant to the field of psychiatry.

2 Mental Distress in the Social Context of the Twenties

2.a. The Social Context of the 20s.

Britain of the twenties was still recovering from the upheaval and changes brought by the First World War, the last to be called "The Great"(1). The poetry and prose written during and after that war attest to some of its shocking effects on its participants(2). The meaninglessness of the war was realized, as well as the more brutal aspects of life. The disconnection between the soldiers at the front and those at home made some people acutely aware of the desirability of basic changes in the existing social reality, while the majority's emphasis was on the return to normalcy.

The war had drained the human and financial resources of the country. However the economic decline of Britain which followed should be attributed to the contribution of several additional factors: The increase in the size of the population; the inability of British industry to compete in the world market; world economic depression and a continuing policy of investing capital in the empire rather than in the country(30).

The number of those unemployed reached its peak of 2.7 millions only in 1932 (out of a general population of 39 millions(4)). Yet unemployment was strongly felt throughout the 20s. Unemployment benefits were far from meeting even basic needs of the unemployed and their families. The Rowntree study bears evidence on the degree of poverty among working-class people at the time(5). Although a period of economic depression, new industries were developing from the mid 20s(6). Wages too rose constantly during this decade, even in real

terms(7). People with secure jobs and in areas
which had not been directly affected by the slump
felt that they were better off economically than
before.

Thus a sharp division emerged between "the
haves" and "the have nots", where employed
working-class people expressed similar interests to
those of the middle class rather than solidarity
with the newly unemployed.

Class conflict and interclass clashes were
expressed frequently. The events of the general
strike of 1926 and its aftermath illustrate best
the classes' relationships and the undeniable fact
that working-class people were exploited and
largely undefended from it by the state. At the
same time it was within the power of the working
class to bring Labour into government not only once
but twice within the decade of 1920-30. Despite
being a minority government it was the first Labour
government which established the 1924 Royal
Commission on mental illness and the second Labour
government brought the bill to Parliament in the
1929-30 session. The connections between Labour,
Liberals and Conservatives' thinking on general
welfare to mental illness policies will be
discussed later.

Questioning the existing order followed
logically as the aftermath of the war: Socialist,
"populist" and Fabianist ideas were debated by left
wing circles(8). Further capitalist expansion,
nationalism, fears of and fascination with the
growing Fascist movement and deep suspicion of
Communism were the concern of the right,
cross-cutting party lines(9).

Several acts related to social welfare
measures were legislated, the best known are the
1920 and 1927 Unemployment Insurance Acts and the
1929 Local Government Act designed to change the
workhouse system. While the Unemployment Insurance
Act did bring some relief it was insufficient and
adhered to the principle of differentiating between
the "deserving" and the "undeserving" even among
the unemployed(10). The Local Government Act was an
attempt to re-implement the 1834 Poor Law
principles(11). Perhaps the most progressive
legislation was the recognition of dependents to
the main bread-winner for the purpose of benefit in
1922.

Most of the social welfare legislation that
was passed had similar effects to the two acts
mentioned above, i.e. of preserving the system and

its values, (e.g. the requirement to work) and containing the poor rather than changing the conditions that led to becoming and staying poor. At the same time the Acts brought relief at various degrees to many and paved the way for further changes. This basically conservative approach is the outcome of the fact that: a.Labour governments were minority governments of short duration, with a curious mixture of conservative and radical intentions which did not lead to actual change. b.Conservative governments were interested in keeping the status quo in the field of welfare and opposed greater state intervention in this field. c.The Liberal government of the early twenties had in fact attempted to introduce major changes in social welfare legislation but its public support and backing was dwindling rapidly(12). The ideologies expressed in the social policy debates are pertinent to the attitudes towards health care and will be discussed later briefly.

2.b.The Mental Distress Scene.

The number of in-patients in 1930 were estimated to be 142,000, in a population of 39 millions(13). The rate of admissions and discharges was very stable: 22,000 were admitted, 10,000 discharged and 9,000 died in hospital every year between 1921-29(14). The number of out-patients was not available as these statistics were not collected by the Ministry of Health (which only came into being in 1919), bearing evidence on the relative insignificance of the out-patients' sector.
    Table 1 (appendix 1) shows the changes in in-patient population size during the decade(15). The statistics presented here were collated from replies of the Minister of Health in the House of Commons and from the annual report of the Ministry. These statistics are far from satisfactory: one set of figures does not fully fit with the others. As mentioned below, the rate of recovery was calculated by the number of admissions and discharges rather than in regard to the total number of in-patients. There are no breakdowns of figures for age, sex, occupation, and education.
    Although length of stay and re-admission figures were not made available at the national level, the degree of chronicity must have been high. This conclusion is reached by comparing the

figures on admission, discharge and death vs the total size of the in-patient population. Such a comparison indicates that the extent of change in the hospitalized population was small - as only 22,000 per year were admitted and slightly fewer patients (19,000) left (either through discharge or death): i.e. about 100,000 of the total in-patient population of 142,000 did not move during the year.

Brenner's(16) well-documented claim that a positive direct relationship exists between the increase in the size of the in-patient population and economic depression in the US is reflected in Britain: the number of in-patients increased year by year until the beginning of the Second World War(17). The increase however was not steep and could be accounted for in more than one way. In addition Jones mentions incidents where people hospitalised themselves to escape unemployment and hunger and the greater availability of auxiliary and nursing staff after 1930(18).

The outcome for discharged persons is unclear, as it is not known how many of these were re-admitted, fully/partially recovered. What constitutes a recovery is a hotly debated issue which this chapter cannot go into. "Recovered" is used here as defined by professional opinion, since this definition formed the basis for the collated statistics.

Officially the figure of 7,119 recovered patients per year is quoted by the Minister(19). The comments made on recovery rates of the period were based on calculation from admission rates by county and borough hospitals, and were left unrelated to the total number of in-patients - a highly doubtful method. According to these sources the rate of recovery was 32% in 1920-9, compared to 40% in 1871-80(20). These figures plus the total number of in-patients, could not have given the impression of a successful and competent professional activity to the lay public or the professionals themselves(21).

The number of patients dying each year was high when compared to the number of discharges or admissions (10,000 per year). At the same time it should be remembered that these figures are not high in relation to the total of the hospitalized population, given the prevailing conditions in hospitals and in general medicine. One wonders what were the reasons for the deaths and what were the public's reactions to these figures. Were mental hospitals used at times instead of general

43

hospitals and workhouses for the poor? Was it a special category of patients that died, i.e. the elderly and/or from specific disease categories? Did more die in a specific type of mental hospital institution? (e.g. the Poor Law hospitals, the private or county ones). How long did those who died stay in the hospital prior to dying? - i.e. were they brought in already seriously physically ill?

In-patients were confined to mental hospitals after a certification process. Only in fourteen hospitals were voluntary patients accepted (or a total of 4,700 placed(22). A tiny minority was receiving psychotherapy outside the hospital. For the majority treatment consisted of hospitalization, use of drugs - mainly bromides and barbiturates - hydrotherapy in some cases and the use of mechanical restraints at times. The atmosphere of most mental hospitals could not have been pleasant as they were located in huge, dark Victorian buildings, suffering from chronic overcrowding and severe shortage of staff(23). Clark (24) points out however that in some hospitals the relationships between patients and staff were friendly and relaxed.

The number of private hospitals in 1938 was 50, compared to 116 in 1900(25). Most of them were small, accommodating about 60 patients. Conditions varied greatly, partly in accordance with the price paid for care and whether the house was aimed at the "educated" vs. the "uneducated" classes . Treatment methods followed usually those used at the time by physicians. Some of the private homes were the first to innovate intervention methods (e.g. the Retreat in York). A number of the small institutions, especially in the rural areas, were run as family homes. Women patients were helping in domestic work and needlework, men working in the garden. The more expensive private houses looked like the boarding schools of the time. Complaints about abuses in private houses were a regular feature in the press and in numerous publications. The complaints and the abuses were not confined to private homes but were equally reported on public hospitals (i.e. county, Poor Law and voluntary hospitals).

Although the statistics available were very incomplete the failure of the existing system of treatment was largely accepted by leading public figures(26) and led in part to the establishment of the 1924 Royal Commission. The Commission was set

44

up by the first Labour government as part of an attempt to initiate reforms in major welfare areas. During the First World War it became apparent to professionals and the public that the asylum system was not working properly. The emergence of psychiatry as a recognised profession within medicine and a concern with the lot of poor patients who went in for very long periods of hospitalization led to the establishment of the Commission. Its mandate was to look at the laws on lunacy as well as conditions of care in regard to the mentally ill and the mentally handicapped(27).

The Commission was composed of ten members, MPs, psychatrists, nurses and lawyers. It conducted 25 visits, of which 23 were unannounced. Ten patients were interveiwed by the Commission compared with 24 physicians and psychiatrists. The estimated cost of the inquiry was £2,385.

The 1890 Act recognised four types of admission, all of them compulsory. Medical recommendations were necessary in all cases, varying between one and two medical opinions. Magistrates had to be involved in two instances, the Judge in Lunacy in the case of "Chancery Lunatics", (i.e. offenders) and the Poor Law Relieving Officer in the case of pauper patients. The Lord Chancellor was in charge of the Act, appointing the Lunacy Commissioners. The commissioners were responsible for inspection and the welfare of all patients, including those confined to their own homes. As befits the period, women were not allowed to be commissioners. Any use of mechanical restraint had to be authorized by a doctor. Patients had the right to address in writing certain persons in authority assured that their letters would not be opened, while all other correspondence was to be looked at. Penalties were laid down for offences such as obstructing a commissioner or aiding the escape of a patient. Patients would normally be discharged only if the medical officer agreed to a suggestion coming either from the person who signed the admission petition in the first place or the local authority in the case of a pauper patient. Three commissioners, however, could veto a medical officer's decision. Usually at least one of them would have been a doctor himself.

The 1890 Act concerned itself mainly with safeguards to the liberty of the citizen as a patient. It did not concern itself with intervention provision, either quantitatively or

45

qualitatively, apart from basic physical conditions. In 1913 the Board of Control was established as the administrative body to carry out the Commission's work.

Individuals had to pay for hospitalization; the very poor were financed by their local authority, though it meant at times being transferred to a remote place which was cheaper than the nearest hospital. The burden on a neither poor nor rich family when the husband or wife became ill must have been very heavy to bear, unless aided by a charity organization. Despite the lack of breakdown of the patients' population by occupation and education the information available indicates that the majority were of working-class origin, as:

1.The majority of patients were hospitalized in county and borough hospitals; relatives were required to pay when they could. The statistics on sources of expenditure show clearly that relatives' payments for the county's hospitals amounted to 19% of the total expenditure. The implication is that the bulk of the patients came from families that could not contribute financially towards their keep in the hospital(28).

2.Those who could afford a private hospital or were recognised as middle class by virtue of their past were in private homes. The cost of stay of the impoverished middle classes was covered by charity organizations(29).

The weekly cost in 1931 for a patient in a mental hospital was given as £3. £10,361,991 were spent on the mentally ill annually(30). Two-thirds of this sum were raised through rates and only £1,281,582 were special government grants(31). The cost of private care in 1920-30 varied considerably from about 5 guineas per week to £1(32).

Prevalent approaches towards mental distress and the mentally distressed.
In the popular press and literature of the 20s the madman was portrayed as someone to be feared and pitied simultaneously(33). The prognosis for the mentally ill was seen as much more hopeless than that of the physically ill. Mental hospitals were perceived as frightening places in which people were locked in for good and being hospitalised implied being removed from ordinary life. Indeed the statistics on the rate of admission and discharge vs the total number of the patients'

46

population presented above corroborate such a belief.

It was claimed that the general public saw mental illness as caused by hereditary factors. This view implied stigmatization not only for the patient but also of all his/her family members. Such a position followed closely the eugenic emphasis in regard to the mentally defective (see chapter 3, section 3.a.i). It comes as no surprise therefore that lay people, especially of working-class origin, were terrified of hospitalization. Due to lack of relevant research it can only be speculated that working-class families would tend to postpone hospitalization as much as they could.

Three main alternative approaches to the issue of the mentally ill were acknowledged by the interested public during the 20s. Fourth and fifth possibilities to be mentioned remained dormant. The legalistic approach(34) embodied in the 1890 legislation emphasized the safeguards against unjustified hospitalization. It neither focused on aetiology and intervention nor attempted to act instead of the clinical-somatic and moral models of madness. The development of this approach coincided on the one hand with the emphasis of individuals' rights vis-a-vis the state. On the other hand it suited the emerging view of the madman as a person rather than as an animal(35). The adherents of this stand were primarily interested in the plight of the sane considered to be insane (see the activities of the League of Friends(36)). Though less interested in the mentally distressed person whose illness was not doubted, the extension in principle of basic civil rights to this category was revolutionary. Its importance should not be minimized despite the fact that it was left to representatives of the middle and upper classes (magistrates, commissioners) to decide on the soundness of mind and living conditions of predominantly working-class patients. The Lunacy Commission duties to inspect hospitals in order to secure adequate physical conditions reflect on the principle of the right of the insane to be treated as ordinary human beings, though it left out the issue of the need for specialized care and did not intervene with clinical decisions.

By the 20s the only new major issue from the legalistic viewpoint was that of giving/not giving legal recognition to the category of voluntary patienthood. To accept this group as a special legal case did not require a transformation of the legal framework but only an extension of it. Apart from the issue of the voluntary patient the legalistic orientation seemed to have spent itself at the time, as it did not advocate any changes in thinking or acting in regard to mental illness. The social disenchantment with the legalistic position was related to the greater prestige bestowed on the 'new' professions - e.g. medicine - which were perceived as less bound by class membership and more by objective, scientific knowledge. We shall come back to this point in the discussion of the objections of politicians to the role played by magistrates in certification.

The _moral_ approach developed during the 18th century, when the slogan "freeing the mentally ill from their chains" became its hallmark. Like traditional psychiatry it emerged simultaneously in England, France and the US(37). It assumed that the person should be understood in relation to his environment. The impact of the latter on the first is primary and vital(38). Thus optimal physical, psychological and environmental conditions can restore a mentally ill person back to sanity and to society. This belief was based on the acceptance of the supremacy of the environment over all the facets which influence human development. In some respects it was derived from Locke's conceptualization of the person as "Tabula Rasa". In its application to treating the mentally ill, elements of early Christianity and reminiscences of the "Good Neighbour" idea were clearly recognizable. Institutions like the Retreat in York(39) were offering sheltered retreat from the world in order to help the person regain his sanity and trust, thus enabling him to return to society. In the French version the re-education process was more pronounced than in the English one(40). At no point was the existing social order questioned or seen as leading to mental illness. Yet the moral level of the society was seen as unsatisfactory. A notion of "sin" was attached to mental illness. While the person-patient was not regarded as guilty he was seen to be morally on the "wrong side" and should be led to see and accept the "right side".

The moral approach was not against the use of medicine in treating the mentally ill but did not see it as the only or the best means of doing so. A number of its protagonists were doctors themselves, but - in contrast to the protagonists of the clinical-somatic model during the 19th century - their views were rooted in lay culture. The leaders in the UK were amateurs and saw lack of professionalism as a virtue rather than as a disadvantage. As a result they did not attempt to construct a theoretical stand of their own that would be differentiated from the acknowledged ideology(41).

The appeal of the moral approach to those individuals and groups interested in social reform should have been greater than that which the approach attracted during the 20s. Thus we are confronted with the question of the reasons leading to the relative lack of attraction of the moral approach when compared to the other orientations. This issue will be discussed below, in the summary of the alternatives before the 1924 Royal Commission and the 1929-30 Labour government.

In contrast to the legalistic and moral approaches the clinical-somatic school was more rooted within a specific professional group. As already described in chapter 1, within the clinical-somatic approach mental illness is defined as a disease, with physical causes for it, even if the manifestations are not physical(42). As a disease it was to be treated by professional doctors. The approach concentrated largely on diagnosis of the disease and treating "it" specifically rather than attempting to understand the whole person and his milieu(43). Hospital medicine - as opposed to bed-side medicine - was gaining its preferred status since the middle of the 19th century(44) and the big Victorian asylum fitted in with this approach. It took a long time for the medical paradigm to become part of the general cultural order. But by the 20s doctors were perceived as part of the new social order(45)

The dominance of this approach in medicine, in psychiatry and in the general public opinion primarily related to the changing attitudes towards science, technology, secular knowledge and the prestige bestowed gradually on "the professions" which took place during the 19th century(46). It had relatively little to do with achievements in psychiatry itself. Scull's analysis (47) shows how psychiatry was used in the previous century to fill in a social gap in containing the mentally ill despite the general recognition of the poor status of its knowledge base and intervention techniques. In this century medicine was hailed as capable of curing a number of mass illnesses, notably tuberculosis and malaria. The only equivalent

discovery in the field of mental illness was made
by Wagner-Jauregg, who found in 1917 what amounted
to a cure for general paralysis(48). It was hoped
that further scientific discoveries in psychiatry
would lead to the same excellent results. The
success in treating post-traumatic neurosis of
soldiers during the First World War by
psychotherapeutic methods was seen as further
evidence for the viability of psychiatry (see
chapter 3, section 3.a). The major implication of
the discovery made by Wagner-Jauregg was that all
mental illnesses may have a single physical cause
at their root and it is a matter of time and effort
within the framework of medical research before the
causes would be located and controlled. This point
of view appealed to the lay person not less than to
the professional psychiatrist or nurse, because of
its simple and straight line of logic, the neat
solution it offered and the prestige carried over
from general medicine. The assumption that medicine
was value free added to the readiness of people
from different ideologies and creeds to accept that
the adjunct model of the person was the "faulty
machine type"(49) which followed the mechanistic
thinking of the period.

A beginning of the search for the role that
social factors may play in leading to and
maintaining mental illness was made in the
twenties(50). It was motivated by the public health
reasoning in regard to physical illness(51), as
well as by the disenchantment with the asylum
system. At that stage this alternative did not
constitute a challenge to the clinical-somatic
model; in part because it was more latent than
manifest. Its protagonists were less articulate and
often came from the elite of the working class,
reflecting on the political reawakening of this
class during the 20s. Re-socialization of the
mentally ill which was (and still is) synonymous
with recovery for most laymen and professionals was
thus related to an improved standard of living by
those interested in the welfare of the poorer
sections of the community. Within this orientation
too mental illness was viewed in similar terms to
those of physical illness. This similarity in
conceptualization reinforced the view that
psychiatry - like medicine - might offer a quicker
cure to mental illness than what might be
potentially available through the application of
the public health approach.

Although psychoanalysis was already practised

in London its impact on the majority of lay people was virtually non-existent. Psychoanalysis attempted a process of reinterpretation and re-socialization but its focus on individual psychology probably prevented it from forming any alliance with those voicing a public health attitude towards mental illness. The fact that it was a very close-knit and elitist movement(52) was another reason for its relatively isolated position. It should be remembered that psychoanalysis was/is an archetype of psychiatric approach which is not somatic in essence.

The three political parties of the time - the Liberals, the Conservatives and Labour - did not pay direct attention to the mentally ill or mental illness in their manifestos. It is only from their ideologies and policies on general welfare and physical health and illness that it is attempted here to abstract their attitudes towards mental illness. Both Liberals and Conservatives linked health to greater national efficiency, a reaffirmed legacy from the pre-First World War period(53).

A part of the Liberal Party and a significant component of the Labour movement were influenced by the Fabians. The latter maintained that social morality needs to and can be restored only when greater justice and improved social conditions will prevail(54). It is quite likely that the Fabians' ideas were linked with the emphasis on national efficiency and nationalism, as claimed by Semmel and Thane(55). The Fabians' approach also fitted well with the pressure in the Labour movement for social reform for the working class and the wish of the political wing of Labour for a gradual change of the existing social order(56).

The assumptions behind the Fabians' orientation and Rosebery's about health were that both illness and health are heavily influenced by standards of living rather than by biological or moral individualistic characteristics. Such an assumption implied that it is within the power of a society and its government to change these standards of living and that it is socially desirable to do so(57). Thus a shift in responsibility from the individual to society became accepted though not without a struggle as the history of social welfare policies demonstrates(58). Such an implication was certainly accepted by socialists though it derived for them from a different analysis of capitalist societies. By further application of these two principles it

51

could be inferred that mental illness - in addition to physical illness - might be the outcome of social conditions and hence could be reduced and ameliorated by the improvement of such conditions. Although it was recognised that the majority of in-patients were poor(59) this knowledge did not have an impact on lay people's thinking on either aetiology or intervention. These data, however, did influence the wish to secure equal rights to paupers as to non-pauper patients(60). One can only speculate as to the reasons behind the narrowness of this approach but it seems plausible to assume that the attraction of the universality of the clinical-somatic approach - where no class differences are acknowledged - appealed to socialists too and thus prevented them from giving social and political meaning to the data confronting them.

The taken-for-granted supremacy of the prevailing model of scientific thinking and method was shared by the majority of all different political shades. Professionalism too became socially desirable, especially by the Labour Party which preferred the new professions to those which symbolized the old order, such as magistrates and lawyers. The occupational composition of Labour MPs shows clearly a gradual shift from workers to professionals(61).

The element of re-education, so emphasized by the moral approach and its preoccupation with the moral character of the society re-appears in the Fabians' orientation. Yet the shift to a collectivist orientation on the one hand and the belief in science and expertise on the other hand were more than counter-balancing the potential attractiveness of the traditional moral approach towards the mentally ill. These relatively new views reinstated psychiatrists as the carriers of a revised moral approach in which they became the reflection of accepted social responsibility towards the mentally ill (i.e. the readiness to provide them with the best available treatment). The fact that the best available methods did not produce satisfactory results could be shelved aside in the hope for a better, progressive future and in the light of the weakness of the other approaches.

Therefore the alternatives before the 1924 Royal Commission and the Labour government at the time and in 1929-30 in regard to intervention and legislation on mental illness were four:
1.To adhere to the clinical-somatic approach.

2.To tighten even further the 1890 legal system of admissions, discharges, patients' and staff's rights, leaving the intervention in the hands of doctors.
3.To apply a public health approach to mental illness and combining it with the medical model
4.A combination of the first three alternatives.

To judge which possibility was selected by the Royal Commission and the government we have to look at the main recommendations of the Commission and at the basic tenets of the 1930 Mental Treatment Act(62).
The Royal Commission suggested that:

1.While mental illness was manifested in the inability of the patient to maintain his social equilibrium the demarcation between mental and physical illness seemed to be increasingly unjustifiable.
2.In addition to certification voluntary admission should be made legally and easily available to ensure: a.patient's co-operation; b.early intervention; c.decrease in the stigma attached to hospitalization; d.patient's liberty.
3.Abolition of the connection with the Poor Law and the legal differences between private and pauper patients was urged.
4.Aftercare should be provided throughout the country. Though to be funded by the local authorities it should be carried out by voluntary associations. Aftercare services were to include out-patient clinics, observation beds in general hospitals and the continuation of the work of the Mental Aftercare Association.
5.Doctors should be defended from the possibility of being sued by patients or relatives, unless there are reasons to suspect acting in bad faith.
6.Patients' and relatives' rights should be brought to their attention by the Board of Control. The Commission's practical suggestion was to put notices in each ward.
7.The Commission found no basis for the numerous allegations of ill treatment of patients. To the contrary, it was impressed by the degree of skill and dedication of the staff in the various institutions visited.

Three of the seven conclusions follow the legalistic alternative: the abolition of differences in legal status which were based on class differences; the creation of the category of voluntary patients and making public patients' and relatives' rights.

The call for the provision of mental health services in the community is the nearest to the public health reasoning in encouraging secondary and tertiary prevention(63). In contrast to physical public health however the commission did not concern itself with primary prevention.

The redefinition of mental illness as another type of physical illness brought the first further than before within the fold of the latter - i.e. into medicine. The prevailing structure of services and its personnel were warmly defended by the Commission, which praised the existing level of care, protected doctors from being sued by ex-patients and relatives and called for the employment of more nurses and psychiatrists. In fact the creation of the voluntary patient category meant that many more people would be referred or self-referred for the available treatment in the existing institutions. At the same time it was hoped that the out-patients system would be developed on a larger scale.

The only exception taken to the system appeared in the Commission's recommendation that the number of beds per hospital should not exceed one thousand. In addition hospital wards should be organised as 'villas' - i.e. as relatively autonomous units. The notion of a one thousand bed hospital as a small institution or that wards could become autonomous given the rigid hierarchical structure of the hospital system seems rather unrealistic, though it reflects on the conditions in hospitals at the time.

The acceptance in principle of the existing system of services including the Board of Control ruled out the possibility for radical changes in the mental illness/health arena.

While the legalistic approach was evident in the Commission's suggestions it became secondary in importance to the clinical-somatic orienation: the major status to be conferred (i.e. that of a patient) was conceptualized within the framework of medical thought. This master status(64) was recognized by the Commission as one which went beyond the boundaries of class, sex and age - re-indicating the attraction of the medical approach as one which transcends the accepted social markers. K. Jones is right in viewing this recommendation as revolutionary(65) in a period

54

where class and sex were used as social dividing lines in everyday practice and theory.

Today's awareness of the likelihood of stereotyping and stigmatizing patients when they are stripped of their social past(66) was unheard of in the 20s. Patienthood as a master status was seen as beneficial to the person in permitting him/her to give up ordinary responsibilities on a hopefully temporary basis in which professional attention was to be given. Alignment with physical illness was seen as providing not only medical expertise but also a major tool in demystifying the demonological meaning attached to mental illness.

Without saying so the Commission gave a vote of no confidence in psychiatry but one of great confidence in medicine, for the reasons outlined above. The public health approach was the least prominent in the Commission's recommendations: while the Commission viewed favourably aftercare services the latter were not given the same unequivocal support attached to the establishment of the category of the voluntary patient. Pre-care facilities - i.e. preventive measures - did not come into the Commission's conclusions. On the one hand this position relates to the positive acceptance of the existing system. The system was built around hospital intervention in acute and chronic conditions of mental disorder and therefore was not geared towards prevention. On the other hand it was linked to the emphasis on the individualistic components of both aetiology and intervention within the medical model.

The Mental Treatment Act endorsed most of the Royal Commission's recommendations. It went further towards the clinical approach by excluding magistrates from being involved in the entry of voluntary patients. The Act moved away from the Commission's suggestion on aftercare services by making them into permissive duties of local authorities. The recommendation to display relatives' and patients' rights on the wards was eliminated. The Ministry's position should be understood as part of the configuration of attitude expressed by the politicians which are described in details in the following chapter.

The 1930 Mental Treatment Act produced three radical changes from the past:

1.The introduction of voluntary admission.
2.The abolition of mental illness as a category

55

within the framework of the Poor law.
3.The appropriation of aftercare facilities to
the responsibility of local authorities.

However, only the first of these changes was
to be implemented in the inter-war period. Even
this innovation was legislated in such a way as to
make it very uncomfortable for the future voluntary
patient to apply for.
To conclude, the 1930 Mental Treatment Act
reflected closely the shift in the educated
public's views towards a positive approach to both
medicine and professionalism.

References
1.Taylor, A. J. P. (1963) The First World War,
Penguin, Harmondsworth.
2.Fussell, P. (1975) The Great War and Modern
Memory, Oxford University Press, London.
3."Only Connect" - it could be said that these two
words, so seductive in their simplicity, so
misleading in their ambiguity, had more influence
in shaping the emotional attitudes of the English
government class between the two world wars than
any other single phrase in the English language.
Rees.G. (1972) A Chapter of Accidents, Michael
Joseph, London, p.95.
4.Cole, G. D. H., Postgate, R. (1966) The Common
People, Methuen, London.
5.Thane,P. (1982) The Foundations of the Welfare
State, Longman, London, p.163.
6.Rowntree, B. S. (1941) Poverty and Progress,
Longman , London, pp.28-9, 103-4.
7.See ref. no.4, p.41.
8.Pimlott, B. (1977) Labour and the Left in the
1930's, Cambridge University Press, Cambridge.
Thane, P. (ed) (1978) The Origins of British Social
Policy, Croom Helm, London.
9.Bauman, Z. (1972) Between Class and Elite: The
Evolution of the British Labour Movement: A
Sociological Study, University of Manchester Press,
Manchester.
10.Brown, J. (1978) Social Control and the
Modernization of Social Policy: 1830-1929. In:
Thane, P. op. cit., ref. no. 8, pp.126-146.
11.Crowther, A. M. (1978) The Later Years in the
Workhouse: 1830-1929. In Thane, ref. no.8,
pp.36-55.
12.Gilbert, B. B. (1966) The Evolution of National
Insurance in Great Britain: Origins of the Welfare
State, Michael Joseph, London.

13.Annual report of the Ministry of Health, Command Paper, 1932-33, XXV, pp.82-84.
14.Hansard, Vol. 237, pp.590, 1456.
15.See ref. no.13.
16.Brenner, M. H. (1973) Mental Illness and the Economy, Harvard University Press, Cambridge, Mass.
17.UK Annual Abstracts of Statistics, 1935-1946, Table 37 and No.13.
18.Jones, K. (1972) A History of the Mental Health Services, Routledge and Kegan Paul, London, pp.253-254.
19.Hansard, vol 237, p.580.
20.Lord, J. R. (1929) The Evolution of the Nerve Hospital as a Factor in the Progress of Psychiatry, Journal of Mental Sciences, 75, pp.307-15.
Leeper, R. R. (1931) Some Reflections on the Progress of Psychiatry, Journal of Mental Sciences, 77, pp.683-91.
21.Lomax, M. (1921) The Experiences of an Asylum Doctor, Allen and Unwin, London.
22.Hansard, Vol. 235, p.961.
23.See ref. no. 21 and: Hansard, Vol. 237, p.1455, Vol. 247, p.1631, Vol. 250, pp.507-8, Vol. 254, p.1455.
24.Clark, D. H. (1964) Administrative Therapy, Tavistock, London.
25.Parry-Jones, W. (1972) The Trade in Lunacy, Routledge and Kegan Paul, London, pp.31-32.
26.Hansard, Vol. 235, p.2544, Vol. 237, p.2530.
27.Lunacy (consolidation) Act 1890 and Lunacy Act 1891.
28.See ref. no. 13, p.84.
29.See for example the history of the 'Crown Lodge' hospital as related in: Jones, K., Sidebottom, A. (1962) The Mental Hospital at Work, Routledge and Kegan Paul, London.
30.See ref. no. 13.
31.Ibid.
32.See ref. no. 25.
33.Hansard, Vol. 235, p.972.
34.Jones, K. (1960) The Triumph of Legalism. In: Mental Health and Social Policy: 1845-1959, Routledge and Kegan Paul, London, pp.7-42.
35.Scull, A. (1978) Museums of Madness, Macmillan, London, pp.59-73.
36.See ref. no.18.
37.Foucault, M. (1967) Madness and Civilization, Tavistock, London.
Rothman, D. (1971) The Birth of the Asylum, Little Brown, New York.
38.Ibid.

39.Tuke, D. H. (1882) Chapters in the History of the Insane in the British Isles, Routledge and kegan Paul, London.
40.See ref. no.37.
41.See ref. no.35
42.Kraeplin, E. (1906) Lectures on Clinical Psychiatry, 2nd revised edition, Bailliere, London.
43.Hunter, R., Macalpine, I. (ed) (1963) Three Hundred Years of Psychiatry, Oxford University Press, London.
44.Armstrong, D. (1979) The Emancipation of Biographical Medicine, Journal of Social Sciences and Medicine, 13A, pp.1-9.
45.Parry, J., Parry, N. (1976) The Rise of the Medical Profession, Croom Helm, London.
46.Johnson, T. (1972) Professions and Power, Macmillan, London.
Peterson, J. (1978) The Medical Profession in Mid Victorian London, University of California Press, Berkeley.
47.See ref. no. 35.
48.Sim, M. (1969) Introduction to Psychiatry, Churchill Livingstone, Edinburgh, p.117.
49.Russell Davies (1970) Depression as Adaptation to Crisis, British Journal of Medical Psychology, 43, pp.109-16.
50.Hansard, Vol. 235, pp.20, 29 .
51.Frazer, W. M. (1950) The History of English Public Health, Bailliere, London.
52.Jones, E. (1957) The Life and Work of S. Freud, Hogarth Press, London.
53.Semmel, B. (1960) Imperialism and Social Reform, Allen and Unwin, London.
54.Pease, A. (1961) The History of the Fabian Society, Heinemann, London.
Pinker, R. (1971) Social Theory and Social Policy, Heinemann, London, pp.80-94.
55.See ref. no. 53 and no. 8.
56.See ref. no. 9.
57.See ref. no. 54.
58.For example see: McNicol, J. (1978) Family Allowances and Less Eligibility. In: ref. no.8, pp.173-202.
59.Hansard, Vol. 235, p.2544, Vol. 227, p.2545.
60.For example, see the Recommendations of the Royal Commission on Lunacy and Mental Disorder, 1926.
61.See ref. no.9.
62.The Royal Commission on Lunacy and Mental Disorder (The Macmillan Commission), 1926.
63.For the definition of these terms in mental

health see Caplan, G. (1959) Concepts of Mental Health and Consultation, Children Bureau Publications, New York. no. 373
64.Becker, H. (1963) Outsiders, The Free Press, New York.
65.See ref. no. 34, pp.111.
66.Garfinkel, H. (1956) Conditions of Successful Degradation Ceremonies, American Journal of Sociology, 61, pp.420-24.
Goffman, I. (1961) Asylums, Penguin, Harmondsworth.
Scheff, T. (1975) The Labeling Theory of Mental Illness. In: Scheff, T. (ed) Labeling Madness, Prentice Hall, Englewood-Cliff, New Jersey, pp.21-33.

3 Professionals' Theories and Value Preference in the Twenties

3.a. Psychiatry and Psychiatrists in the Twenties: An Overview.

Scull(1) has documented the coming into power of psychiatry in the second half of the 19th century, a move which was consolidated in the 20s. For example, the Association of Medical Officers of Asylums and Hospitals for the Insane changed its name to the Medico-Psychological Association in 1865. Its official journal (The Journal of Mental Science) appeared first in 1858.

Nevertheless the working conditions of the majority of psychiatrists during 1920-1930 were still poorer than those of physicians. The asylum psychiatrists lived in tied accommodation, had to ask permission to get married and earned a third of a physician's salary(2). The superintendent of a hospital had the right to dismiss instantly every employee, including psychiatrists.

The major views expressed during the period were neurological and psychoanalytical in orientation. While the first was the dominant trend the latter was trying hard to be heard. Even when expressed, the psychoanalytic position was often either distorted or ignored(3). The neurological point of view approached psychiatric syndromes as diseases of the brain. Research at Birmingham University on the function and structure of the brain, on drugs and hypnosis(4) was upheld as the archetype of promising research. The focus was on diagnosis as a key factor to successful intervention and research and on the hospital as the right setting for both. The "pro neurology" lobby did not oppose out-patient clinics but favoured their location inside hospitals(5), thus securing control over them for the medical profession.

Despite the inclusion of psychology in the title of the Medico-Psychological Association, the impact of any type of psychology is not easily found in the professional literature. Even the idea of a range on which the normal and the abnormal co-exist - typical of most psychological approaches - was rejected by the majority of psychiatrists. Following 19th century psychiatry it was restated that the differences between the normal and the abnormal were a matter of drastic qualitative and quantitative differences and therefore could not be contained within one range.

Rarely were social factors mentioned in regard to psychiatric illness. When mentioned, the aim was to state that they merely reflect the existence of somatic causes. For example, Dr. Carswell from Glasgow spoke about a survey on the incidence of mental illness in the city(6). The fact that most patients were poor was seen by him as proving the case for hereditary factors. Therefore he concluded that caring for these groups would merely reinforced the survival of the unfit. The Eugenics Society was helped by the Medico-Psychological Association in preparing an educational film on the mentally ill and the mentally handicapped(7). This cooperation and Dr. Carswell's views indicate that there was no basic disagreement between the Eugenics Society and the psychiatric association. (For a review of the aims and methods of the Eugenics movement, which was devoted to the improvement of the genetic base of Britons, see ref. no.8.) Instead, psychiatrists were unhappy about the state of the huge Victorian custodial hospitals which were quite unlike ordinary general hospitals. The transformation of these institutions into "proper" hospitals would allow psychiatry to be more integrated into medicine and to move out of the public assistance system. Their suggestion how to bring about this major change will be discussed in the section on contributions to journals.

The experiences of shell-shocked soldiers during the First World War focused professional and public attention on the neuroses. While before the war neuroses were recognized as a distinct diagnostic category, neither explanations nor methods of intervention were specifically related to it within the mainstream of British psychiatry. When sufferers from neurosis could not hide it any more they were treated like those who suffered from a psychotic illness. Professional intervention with soldiers suffering from the effects of shell-shock was initiated first by a psychologist (C.S. Myers) who was ready to accept the lack of somatic causes while endorsing the impact of psychological stress. He was followed by a group of British psychiatrists who were sympathetic to Freudian ideas but who refrained from using psychoanalytical methods with shell-shock sufferers. The treatment included: 1.Removing the soldier from the front. 2.Demonstrating sympathy and understanding particularly in a group situation. 3.Use of hypnosis and suggestion. 4.Attempting to send the soldier back to active service as soon as possible. This type of intervention has been repeated with minor variations during the Second World War and is practised in active combat situations today too(9).

In the 1914-1918 period the army could have hardly afforded to have so many soldiers running away from the battlefield in terms of its reputation and efficiency. According to Henderson and Gillespie the annual number of such soldiers during the war was 6,000(10). The new approach to shell-shock sufferers offered a neat solution to the legitimation and motivation crisis which was felt during the war. By attributing the label of illness unintentional irresponsibility of individuals is imputed which removes the blame and doubts from the collective. The image of the soldier as psychiatrically disturbed rather than as a deserter implies lack of badness and guilt on the one hand. On the other hand personal vulnerability and weakness are suggested.

There is no doubt that sick soldiers received a more humane treatment as the result of the change in the labels: to be sent to an army psychiatric hospital was an infinitely more humane intervention than to be shot. However, one wonders why the army chiefs were ready to accept the psychologists' redefinition: was it because of the unexpected magnitude of the problem? Was it because of the prospect of having the soldiers back was an improvement on shooting them from the perspective of personnel demands? Was it the impact of the fact that upper-class recruits suffered too from shell-shock and publicized it? (see S. Sassoon's memoires(11)). The solution offered by clinical psychology provided the army chiefs with a way out of one of their stumbling bloks.

The image of restoration embedded in this case is fairly explicit: a recovered patient is a soldier able to fight again. As such it goes beyond the removal of symptoms, into the realm of social functioning. Thus it moves a long way towards emphasizing one's obligations towards the collective rather than one's own needs. In this way subjective experiences received an objectivized meaning, which was then fed back to the individual and his relatives. The fact that this new meaning is delivered by professional people adds to its aura of authority and objectivity, leaving the rather confused individual with virtually no other option but to accept the judgement and to bury his doubts about the collective.

A clear role of an intermediary emerges here: the psychologist/psychiatrist speaks about the patient-soldier to his chiefs and society on the one hand, interpreting in a new light a well known and socialy undesirable type of behaviour. He is also advocating a new mode of social attitude and intervention. On the other hand he comes to the patient as his supporter against the rest of the system, offering him sympathy where before only abuse and punishment descended. At the same time the professional comes as a social agent, ensuring that the recovery of the patient is channelled into a socially desirable form.

Although somatically-oriented psychiatrists were not involved in the intital stage of re-interpretation and the battle for its social acceptance, they too followed in the end the guidelines of management it implied. Thus the confrontation between the new explanation and intervention and that of the clinical-somatic approach were swept under the carpet. Moreover, psychiatrists annexed this unexpected bonus as if it was an achievement of medicine(12). None of the psychologists or psychoanalysts involved protested against this annexation, perhaps because they too welcomed the affiliation to medicine.

Thus the new intervention in regard to traumatic neuroses offers a pertinent illustration of the importance of uncovering the unsaid. At the conceptual level, however, the army psychiatrists and the majority of civilian psychiatrists denied the validity of the alternative perspective(13).

Within the psychoanalytic camp the impact of the war led to rethinking. Freud reformulated his view on aggression, the death instinct and the treatment of traumatic neurosis in the light of the shell shock phenomenon and the whole war experience(14). The opening of the Tavistock Clinic in 1920 followed directly from the devlopments during the war in regard to neurosis(15). The group which initiated the Tavistock consisted of professionals who were active in the work with shell-shock soldiers. The clinic signified a major departure from accepted psychiatric tradition in terms of the organizational and theoretical framework as well as in the mode of management of patients. The assumption that many people with psychiatric symptoms do not need to be locked up was a confirmation of the general public's threshold of tolerance, as the latter usually did not refer people with neurotic disturbances to psychiatrists or asylums. At the same time it expressed a major departure from public opinion in suggesting that relatively minor behavioural and emotional problems require professional intervention. Thus the scope for psychological and psychiatric intervention was considerably extended. It led to new definitions of tasks and roles for psychiatrists, clinical psychologists and social workers. It also led to the exclusion of nurses from the new avenue of practice, an issue which will be discussed in the section on nurses. The emphasis on an out-patient clinic stands in contrast to the one expressed by the majority of psychiatrists at the time on the need for more hospitals, for separate institutions for compulsorily and voluntarily admitted patients(16). Moreover, the construction of a setting independent of a hospital went against the preferred mode of operation within established psychiatry which could not envisage itself outside the realm of the hospital.

The focus on psychoanalytic psychotherapy was another feature which stood out in contrast to mainstream psychiatric practice. Psychoanalysis shuns giving advice, telling people how to regulate their everyday life and attempts not to rely on drug therapy. Psychoanalysis provided a challenge to the existing paradigm of psychiatric thinking and practice. The response to this challenge ranged from: 1.Almost denying its existence; 2.Attacks on its assumed unscientific base and its lack of relevance to the majority of the mentally ill, i.e. those suffering from psychosis; 3.A polite dismissal of its significance(17).

In part such a situation was possible because of the relative weakness of psychoanalysis as a pressure group. Their wish to remain affiliated to medicine and their disinterest in social policy prevented them from attempting to put their case to the politicians and other influential components of the general public.

Following the line of non-provocation the founders of the Tavistock Clinic stressed that they did not neglect the neuro-physiological aspect either at the diagnostic stage or during intervention(18). As an institution the Tavistock merits our attention for several reasons. It was the first clinic unattached to a hospital with the aim of working with neurotic clients and offering psychotherapy. In addition it was also the first setting which developed a multi-disciplinary team including social workers and psychologists. Services were offered to both adults and children.

The clinic did not get the blessing of the psychiatric profession, but got that of the government. For example the Conservative Prime Minister's wife was a member of the board of governors. Miss Macdonald - the Labour Prime Minister's daughter - stressed in a ceremony at the Tavistock the aim of "redirecting the mentally ill deviants towards ordinary social functioning"(19). Thus the politicians' circle seemed to have grasped the new setting's potential for social control and care.

The only attempt from within established psychiatry to offer a similar service to the one provided by the Tavistock clinic took place at the Maudsley Hospital. The latter was an exception in the asylums scene in more than one way(20). It was the only hospital in England to treat many acute cases on a volunary basis already in the 20s. Its policy of intervention followed more closely that of mainstream British psychiatry at the time than the Tavistock ever did.

M. Klein's revision of Freud's views on child development, the reasons for psychosis and neurosis began during the 20s(21). They paved the way to original British contributions to psychoanalysis during that period and later.

To summarize, the decade between 1920 and 1930 saw the beginning of the expansion of British psychiatry in this century, an expansion which was often diversified and contradictory.

3.a.i.The analysis of psychiatric textbooks.
Craig and Beaton's "Psychological Medicine" reached its fourth edition in 1926. Several of its chapters had been rewritten specifically for this edition. The book aimed at the audience of postgraduate

65

medical students. The sequence of presentation moves from description to aetiology, diagnosis, prognosis and treatment. Prognosis is based only on frequency and severity of clinical symptoms. Kreplin's diagnostic scheme is adopted with minor changes but without explaining its principles or the justification for using it. The unit of description and analysis is the individual patient's clinical symptomatology. Apart from patients' gender no other background variable is taken notice of. "The Patient" is therefore a highly generalized entity, which exists ouside an identified social context.

The book expresses a tolerant and commonsensical approach for its period. For example masturbation is described as the most prevalent sexual perversion but one which "in itself has no particular effect on either the mental or physical condition but if carried to excess or continued beyond adolescence it indicates a failure to develop normally"(pp.106-7). Throughout the text the authors state firmly their belief that mental disorders are biogenic in origin, inclusive of neurotic states. Thus "the causes of the anxiety state are the causes of anxiety but certain people seemed to be innately predisposed to it especially those of neuropathic inheritance" (p.257). The emphasis on the somatic perspective resulted also in a chapter on insanity and physical diseases (chapter 19). The chapter includes such headings as "Phthisis and Insanity", "Rheumatic Fever and Insanity", "Influenza and Insanity", "Renal Disease and Insanity" among the less traditional possibilities. While no specific relationship between heart disease and insanity is proposed, "Rheumatic fever is another disease closely connected with mental disorder, it may alternate with insanity in the same way as gout and diabetes" (p.304). Whether this possibility was due to problems in controlling delirium states or not is difficult to judge. It exhibits however a tendency to carve a wide empire for psychiatry.

A description of psychological processes is provided in the book. Emotions are described from McDougal's learning theory viewpoint. But this perspective is not linked to any other component of the book (e.g. diagnosis, aetiology, prognosis and treatment) leaving one to wonder whether there was a place for psychology in a book on psychological medicine. Psychoanalysis too is politely presented only to be shelved off without discussion.

Throughout the text the terms "medical psychology" and "psychiatry" are used interchangeably. As both terms are not defined the authors' views on the differences between them are left uncovered.

Under the section "Miscellaneous" we find a chapter on treatment (pp.346-367). Its sub-headings illustrate best its concerns: "General - in which the need for patience and winning the confidence of the patient is stressed. Bed treatment, diet, compulsory feeding, bowels, intestinal disinfection, exercise, violence, suicide, homicide, moral treatment, correction, psychotherapy, correspondence, visits of friends, religious services, special duties of nurses, drugs, baths, electrotherapy, convalescence."

In the section on drugs the position taken is that "few drugs apart from narcotics have any specific action, but medical officers of mental hospitals are apt to forget that most laymen have a firm traditional belief in the omnipotence of the physic" (p.366). Thus lay culture is taken into consideration as a matter of fact, even if viewed as inferior to medical understanding. Looking at a specific example it is suggested that in anxiety states the patient should be advised that "He must give up late hours, regulate his work, take fresh air, adequate diet and moderate exercise, and correct any faults of living." We are told that the patient "suffers acutely in his self-esteem." The remedy to this problem is for him to become convinced by the physician that "his instability is a sign of physical disturbance not of the deterioration of his personality" (p.261).

The intervention offered is one of total management of the person's life - a repetition of the moral approach without admitting it yet labelling it "scientific". Available physical treatment methods were not believed to be useful apart from their psychological impact or as means of decreasing restlessness. Yet again this admission is presented in such a way that its significance vis-a-vis the firm belief in somatic aetiology is masked.

A contradictory picture emerges in regard to the relationships between understanding a given clinical entity and the intervention prescribed. In the case of anxiety states, for example, psychological reasons and a biological basis are postulated only to lead to the suggestion that the patient will recover more quickly if he would be made to believe that he is physically ill. On the whole intervention methods seem to be unrelated to the stated explanatory position but the authors seem unaware of this inconsistency and its possible significance. Acknowledgement of insufficient knowledge in regard to the majority of the phenomena presented reoccurs. Nevertheless the authors do not express any doubts as to the reliability and validity of their preferrred perspective, namely the overriding primacy of biological factors in the causation of mental distress. Despite the admission of lack of knowledge we are not told what are the questions to be asked and/or the methods to follow in the pursuit of answers. As already mentioned brain research was seen as the most promising research direction. However its possible connection to the many admissions of lack of knowledge and certainty were not specified.

Craig and Beaton's book seems to have been written from a prescriptive stance, offering pragmatic knowledge. Such a perspective takes for granted what most theorists would view as assumptions to be made explicit and questions to be formulated. In addition it does not aim to provide the reader with analytic tools but with an overall descriptive view and commonsensical intervention methods. Portrayed as "commonsense knowledge" prescriptions are rendered as unproblematic(22). As long as the authority of the prescribers was not doubted this aspect became an additional advantage in the battle for the social acceptance of psychiatry.

The attitude to popular beliefs about madness promoted by the authors is intriguing. They seem set out to win the lay public by providing it with the type of explanations and interventions assumed to be acceptable to the latter. Yet the writers claim to adhere to different concepts and beliefs. However the wish to make the public use psychiatry seems to be overriding.

The portrait of the patient is of a person without qualities apart from an inherent vulnerability to withstand the pressures of life. Few case descriptions appear in the book; people's background is omitted from the descriptions as well as their feelings, their original utterances or those of their family members. "The Patient" is a clinical, abstract concept, without even a hint of a subjective dimension. It is difficult to delineate their images of the restored patient-person apart from the removal of psychiatric symptoms.

The authors' value preferences will be summarized together with those of the writers of the other textbook.

Henderson and Gillespie's "A Textbook of Psychiatry" appeared first in 1927. By now it has become a classic, with a fourth edition in 1936 and an eighth in 1956. The book has survived as a basic textbook for many years, a feat which Craig and Beaton have not managed to achieve. An intriguing sideline would be to attempt to explain why this book succeeded where others failed. As a popular textbook it should reflect the major preoccupations and solutions of British psychiatry during this century.

Its aim is: "To present psychiatry as a living subject, with important relations not only to general medicine but to the social problems of everyday life"(preface). While it is unclear what is meant by a "living subject" it will be pertinent to observe throughout the book: 1.If the relations to social problems are indeed explored; 2.the proposed type of relations with general medicine.

Following A. Meyer, mental illness is defined as "the cumulative result of unhealthy reactions of the individuals's mind to its environment" (pref. viii). Thus illness is exchanged for unhealthy reactions. Health is defined much later in the book as "the healthy attitude to life's difficulties and problems is a direct, aggressive, matter-of-fact one, designed to overcome the difficulty once and for all, with the result that the individual feels satisfied, and can proceed confidently to his next problem"(p.195). Therefore unhealthy reactions would include behaviour, thoughts and feelings which frequently do not demonstrate directness, aggression and matter-of-factness. The value base of this definition of health and unhealth becomes quite clear: it is one which plainly typifies success in our society and which would not put its seal of approval on poets, artists and shy people.

A qualitative jump is taken when the text focuses on specific categories of mental disorder. Regarding manic-depressive psychosis Kreplin's formulation is adopted: "In this group he included the whole domain of periodic and circular insanity. He considered that all these conditions were representations of a single morbid process" (p.124). "Schizophrenia, in its typical form, consists of a slow, steady deterioration of the

entire personality ..it involves principally the
affective life and expresses itself in disorder of
feeling, of conduct and of thought, and an increase
in withdrawal of interest from the environment"
(p.192). A clinical, rather than an ethical or
normative, language is employed to describe
specific categories of mental illness. This
language focuses on severity and scope of
deterioration of functioning and on whether a
category represents one process or more. Only in
the case of neurosis does the assumed aetiology
play a major role in the definition. It is also
with this category that patients' subjective
perceptions are incorporated into the definition.
The difference in the conceptual level of the
definition of psychotic vs. neurotic disorders may
lie in the need to explain the lack of severe
deterioration in the functioning ability of those
suffering from neurosis. The two other definitions
remain largely at the level of reiteration of the
list of symptoms.

Although the criteria for formulating
definitions are not made explicit a major emphasis
is put on classification. The latter is to be based
on symptomatology, aetiology, psychology and
physiology. General aetiology receives attention in
a chapter devoted to it. However, when it comes to
specific categories the issue of aetiology often
merits only a short paragraph in the section on
diagnosis. Nearly two-thirds of the book deal with
symptomatology, with less than a quarter on
treatment.

Aetiology is described as "the most important
question in psychiatry ..the hope of the future
lies in preventive measures that may be deduced
from its study" (p.24). The major aetiological
factors mentioned, in order of importance the
authors ascribe to them, are: heredity, alcoholism,
toxication and infections, fatigue and exhaustion,
trauma, mental states, age, race, culture, climate,
sex, endocrine influences. Under the title "general
psychopathology" we find an exposition of Freud's
theory on the production of symptoms. This approach
is presented not as an aetiological position but as
a description of the processes involved in creating
symptoms and is later dismissed as too complicated
for use. Thus the chapter on aetiology has
virtually nothing on psychological and social
factors, despite the claim made in the preface and
in the introductory chapter. The existing section
on culture amounts to citing statistical

70

differences on the prevalence of mental disorders in different societies wihout attempting to make sense of the figures.

The long section on heredity (15 pages) attempts to describe the various approaches to the issue. It demonstrates that not much was known about the possible processes at work and that the validity of what was known was rather doubtful. This state of affairs, admitted by the authors, does not detract them in any way from the position that "the role of heredity in relation to mental disorder is of fundamental importance and demands the closest study and investigation. Few definite formulae can be yet laid down. But there is evidence that every civilized nation, owing to the economic and social burden of caring for the unfit, is paying more attention to racial qualities" (p.27). While once more the emphasis shifts from possible scientifically accummulated evidence to the realm of moral and social decisions, this shift is made without an awareness of the gap between the two levels of the argument. It is subtly implied that the evidence available is sufficient as a basis for social decisions while the paragraph in fact admits that this is not the case. The influence of the Eugenic movement can be detected in this section as well as in others, some of which will be mentioned specifically later.

Case descriptions list mental disorder and "unhealthy" features of family members other than the patient, wherever such characteristics were known, especially in cases of mental deficiency. No doubt is raised as to whether mental deficiency is a case of mental distress or not. Yet in the diagnosis section of every category heredity occupies a much lower explicit profile, with the exception of schizophrenia and mental deficiency. Instead the emphasis is put on toxic factors and the stage of physiological development (p.169). The environment is given the status of a predisposing factor for involutional psychosis while faulty habits and influenza are seen as relevant factors for schizophrenia (pp.169, 195, 200).

As for the neuroses, Freud's views are given an airing but the favoured explanations are those put forward by Dejerine and Ross. Dejerine postulated that there is always an emotional cause in the genesis of psychopathic (sic neurotic) states (p.426). These causes - which remain unspecified - lie at the core of pyschic and physical disturbances. Conscious inferences are

71

made but they are mistaken and autosuggestion of physical disease results. In hysteria a "peculiar emotional constitution" acts together with an emotional disturbance to bring it about (p.426). According to Henderson and Gillespie, Ross clarified further Dejerine's formulation by applying Pavlov's concept of conditional reflex to the theory of emotional origins of neurotic symptoms. Thus the preference for behaviourism over psychoanalysis as a system of explanation is already noticeable. It seems that Dejerine's position is preferred to that of Freud because it is "less involved" (p.426), although it is acknowledged that the first perspective is less elaborated and less detailed than the second approach. Thus a simple conceptualization is favoured over a complex one. But to use simplicity as the sole criterion sounds rather naive when a claim for the status of a scientific discipline is at stake. Symptomatology usually follows the aetiological section, described by numerous short vignettes. Case studies include: 1.Reference to family history of mental ilness. 2.A description of social assertiveness or lack of it by the patient. 3.Educational and occupational indicators. 4.The culminating event of the outburst of the illness. 5.Behaviour in the hospital. 6.The patient's own account of his/her problem. 7.Evaluation of mental abilities. 8.Final outcome at the time of writing.

As the list demonstrates, symptomatology covers much more than the description of symptoms. It implicitly incorporates notions about aetiology, normative behaviour and outcomes (e.g. by giving prominence to social assertiveness and to the prevalence of mental illness in the family while omitting variables such as family relationships).

The section on symptomatology allows us to understand which features of the patient are moved to the foreground. Gender counts in so far as the major difficulties encountered by men and women are described as essentially different: men's problems are located in the educational and occupational sphere while women's issues are focused on their relations with men (such as husbands, fathers, lovers, but not with male children). These areas reflect on the social conceptualization at the time of likely fields of difficulties for men and women. However the problems are not presented as an outcome of a reflection of social emphasis but as an individual's pathology, since we are looking at cases of failure to achieve socially required standards. Thus despite the promise in the introduction to link psychiatry to social problems this line is left largely untouched, with the exception of sterilization, to which we will come later. Social behaviour of patients is another major layer which receives attention. An implicit comparison is being made between the ideal of the assertive and matter-of-fact problem-solving man and the index patient who does not measure up to this ideal. Attitudes to one's family are described when they form part of the patient's complaints or misbehaviour but not otherwise. The reactions and views of family members are hardly ever mentioned. The only other level of relating to people which is frequently discussed is behaviour towards the staff. Other patients, however, are not seen as a component of the system which merits atention.

We get a glimpse of people's hopes, desires and fears from the description of precipitating events and subsequent developments. When patients' class background is mentioned it becomes a sign which confirms either the heredity factor when it relates to "the poor" or a sign of the degree of personal exceptionality when discussing middle-class clients.

Prognosis is the component which comes nearest to prediction since it attempts to predict the course of development of the illness and the person. Usually not more than half a page was written about this section. Several factors are listed as prevalent in favourable prognosis: 1.The existence of external factors. 2.A reasonably adopted pre-morbid personality. 3.An acute onset. The paragraphs on prognosis stress the variability of outcomes and therefore the uncertainty of such a prediction. We are not told how it would be possible to improve on this state of affairs and no worry is expressed about the low level of certainty of these predictions. The ideal of restoration is of a person conforming to social norms and content with his/her lot in life. The restored person is falling behind the ideal of the healthy one. It is logically consistent to assume that if heredity plays a major role in leading to mental illness then even a recovery would still leave the person behind the ideal of health since the assumed defect has not been removed or altered, only subdued and controlled.

The war experience is described in a chapter devoted to it (ch. xv). Its gist is that the war "proved that purely psychological factors can produce mental illness" (p.488). However this statement is qualified later to be correct only for the neuroses. For psychoses, personality or inheritance disposition remained the most important factor (p.488). War neurosis is perceived as a failure to adjust to the war situation (p.495) i.e. as a personal characteristic unrelated to a social crisis. While the majority of shell-shocked soldiers recovered from their neurosis, according to the authors most of them did not return to the front, or when returned were likely to relapse back into the neurotic state (p.498). The writers express scepticism about the possibility that the aetiological factors involved were indeed purely psychological even for the neurosis. The success in intervention is put down to suggestion and early removal from the front, while "the pansexualism of certain psychoanalysts received a severe blow" (p.488). The chapter is informative in providing statistics on the prevalence of shell-shock casualties in the UK, US and Ireland. It does not, however, tell us what are the implications of the war experience for the explanatory and intervention system of psychiatry.

Modes of intervention

Decisions on intervention depend primarily on whether an illness is seen as psychotic or neurotic in nature. For the first category prognosis is poor from the beginning, almost regardless of the features of the specific case. The actual intervention does not differ among the various types of psychoses, and includes the following:

1. Reducing life to the simplest level.
2. Hospitalization should start as early as possible.
3. Treatment in bed, preferably in the open air, should be adopted from the beginning.
4. Attention to the physical condition of the patient is advised, inclusive of "it is wise to start artificial feeding without much delay" in the case of the depressed patient who refuses food (p.164).
5. Sleep and a bath are recommended as forms of relaxation, together with tonics (described as helpful in the stage of convalescence).
6. "Perhaps the most important thing of all in the way of treatment is to give the patient some better understanding of the factors which have been responsible for the illness so as to prevent

a possibility or recurrence" (p.166). However little is mentioned about the forms of providing such better understanding and what its value would be in the large number of cases where heredity is assumed to be the main cause.

Only one page is given to the treatment of schizophrenic reactions (p.233-4). Tellingly this page focuses on the desirability of early detection and prevention and on occupational therapy within an institution. In contrast four pages are devoted to the discussion of anxiety states (pp.441-445). Following Ross, history taking and a physical examination are recommended as preliminaries. The provision of a psychological explanation and its acceptance by the patient are seen as the core of the intervention. The appearance of specific symptoms is viewed as related to an actual traumatic experience. Thus the set of symptoms and corresponding traumatic events has to be worked out for every patient, a device similar to the one used in psychoanalysis before the war and in behaviour modification today. How far the psychiatrist should probe into the past depends on the patient's needs (as defined by the psychiatrist). Dreams and their interpretations are mentioned too as a valuable tool but one which has to be handled with care. For the first and only time in the book the possibility of bias by the professional person is raised (p.455). However it is not suggested that those who offer psychotherapy should undergo special training.

The only illness category where a detailed description of intervention by drugs is presented is that of general paralysis (pp.323-326). Such a description could be provided because general paralysis was the only diagnostic category for which a single biochemical cause has been identified. The range of intervention suggested for psychotic disorders amounts to that offered to a highly strung person at the stage of convalescence from a physical illness. While the majority of strategies would have done no harm they are tactics to be found on the basis of commonsensical understanding.

Classification becomes the main outcome of the psychiatric enterprise together with the application of practice wisdom. The authors however continue to speak about "the real developments in psychiatry" at the time and do not express concern or unhappiness about this state of affairs. They are confident about the positive contribution of psychiatry to the treatment of the mentally ill and therefore to society at large. The lack of awareness of the gap between the claims for psychaitry and the prescription it offers is similar to that already mentioned about Craig and Beaton's book.

The place of ethics

The authors present initially an attitude of tolerance and benevolence towards the mentally ill. For example in the discussion on sterilization they suggest that such a difficult decision should be left to the individual, despite their preference for a less vague British law, but rather one like the German law. However their final solution to the issue of reproduction of the mentally ill and handicapped is one of forced segregation: "Segregation in colonies ..or in mental hospitals is the accepted and recognized mode of dealing with the majority of those who are so defective or so mentally incapacitated as to be unable to care adequately for themselves or their offspring. This is a humanitarian and helpful way, not only for caring for those who are incurable but of benefiting and curing those who may still have the capacity to adjust" (p.41). This stand reveals that one of the main aims of hospitalization is segregation not for the sake of the patient and not out of fear of violence but out of beliefs in society's right to control human reproduction. Thus the apparent tolerance seems to have a thin threshold.

The ethical and social issues involved in decisions on segregation and sterilization are not discussed, despite the promise of the authors to relate psychiatry to social problems. One wonders why they wished initially to make such a connection and what prevented them from following this path in the book. Psychiatry was linked to social problems whenever it was considered from the social policy angle. In the eyes of politicians and administrators this link was assumed to exist a priori. In the wake of World War I it was logical to follow a line that gave power and social credit to psychiatry. Yet what psychiatrists wanted most was to be an integral part of medicine. The world of medicine is assumed to be neutral of value-laden issues such as social problems. Hence when it came to spelling out the possible meaning of such links emptiness descends.

Several value judgements emerge from the two books which enable us to reconstruct their belief system:

1.Psychiatry is a scientific activity, in the same way that general medicine is.
2.The explanations offered by psychiatry are objective. The description of a mental disturbance by the person has to be translated into the objective langauge.
3.The mentally ill are unhealthy people. The healthy ones are those who are aggressive, assertive and with a matter-of-fact mentality. They are achievement motivated and do well in their education and occupation. In contrast the mentally ill lack in self-confidence, are suspicious of others and blame others for their failures (relevant only for Henderson and Gillsepie's book).
4.Mental illness is an affliction in the sense of lack of personal responsibility in bringing it upon oneself.
5.The main cause for mental disturbance is faulty heredity.
6.It is taken for granted that psychiatrists act on behalf of society in many ways, including the control over the fertility of its clientele. Likewise it is assumed that psychiatric knowledge and practice serve positively both society and the mentally distressed.
7.The core of psychiatric practice lies in diagnosis, which is the process of giving meaning to seemingly meaningless events. The essence of intervention is in hospitalization which offers a refuge from everyday life.
8.Psychiatry should relate itself to social problems, though it is not speficied how it should do so (relevant only to Henderson and Gillespie's book).

Overall comparison of the two textbooks.
Three major differences are apparent between the two books reviewed here. Firstly, Craig and Beaton's book does not aim at incorporating the relationships between psychiatry and social life, as Henderson and Gillespie's book claims to do. Secondly, the latter's text includes a long chapter on psychoanalysis which does not appear in the other book. Instead Craig and Beaton provide us with a chapter on McDougal's psychological approach. Thirdly, Henderson and Gillespie's

textbook gives ample case descriptions while the second text includes only a few.

However the first two differences are more apparent than real. As already mentioned Henderson and Gillespie's text does not actually address itself to the relationships between social life and psychiatry, although it passes judgement on social issues and describes an unusual social experience such as the war. Yet this book does pay more attention to some sociological variables, such as educational and occupational background. Likewise Freud's ideas are presented only to be later dismissed in favour of those of Dejerine and Ross. Ross's adaptation of Pavlov is much closer to McDougal's writings than to Freud's. In both books psychological understanding is applied almost exclusively to neurotic clients, leaving the bulk of the patients outside the scope of the psychological approaches.

The third difference is more a matter of style of teaching and may be one of the reasons why Henderson and Gillespie's text became and remained a popular book. It certainly managed to present psychiatry as a lively subject.

Both texts present psychiatry as a body of pragmatic knowledge leading to prescriptions. It is described as a discipline without internal contradictions and without large areas of lack of sufficient knowledge. The possible failures of psychiatry are never mentioned. When the poor recovery rate from certain diagnostic categories is hinted at, it is put down to the patient's inherent defects. Thus the lack of a critical stance towards the subject matter makes these books into prescriptions to be followed by the newly initiated.

None of the other professions is mentioned in the book, with the exception of occupational therapy.

The stand on the place of psychiatry in society follows the pattern of utilitarian thinking, as does the preference for behaviouristic explanations of mental disturbances which are assumed to be non-hereditary.

3.a.ii.Contributions to Psychiatric Journals.

The content of journals indicates that two major concerns preoccupied psychiatrists during the twenties: 1.Ensuring a more suitable treatment and admission procedure for voluntary patients. 2.The social and inter-professional standing of the profession.

It was widely recognized and accepted within professional circles that the less disturbed patients were not getting the attention and care required. Consequently it was believed that their chances for earlier recovery were jeopardized. Letters to the editor and an editorial endorsed this argument(23). The remedy suggested was to establish separate institutions for voluntary patients. The mild character of the disturbances of these patients which seem to coincide with their respectable social background were stressed by the psychiatrists. Civil rights for this category were demanded infrequently too, but not for the more severely ill patients.

Together with the request for separate institutions came the demand to allow voluntary admission to enable early treatment and to minimize stigmatization. The concern for the voluntary patient combines the interest in patients who are more like the rest of us with the likelihood of enhancing the rate of recovery.

Psychiatrists were offering a restructuring of the organizational framework of their practice and not a new intervention method based on psychiatric knowledge.

To compensate for the lack of innovation, they emphasized the stigmatizing effect of hospitalization and the positive value of already used intervention methods provided these were applied early on in the course of the illness. The inclusion of stigmatization as a crucial factor in recovery - or lack of it - stands in contradiction to the dismissal of the relevance of social factors in understanding mental distress or the insistence on the goodness of hospitalization. This inconsistency in approach was never mentioned and seems to have remained unrecognized by the professionals involved or by the general public. The fact that hospitalization on its own led to stigmatization and that therefore having separate institutions was unlikely to resolve this problem was not analysed for what it meant: fear of what went on in hospitals and the wish to dissociate onself and one's group from those put away. The wish to have people suffering from neurosis in the hospitals was related to the growing awareness of its existence since the war and the lack of new intervention methods. The opening of out-patient clinics unattached to hospitals which offered a qualitatively different approach from traditional psychiatry provided an additional incentive to ensure that this potential clientele would come under the wings of traditional psychiatry.

Psychiatrists' Social and Professional Standing.
Psychiatrists were unhappy with their social status and their standing within medicine. The case of Dr. Band(24) who was tried and found not guilty of mishandling his patients, was mentioned several times as an illustration of the misleading public image psychiatrists were subjected to. The public was also accused of wrongly assuming that psychiatrists hospitalized people unjustifiably and of refusing to accept that mental illness is a physical disease and therefore unjustly stigmatizing patients. These last two issues were seen as closely related: it was believed that if only ordinary people would see the mentally ill as suffering from a physical illness then stigmatization would be considerably reduced.

Psychiatrists saw themselves unequivocally as physicians. The fact that they earned less and were on a lower grading scale than other doctors implied that the government and the dominant elements of the medical profession did not see them as equals. However this argument was never put in writing by either side. Several attempts were made to achieve equalization by:

a. Expressing preference for physical reasons for mental distress, hospital work and research(25).
b. Strengthening the ties with the general hospital. A psychiatric ward was established in Edinburgh already in 1924. This move was praised and viewed as the preferred direction for the future of the service(26).
c. Expressing envy of the relatively independent position of American psychiatrists who were not in a "lawyer ridden land"(27).
d. Teaching psychological medicine at graduate level.
e. Establishing the Royal Medico-Psychological Association in 1926.
f. Pressure towards legislation which would broaden the circle of those treated by psychiatrists.
g. Providing extra legal defence against complaints by patients and relatives.

This last point was a test case of the value of psychiatry for legislators and the ruling groups. It symbolized the point of equality with other physicians who had already achieved such a protection - i.e. the requirement to prove in court that there is a case to be answered prior to initiating an ordinary hearing of a lawsuit. This device was perceived as part of protecting the autonomy of clinical-professional judgement as against the laity. It was assumed that professional logic offered an improvement on the commonsensical one but that this fact may not be accepted by everyone. This measure was a reflection of existing social ambivalence and attraction towards the profession.

The wish for extra legal protection has a double edge attached to it: on the one hand the doctor's authority was perceived as being above the ordinary, on the other hand it was strongly believed that being the subject of any lawsuit, even an unsuccessful one, could still ruin a doctor's reputation.

Other professions were infrequently mentioned in the psychiatric publications. Social workers were perceived as having a positive contribution to make yet as lacking in knowledge by some psychiatrists. Others preferred social workers not to study psychology but instead to be "good and practical"(28).

Apart from acknowledging fears of stigmatization, patients' family members' concerns were not commented upon. Implicitly it was taken for granted that psychiatrists knew what they were doing, were committed to support and cure their patients and knew better than anybody else what was good for patients. These assumptions make intriguing reading when it is remembered that: a.The knowledge base was fairly limited. b.Only a few clear connections could be made between the explanatory framework and intervention. c.The rate of recovery was perceived as unsatisfactory. d.Psychiatrists themselves thought that the mildly disturbed were getting a rough deal.

It is argued here that this state of affairs could be tolerated and accepted both by the profession and by the general public because the same value preferences were shared by the majority of the professional group and those in control over resources.

The set of preferences included:

1.A belief that mental disturbances were diseases, located in the individual's body and mind. No qualitative difference was made as to the demarcation between physical and mental illness.
2.The physician-psychiatrist is responsible for the care and control of the mentally distressed. No unhappiness was expressed by psychiatrists at the time about the removal of patients from the community, or at forced feeding in psychiatric hospitals.
3.The patient's welfare included mainly his/her physical well-being. Psychological well-being was considered too, but as of secondary importance. The social existence of clients, including their material existence, was not seen as part of the brief of psychiatrists, or as a possible reason for the person's mental breakdown.
4.Patients were thought of as primarily vulnerable and inferior to others. Hence they were entitled to care due to the vulnerability which was seen as not of their own making. Given this assumption expectations of recovery were couched at a fairly low level to start with.
5.The role specifications of psychiatrists were to examine the person, diagnose the condition and suggest methods of intervention. Most of the actual treatment was to be carried out by nurses and aides. The psychiatrist was therefore set up in the role of the overseer in regard to any other occupational group within the psychiatric service.
6.Psychiatry was a branch of medicine. As part of the medical sciences (the term used by Craig and Beaton) it was to be committed to the pursuit of scientific knowledge as defined in medicine. Social science approaches were not even considered as complementary possibilities. The faith in the evolutionary progress of science, in the value of experimental trial and error typified the world of medicine. Seen from such a perspective it became comfortable to accept that developments in psychiatry were bound to be slow, without it detracting from the belief in the goodness of the final outcomes.

Psychiatrists and politicians shared the view that what psychiatry offered was more beneficial to patients and more humane than what was provided before. Similarly they shared the faith in the supremacy of the rational over the irrational, the social over the a-social, the productive over the unproductive members of society. The fear of human aggression and the tendency to view it as innate have become stronger in the wake of the war. Most of the discourse in which psychiatrists were engaged was primarily an inter-professional one between psychiatry and medicine, in which the first attempted to ally itself to the second. In response to criticism from the outside - notably from MPs as chapter 4 will show - the profession was forced to enter a dialogue with the ruling groups. The profession's claim to protect patients could be seen as an attempt to speak for patients or on their behalf. However it treated patients as clinical entities, suitable for inquiry and investigation. Compassion or pity do not appear in the professional psychiatric literature of the period, no doubt because such features were deemed as "unscientific" and unprofessional. Thus the profession spoke for clients only after transforming their experiences into acceptable professional concepts and vlaues.

3.b.Nurses' Theories and Value Preferences.

Although nurses outnumbered psychiatrists considerably they did not develop their own conceptual framework or a crystallized approach towards their practice. On the whole nurses tended to accept the psychiatrists' views and to see themselves as auxiliaries to doctors. A striking class difference in the composition of the two groups existed: nurses were recruited primarily from working-class populations and did not receive formal training(29). Doctors came from upper middle-class backgrounds and had a long period of professional training. Hence nurses lacked the training in the conceptual language necessary for the construction of theories. Given the type of intervention methods described in the two textbooks reviewed above there was little to distinguish pyschiatric nursing from any other institutional care and control. The fact that psychiatric nursing was using little of the available medical technology was one of the reasons for its lower status compared to that of general nursing.

In terms of the volume of contributions nurses' publications gave much less space to mental illness and the nursing of the mentally ill than psychiatrists'. The nature of the contributions varied from a theoretical paper, through descriptions of mental hospitals and nurses' working conditions to letters on the quality of food in the hospital. Both the form and the content of the contributions differ considerably from those of the other professional groups.

The classification system used in British psychiatry was taken for granted by the nurses. Several aetiological alternatives were mentioned, with hereditary factors and those related to psychological relationships between the person and his environment being given priority(30).

The psychoanalytical model was presented as a general psychology and philosophy of life as well as an approach to psychiatry in a series of short articles(31). The presentation indicated the relevance for the practice of psychiatric nursing in an uncritical way. On the whole, however, mental distress was seen as a disease, a view perceived as less sitgmatizing than other perceptions. The awareness of the stigma attached to hospitalization is more noticeable in nurses' writings than in those of other professional groups(32).

However, no alternative was put forward. To the contrary, the nurses too supported early hospitalization. The only innovation they favoured was the establishment of cottage accommodation for patients at the point of leaving the hospital, following proposals by the Mental Aftercare Association(33).

Despite the acceptance of the then current psychiatric thinking on the abnormality of the mentally ill the advocated attitudes towards them were relatively open-ended and in line with treating them like ordinary people. For example it is recommended to be honest with patients. It is argued that although they may be suspicious towards their family members they may not feel the same about their nurses and hence merit an honest approach from the nurse(34). Such an attitude may also have an educational value in demonstrating to the patient that honesty and therefore trust still exist in the way he/she is treated by others.

Several cases of harm and neglect of patients by nurses, including court cases, are discussed. In all of these discussions the act is condemned even if there were mitigating circumstances for the action taken by the nurse(35).

Issues such as sterilization of the "unfit"

were mentioned. While a stand which favours it was suggested the issue was treated as of minor importance compared with the preoccupation with nurses' working conditions. Psychiatric nurses wanted to be equal to those working in a general hospital - i.e. a similar wish to that expressed by the psychiatrists vis-a-vis physicians. However the nurses in the general hospitals and in the training colleges were not interested in a move towards equal status. It seems as if the majority of psychiatric nurses too were not keen to train, while the leadership was urging them to do so.

Descriptions of mental hospitals contain more information on the staff's working and living conditions than on those related to patients(36). The descriptions testify to the attempts to recruit more nurses, especially of middle-class background. Working conditions were discouraging in terms of long hours (66 per week), poor ratio of staff to patients (the figure of 40 nurses for 300 patients was given as an example of a good ratio), poor quality of food and a low salary(37), though it could be argued that most other available jobs for people with the same educational background were not offering better conditions. Interestingly the frustrations due to the work with the mentally distressed were hardly ever mentioned. At the time nursing was not a predominantly female occupation. Soon after the First World War discussions on whether female nurses could work in male wards appear in the journals, raising strong feelings.

Despite the call for more basic training the impression is of a group which did not attempt to achieve the status of a profession. Instead it aimed to reach the position of a protected group of workers. Thus no effort is made to outline the uniqueness of the nurse's role and knowledge. The occupation is presented mainly as a job, but one which could and should be skilfully applied. The qualities of care which are subscribed to are those of understanding the patient's misery, its causes, of expressing overtly kindness and sympathy in a world largely devoid of such expressions.

Thus the contrast in the self-image of nurses and psychiatrists could not have been greater, despite the acceptance of the same knowledge base. The wish for occupational autonomy therefore is vis-a-vis other types of nursing and not from the medical profession. The inferior position of nurses to that of doctors is taken for granted.

There is no debate about the controlling

function of nursing and of hospitals; this function too is taken for granted.

The patient is portrayed primarily as an unhappy, somewhat confused and misguided person who is more harmful to himself than to others. Therefore he has to be protected in a kind way. Few, if any, references are made about the personal and social background of the person. Yet he/she is described in terms kept for ordinary people. With the exception of diagnostic categories the clinical language so typical of psychiatric writings is left unused by nurses. The image of the restored patient is that of someone who is working cheerfully, either inside or outside the hospital boundaries(38). The emphasis on being productive as a worker comes across clearly as the core of the recovered ex-mentally ill person's life and is in line with the emphasis on work in the nurses' self-image. Nursing treats itself as a technology concerned with the total management of hospital residents.

The nurses' publications do not mention the fact that nurses were excluded from the newly developing outpatient clinics. The lack of role for the nurse in this sector related to the identification of the nurse with institutional and physical care. Rethinking and redesigning the nurse's role did not take place for many years to come. Thus nurses were kept out of the more innovative part of psychiatry in the twenties, an indication of their low professional status and power.

A curious value preferences system emerges:

1.Mental illness is a disease, caused by either hereditary factors and/or environmental relationships.
2.Intervention should consist of medication but primarily of taking over the total management of the person's life. Following psychiatrists, nurses too know better than the patient what is good for him. The management has to be provided in a kind way and has to use expressions of sympathy with the patient's plight. Although hospitalization is stigmatizing, there is no other way of providing the required total care and control.
3.Nursing is an occupation, not a profession.
4.Psychiatric nursing should be given the same status as general nursing.

The list implies that although mental illness may be a disease the modes of understanding it and reacting to it are much more in line with an illness concept. This set of preferences demonstrates also the oscillation from a clinical-somatic approach to a psychological model(39).

3.c.Psychologists' Theories and Value Preferences.

The contribution of psychology to the intervention with shell shock sufferers has already been discussed. The administrators at the Ministry of Pensions did not like the increasing number of ex-soldiers on pension due to psychological disabilities. Subsequently they did not view the contribution of psychology to the war effort in a positive light(40).

Clinical and educational psychology did not exist as a professional group to reckon with outside academic circles in the twenties. In part the rejection of the conceptual significance of the war experience by the majority of British psychiatrists prevented such a recognition.

The first psychologist to be employed in a psychiatric setting was appointed only in 1928. She was Ms. Baldwin, a student of C. Burt. Not accidentally she was appointed to the Tavistock clinic - i.e. to a setting outside the mainstream of British psychiatry at the time.

Within the academic discipline of psychology the study of mental disorders became a focus of interest to a number of eminent psychologists in conjunction with the war experience. Rivers, McDougal, Pears, Brown and Myers were some of the scholars who showed this interest(41).

The main thrust of psychological approaches to psychiatric issues was absorbed though psychiatrists, in particular those of psychoanalytical inclination. The British Journal of Medical Psychology - published by the British Psychological Society and not by the British Medical Association - provides us with a very interesting example. It first appeared in 1921 edited by Dr. T. W. Mitchell, a general practitioner. The majority of its contributors were psychoanalysts, including a number of eminent figures (e.g. C. Jung, E. Jones, E. Glover). The topics read like a collection from an early psychoanalytic conference: "The revival of emotional neurosis and its therapeutic value"; "The instinct and the unconscious"; "The question of the therapeutic value of Abreaction". Few experimental studies were reported, such as on the mechanism of hallucination or on the influence of the endocrines in psychoneurosis.

The impression gained is of psychoanalytically oriented psychiatrists publishing in a medical psychology journal perhaps because the latter was more tolerant of their deviating position than the BMA's journals.

As hospitals did not employ psychologists but child guidance clinics did, it seems reasonable to assume that clinical and educational psychologists at the time were mainly following psychoanalytical ideas. The tenets of this approach in the twenties included:

1.Focus on the individual, his unconscious, his emotional life.
2.Focus on the child's interpersonal relations with his parents as the archetype for all future relations.
3.Mental disturbance was perceived as the result of unresolved emotional issues within the individual, which may or may not have been caused by the attitude of significant others.
4.While mental distress was viewed as pathological it nevertheless was seen as occurring on the same range of behaviour as normality.
5.Hereditary factors or biological predisposition were accepted as one basic condition on which mental illness was likely to develop.

The dominancy of the experiential facet of our existence over all other facets was taken for granted. Mental illness was not seen as a disease or a medical problem, but primarily as a psychological problem of living. The body was perceived as functioning in a way largely subjected to the psychological needs of its owner. Rational man was Freud's ideal. Yet the qualities he endowed rationality with differed from the notions of neurologists or positivist philosophers. He primarily emphasized the ability of balancing the three components of the personality (id, ego, superego) in such a way that the ego will be given a free hand without the suppression of the two other components. As already mentioned civilization was conceived as a repressive power yet as a reasonable price to be paid by individuals for social co-existence.

In the field of child guidance the rivalry between Anna Freud's and Melanie Klein's approaches only started to develop in the late twenties, focusing on the relative importance of the first year of life and on the nature of the ego(43).

Psychoanalysis saw itself as a science in the tradition of the natural sciences, although it advocated very different methods of inquiry. Its research methods, based on the analysis of individual cases from a psychoanalytic viewpoint, depended considerably on the researcher/analyst's interpretation of the patient's utterances and the processes attributed to his problem. The methodology is therefore much more akin to that of Weberian social science than to a natural science version. Thus the insistence of psychoanalysis on being seen as a science is indicative of some of the ambiguities of this approach.

There is no evidence that British psychoanalysts in the twenties were interested in the possible relationships between psychological and social factors. The fact that most of their patients came from the middle and upper classes was neither mentioned nor discussed. Psychoanalysts were defensive about what they could offer the bulk of inpatients diagnosed as suffering from psychosis. But the defensiveness did not lead to questioning the value of what was offered or to modify it for a long time to come. The direction of development was more and more towards internal representations of experience and less to do with the real world in which those experiences took place.

The conditions and fate of the mentally ill during the period, relevant legislation, public opinion and evaluation of intervention outside individual therapy do not appear as topics worthy of attention. Confined to psychoanalysts the discourse within clinical psychology was almost exclusively intra-professional despite the fact that it involved both psychologists and psychiatrists. The concern with the scientific standing of the new approach contributed to the exclusion of authentic patients' voices. These were heard only after being transformed into the conceptual language of psychoanalysis, despite the belief by psychoanalysts in the value of subjectivity.

This exclusivity can be understood against the background of a minority group at the very beginning of its formation where the rest of the professional world was predominantly hostile and ignorant. Like psychiatrists and nurses, psychoanalysts claimed to know better than the person the meaning of his/her experience. Unlike traditional psychiatry, however, psychoanalysts were in the process of building up a theoretical framework. Their method of intervention was so closely linked with the conceptual framework that it carried the same name.

Psychoanalytic intervention methods need not be described here as those typical of the twenties have been amply documented in classical case descriptions(44). Suffice to remind us that they are based on: encouraging free association; the provision of interpretation by the analyst; the patient's strong emotional relationships with the analyst; and reworking past and present emotional internal conflicts and relationships.

The alliance with psychoanalysis offered practising psychologists an opening into an intermediary facet between medicine and psychology, which must have been very attractive to a small and powerless group. Confined to their settings the psychoanalytically oriented psychologists enjoyed a high degree of autonomy from the outside. Inside however a fairly rigid hierarchy developed, based on the process of supervision and the closeness to leading figures. A measure of criticism and doubt was tolerated, provided it was expressed internally and in prescribed ways.

The image of the restored person was of one who can balance better the three components of his personality and whose degree and mode of repressing impulses need not be reflected in psychiatric symptoms.

The social control function was not acknowledged as such. Psychoanalysts saw themselves as rebels and innovators and therefore could not see themselves as controlling people but rather as liberating them from the slavery to their instincts. However the recognition of their role as intermediaries did not follow, perhaps because of the lack of a sociological perspective concerning their own activities.

3.d. Social Workers' Theories and Value Preferences.

Only a few psychiatric social workers were employed as such during the twenties(45). They worked in those few child guidance clinics which emerged since 1920 and in the Mental Aftercare Association. Social work was not practised in mental hospitals. Macadmam,(46) writing in 1934, says: "Unless they are the members of authorized committess the intervention of the voluntary worker is not much encouraged in lunatic asylums or mental homes. ..when allowed to have a role in a mental hospital the focus was on securing that the law is followed rather than abused in the institutions."

The first academic psychiatric social work course opened in 1929 at the London School of Economics. The course was primarily psychoanalytical and medically oriented, in contrast to the more sociological framework of the courses already in existence.

The bulk of social workers did not express a specific interest in the mentally ill but saw them as one element among the many destitute, poor and unemployed people whose numbers were growing at an alarming rate during the twenties. The majority of workers were single women of lower and upper middle-class background. Some were trained by the Charity Organization Society (COS) in a training programme which was based on the apprenticeship model(47). The COS training emphasized the importance of the assessment of needs and abilities of individuals and families. In addition the social worker had to judge whether the applicant was deserving support on the basis of evaluating his "moral character". The majority of needs looked at were material in nature, but often had implications for health and education too. The focus on assessment related to a rationalized use of resources based on the value preferences of the period, of which the fear of fostering dependency was prominent. In addition the wish to gain a quasi-scientific status based on an approximation to the clinical model was a likely latent motive.

The social worker's main task was to ease the economic burden and the physical deprivation of families. The emphasis on the family and on conforming behaviour were seen as both the aim and the justification of the social worker's role. The reasons for the misery of the clients were located in individual irresponsibility by the poor as well as ill consideration by the rich. The COS was against greater state intervention in the welfare

field.
Purely psychological explanations emerged slowly during the twenties and were accepted by the minority which worked with psychiatric patients(48).
In contrast to the very few qualified graduate psychiatric social workers, those who worked in the Mental Aftercare Association were usually unqualified(49). Their work focused on rehabilitation of the ex-patient and was more similar to mainstream social work than to the newly emerging psychiatric social work. They concentrated specifically on the provision of housing and sheltered work.
In the debate within social work between the protagonists of social action vs. those who promoted professionalism, psychiatric social work followed the latter which was then embodied in casework(50). In casework the emphasis was on client-worker relationships as the main tool for change. While this focus was shared with psychoanalysis it developed independently of the latter.
During the twenties British social work, including its psychiatric wing, did not claim to possess a unique body of knowledge. Instead PSW were arguing that they had specific skills to offer. These abilities were located at the interface between psychotherapeutic work and relationships with the social environment(51). Working within psychoanalytically oriented settings they were usually allocated tasks related to social functioning and psychotherapeutic work with significant others, rather than with the identified client, such as the parents of a child who was identified as the primary client.
Likewise the belief system of the PSW was similar to that of psychoanalysis with the notable exceptions of viewing the present to be as important as the past and the material base of existence as relevant as the psychological facet.
PSW were more ready than other social workers to accept the view that the source of difficulties which people with psychiatric problems have lay primarily in the person's attitude and interpretation and not in the mutual relationships between the environment and the person. Such a perception altered the role of the social worker and questioned its uniqueness. The supremacy of the psychiatrist or psychoanalyst was taken for granted by social workers at the time.

92

In contrast to other professional groups social workers were explicit about having a value base, to the point of being proud of having it(52). They did not view social work activity as scientific but primarily as an art in the service of society and those individuals who have fared less well than the majority. While accepting the desirability of conformity and the essential goodness of society they also assumed that it was the duty of the rich to give to the poor and believed firmly in collective responsibility. Within the brief of such a responsibility they saw themselves as carrying out the role of the intermediary. Social workers acted as go-betweens for both their clientele and the establishment, including the professional layer. Indeed they perceived themselves as representing one group to the other(53).

In the process of acting as intermediaries, clients' subjective communication and that of the ruling groups were translated into an intersubjective language. It was hoped that this meta-language would be acceptable to both sides. As Philp(54) has pointed out, the essence of the rewritten image of the client is the attempt to convince the others of the lack of personal responsibility and in the existence of potentialities. Instead the person's "objective" background was made to carry the brunt of the responsibility for his present state. These assumptions fitted well both mainstream and psychoanalytically oriented social work, even if the features of the background and the qualities of the restored person differed.

Summary
Diverse issues and approaches were expressed in the writings of the four professional groups. None of the groups came up with a full theoretical framework on mental distress. Psychoanalysis came perhaps nearest to such a framework followed by mainstream psychiatry. The claim for scientific status and for securing objective knowledge go hand in hand with the attempt to create theoretical formulations.
In all of these frameworks the social dimension is either missing or treated as of very minor relevance. When it is included, as in social work, it is as a part of the value preferences rather than as a part of the conceptual system.

While lacking their own theoretical framework, social work and nursing preserved more of the subjective and intersubjective perspectives of mental illness than was the case for psychiatrists and psychologists.

Value preference systems were traced in the writings of all four groups. Only social workers admitted to having a value base without being apologetic about this fact.

All four groups did not view themselves as social control agents. However once more only social workers were aware of their role as intermediaries, although all other groups did not doubt their positive social contribution.

Only psychiatrists expressed a keen interest in the organizational perspective of the services for the mentally distressed, although psychoanalysis was instrumental in the creation of a new setting (child guidance clinics).

Nurses and psychiatrists were preoccupied with their working conditions. Perhaps the small numbers of psychologists and PSWs made such an interest premature.

A critical approach is lacking in most of the writings of professionals. This aspect appears more bluntly in the writings of psychiatrists where the gap between the claims made in the name of the profession and what was actually offered on theory and practice is striking.

In chapter 4 we will see which of the perspectives described in this chapter appealed more to the politicians.

References
1.Scull, A. (1979) Museums of Madness, Allen Lane, London.
2.British Medical Journal (1920) 2, p.371.
3.Lancet (1924) 2, p.613.
British Medical Journal (1924) 2, p.1005.
British Medical Journal (1923) 1, p.542.
Lancet (1924) 1, pp.488, 571.
4.British Medical Journal (1924) 1, p.1105.
British Medical Journal (1930) 2, pp.334, 880.
5.British Medical Journal (1924) 2, p.710.
British Medical Journal (1930) 1, p.613; 2, p.1058.
Lancet (1930) 2, p.137.
6.British Medical Journal (1924) 1, p.874.
Lancet (1924) 2, p.613.
7.British Medical Journal (1925) 2, p.874.
8.Tredgold, A. F. (1908, 1952) A Textbook of Mental Deficiency, Bailliere, London.

9.Jacobson, P. (1983) Psychiatry in the Front Line, The Sunday Times, 13/3, p.14.
10.Henderson, D. K., Gillsepie, R. D. (1927) A Textbook of Psychiatry, Oxford University Press, London. p.410.
11.Bell, J., Sassoon, S. (1935) We Did Not Fight: 1914-1918, Bailliere, london.
12.British Medical Journal (1920) 1, p.851. Lancet (1930) 2, p.136.
13.See ref. 10, chapter 19.
14.Freud, S. (1920) Beyond the Pleasure Principle, Collected Papers, The Hogarth Press, London.
15.Dicks, H. (1970) Fifty Years of the Tavistock, Tavistock, London.
16.British Medical Journal (1920) 1, p.851; 2, p.323.
British Medical Journal (1924) 1, p.1060.
17.Craig, M., Beaton, T. (1926) Psychological Medicine, Bailliere, London.
18.British Medical Journal (1930) 1, p.880.
19.Ibid.
20.Lancet (1924) 2, p.1214.
21.British Medical Journal (1930) 2, p.542.
Klein, M. (1937) Love, Hate and Reparation, Institute of Psychoanalysis, London.
22.Habermas, J. (1972) Knowledge and Human Interests, Heinemann, London.
23.Lancet (1924) 2, pp.393, 1273-5.
24.British Medical Journal (1924) 1, pp.549, 982.
25.Lord, J. R. (1926) The Clinical Study of Mental Disorders, Journal of Mental Sciences, pp.1-79.
26.British Medical Journal (1924) 2, pp.551-3. Lancet (1930) 1, pp.883-4.
27.British Medical Journal (1930) 1, p.740.
28.Abel-Smith, B. (1960) A History of the Nursing Profession, Heinemann, London.
Carpenter, M. (1980) Asylum Nursing before 1914: A Chapter in the History of Labour. In: Davies, C. (ed) Rewriting Nursing History, Croom Helm, London. pp.123-146.
Bellaby, P., Oribabor, P. (1980) Determinants of the Occupational Strategies Adopted by British Hospital Nurses, International Journal of Health Services, 10, 1, pp.291-310.
30.Nursing Mirror (1926) p.393; (1930) p.488.
31.Nursing Mirror (1926) pp.488, 499; (1930) p.294.
32.Nursing Mirror (1922) pp.55, 498.
33.Nursing Mirror (1920) pp.354, 452.
34.Nursing Mirror (1929) p.294.
35.Nursing Mirror (1922) p.120; (1920) p.12.
36.Nursing Mirror (1920) p.64; (1922) p.67; (1924)

p.323.
37.Nursing Mirror (1922) p.408; (1929) pp.515-7.
38.Nursing Mirror (1922) pp.521-23; (1930) p.476.
39.Nursing Mirror (1924) P.488 and ref. 3o.
40.Stone, M. (1982) The "Problem" of Neurosis
during World War 1 and World War 2 and the
Development of Psychiatry and State Mental Health
during the 20th Century. Conference on the History
of British Psychiatry, May 15th, London School of
Economics.
41.Hernshaw, R. (1973) The History of British
Psychology, Allen and Unwin, London.
42.Wollheim, R. (1971) Freud, Fontana, London.
43.See ref. 21 and Freud, A. (1937) The Ego and its
Mechanisms of Defence, Institute of Psychoanalysis,
London.
44.Freud, S. (1977) Dora. In: Case Histories I.
Pelican, Harmondsworth, pp.31-136.
Klein, M. (1961) Narrative of a Child Analysis, The
Hogarth Press, London.
Winnicott, D. (1975) The Piggle, Penguin,
Harmondsworth.
45.Jones, K. (1960) Mental Health and Social
Policy, Routledge and Kegan Paul, London.
Ashdown, M., Brown, C. (1953) Social Service and
Mental Health, Routledge and Kegan Paul, London.
46.Macadam, F. (1934) The New Philanthropy, Allen
and Unwin, London.
47.The Charity Organization Society (1898) Ist
report of the Committee on Training, occasional
paper no. 11, 2nd series and subsequent reports.
Jones, C. (1983) State, Social Work and the Working
Class, Macmillan, London. chapter 4.
48.Yellowly, M. (1980) Psychoanalysis and Social
Work, Van Nostrand, New York.
49.See ref. 45 and also the British Medical
Journal (1920) 1, p.643; (1930) p.1058.
50.Garrett, A. (1949) Historical Survey of the
Evolution of Casework, Journal of Social Casework,
30, 6, pp.219-229.
51.Hill, O. (1893) Trained Workers for the Poor,
COS, London.
Robinson, V. (1931) The Changing Psychology of
Social Casework, COS Review.
52.Loch, C. S. (1910) Charity and Social Life,
Macmillan, London.
53.Woodroff, K. (1962) From Charity to Social Work,
Routledge and Kegan Paul, London.
54.Philp, M. (1979) Notes on the Form of Knowledge
in Social Work, Sociological Review, 27, pp.56-78.

4 Politicians' Concerns and Attitudes in the Twenties

4.a.The Participating MPs.

Between January 1927 and December 1932 fifty MPs
participated in the debates on mental illness. The
figure of fifty MPs constitutes less than 10% of
the House of Commons membership. It should be
remembered that several of the participants had to
do so as part of their parliamentary brief (e.g.
the Minister and his secretary). Nearly all of the
other participants were backbenchers; few of the
well-known political figures of the day cared to be
involved in these discussions. When it came to
voting either on amendments or on the next
procedural step between 170 and 350 MPs were
present. Voting did not follow party lines, and
usually the opposition to the Minister's position
came from his own party, i.e. from Labour MPs (see,
for example, voting results in H.238,1757-62).
    Thus from the start we are presented with a
clear cut case of self-selection. This process of
self-selection can be taken two steps further in
terms of the information available to us. The
majority of the fifty MPs were Labour MPs (Labour:
32, Unionist: 8, Conservatives: 9, Prohibition: 1)
and the more active among them tended to come from
the circles left of the centre of the party. To get
an impression of the main actors involved it may be
useful to look at some of the autobiographical
notes submitted by these MPs to Who is Who(1) as a
measure of self-description and projected public
image.
Mr. Greenwood, A.: Labour MP, Nelson and Colne
since 1922. Minister of Health 1929-31; Secretary
of the Labour Party, heading the research and
information department of the party. Education:

97

Victoria university; head of the, department of
Economics at Huddersfield Polytechnic; lecturer in
Economics at the University of Leeds; honorary
Ph.D., University of Leeds, 1930; chairman of the
Yorkshire division of the Workers Education
Association, vice president of the National
Association. Assistant secretary of the
Reconstruction Committee in 1917, in the Ministry
of Reconstruction, 1917-19. Parliamentary Secretary
to the Minister of Health, 1924. Joint Secretary to
the Committee of Relations between Employers and
Employees; Secretary to the Labour Committee to
Ireland.
Publications: Juvenile Labour Exchanges and
After-Care; The Health and Physique of School
Children; The War and Democracy; An Introductory
Atlas to International Relations; The Education of
the Citizen; The Labour Outlook (1929).
Mr Jones, J. J.: Labour MP, West Ham since 1981.
General Organiser of the National Union of General
and Municipal Workers; member of West Ham local
council since 1904. Christian Brothers school.
Active in Socialist and Trade Union movement for
the last 25 years. Helped in the organization of
unskilled labour in London.
Publications: My Lively Life.
Recreation: Football, cricket, etc.
Mr Sorenson, R.: MP (Lab.) West Layton, 1926;
Member of Essex County Council and Essex Mental
Hospitals Committee; Minister Free Christian
Church. Education: Elementary School; later
studied for four years in a religious community.
Employed in factory, office, and shop; then joined
Order of Pioneer Preachers; appointed to Free
Christian Church, Walthamstow; early member of
Fellowship of Reconciliation (ex-committee);
experimented with farming community life in Essex;
Ex-President Walthamstow Labour Party; Ex-Member,
Walthamstow UDC; Ex-Chairman, Walthamstow Education
Committee and High School Sub-Committee;
Ex-chairman of Socialist Christians League; Labour
candidate for Southampton 1923 and 1924; WEA tutor;
Editor, W Leyton Citizen.
Publications: God and Bread; Men or Sheep; The New
Generation; Religion and Socialism; 1848; Marley's
Maid; Tolpuddle; Modern Problems, etc., plays.
Recreation: Amateur drama.
Sir Wood, K: Rt. Hon. Union MP for Woolich West
since 1918, son of a Wesleyan minister, circuit
steward, Wesley's Chapel, City Road, Civil
Commissioner, Northern division, general strike.

98

Commissioner, Northern Division, general strike. JP, solicitor, senior partner of K Wood, Williams and Co. Euston Square. Member of the London County Council for Woolwich, 1911-19. Chairman of Building Acts Committee, 1913, 1914. Chairman of the London Old Age Pension Authority, 1915. Chairman of London Insurance Company 1917-18. Chairman of Faculty of Insurance, 1916-19 and its President, 1920, 1922-23. Parliamentary Secretary of Health, 1919-1922, 1924-1929. Parliamentary Secretary of Education, 1931. Introduction of Early Closing Bill (1924) and Summer Time Allotments (1924). Chairman of Executive Council of National Conservative and Unionist Association.
Publications: Law of National Insurance, Law and Practice of Housing, National Health Insurance, Relief for the Ratepayer.
Clubs: Carlton, Constitutional, Roehampton, Pratts.

The biographies help to understand the experiences leading some MPs to adopt Labour's ideology on the one hand. On the other hand it shows the multitude of origins of the interest in mental illness of MPs as different from each other as Sir Kingsley and Mr J. Jones. However, the biographies do not shed light on the possible reasons why these MPs would care for the mentally ill more than the majority of MPs. Indeed, why would an issue declared repeatedly to be above party politics and offically introduced as a bi-partisan law (H.235,957) be the concern of so few MPs? Why would a realm of primarily humanitarian concern be excluded from the range of interest of the majority of MPs, all of whom pride themselves as protectors of the weak in their constituencies?

Putting aside issues perceived as "purely" political, we have to ask ourselves why would debates on issues such as women's franchise, divorce and in later days abortion, lead to massive participation of MPs but not mental illness? While the first were (and still are) viewed as moral dilemmas, mental illness seemed to be excluded from the range that requires a primarily moral stand by a logic that will be made explicit below.

There was never much to be gained politically (here defined as gains in power within a political structure, e.g. party, ward, constituency, etc) from advocating the case of the mentally ill. As a social group the latter were a very weak collective in terms of social leverage and desirability. They

99

demonstrated form, unlike criminals. In numbers the mentally ill were a much smaller group than the poor and as such constituted less of an overt threat to any existing social order. As already mentioned it was during the 20s that the mentally ill were finally and unequivocally allocated to the brief of medically qualified professionals. It was by virtue of this allocation that they were taken away from the realm of moral values into that of professionalism which was assured to be value-free yet based on an accepted code of ethics.

Thus those MPs still concerned with the mentally ill were likely to come from among those particularly moved by the plight of the unfortunate rather than from among those more interested in the successful ones. They were also likely to come from among the more ideologically committed MPs of whichever creed (e.g. Mr Scrymgeour, Prohibition MP for Glasgow).

The professionalization of the field of mental distress implied contracting away from the arena of public debate. By providing what was perceived as the best available care the problem was neatly disposed for the rest of the nation. Thus professionalism fitted well the tendency to segregate the mentally ill.

Labour MPs in the 20s were socialists of different grades; all sharing the conviction that the lot of the working class had to be improved and its exploitation by members of other classes should be minimized(2). For this group the mentally ill were included among the exploited poor, and as such they deserved attention and concern.

The acceptance of the concept of "illness" implied the right for special concern because of the element of helplessness involved in it. The notion that the MPs interested in mental illness came forward because of a relevant personal experience has been expressed by only one MP in the debate. Mr J. Jones said that he was once mentally ill and treated by doctors. "I myself might have been certified years ago but still I think that I was as sane as anyone who has spoken tonight" H.235,1095). In fact, Mr Jones was one of few in the House to suggest in no uncertain terms that mental illness was the result of poverty. He took a highly negative view of the Board of Control and a slightly more positive one towards the professionals. The House did not react at all to Mr Jones's confession (H.235,1053). Instead of being hailed as an example of successful recovery he was later treated as an oddity of dubious character. This attitude should be seen on the background of Mr Jones's long standing career as a trade union organiser. Major sources of MPs' knowledge and beliefs were their experience as members of hospital boards and/or as JPs. Several doctors who were MPs at the time participated (Dr Morris-Jones, (Lab.); Dr Davies, (U); Dr Hastings, (Lab.); Dr Bentham (Lab.); but none of them was a psychiatrist or interested specifically in mental illness. The insurance companies and friendly societies were represented to an extent by Sir Kingsley, the Unionist MP who was twice Parliamentary Secretary of Health. As mental illness was not one of the categories covered by the insurance companies (because of the chronicity component) the latter's interest in the debate was indirect. Sir Kingsley professed his wish for change in the existing system and suggested organizational means for doing so. He rigorously defended doctors and was against the involvement of magistrates in certification processes, taking the position advocated by the Ministry of Health. Only on one occasion did he lose his temper and accused a fellow MP of slander when Mr Kinley required an inquiry into the number of dying patients per year in mental hospitals (H.235,1343) (which amounted to 40 per cent of admission rates, as mentioned in Chapter 2). It is easy to understand what enraged Sir Kingsley. Such an inquiry might have examined profits made by insurance companies through delaying hospitalization, or cast doubts on the quality of medical care provided by them.

A number of MPs expressed a consistent interest in specific aspects. For example, Mr E Davies persistently asked for information on the way physical illness of the mentally ill was encountered (H.236,1346). Mr Kinley repeatedly asked on allocation of money and patients (H.245,643;247,2108.;248,877). Mr Sorenson was interested in married patients hospitalized for prolonged periods and the physical conditions in institutions (H.233,937; 235,1406, 1581). Colonel Wedgwood consistently pursued the idea of separate institutions for voluntary patients (H.237,2597; 23;2538, 2544, 2547).

4.b.Tactics.

"Of political parties claiming socialism to be their aim, the Labour Party has always been the most dogmatic - not about socialism but about the Parliamentary system"(3).

The majority of MPs taking part in the debate shared the same views. Yet there were only a few instances of overt collaboration and lobbying. For example, Mr Kinley and Mr McShane (two Labour Left MPs) asked for an inquiry into the number of dying patients (H.237,2535); Mr Gould and Mr Kinley requested information on the number of beds and patients in the mental hospitals of their constituencies on the same occasion using exactly the same wording (H.247,1174-5).

There is no clear answer to the question why we do not see a lobby at work though a basic agreement among the critics of the existing system is evident. In principle it would seem that the lack of a crystallized alternative to the existing framework on the one hand and to the changes proposed in the new legislation on the other hand was the main contributory factor. Without an alternative in mind it was difficult to form a united front as the aim for the fight seemed to be missing even though the causes for it were there. The possible reasons for not forming an alternative were mentioned at the end of the section on the background of the 20s.

The impact of the fact that Labour MPs were criticizing a Labour ministry's legislation of a minority government is difficult to assess but it might have been an additional dimension in preventing a collective action.

Repetition of questions was one of the most frequently used techniques of bringing attention to an issue (H.247,1631, 21029; 248,877).

Requests for statistics on allocation of money and staff (H.211,683; 232,1646; 235,2584; 237,1789), the breakdown of the activities of the Board of Control (H.227,1142, 1286, 11564-5, ;234,2072; 235,988,995), movements of patients' population (H.247,2109; 248,877), were regularly made as means of directing attention to a problem. Similarly individual cases were described partly in request for a specific action as well as an illustration of a more general concern (H.246,1428; 250,507; 235,890; 237,2580). Outright criticism was hardly made.

Shaming MPs was an uncommon tactic, but was used twice: firstly when the Minister stated that an MP had misplaced a hospital by inventing a

non-existing county (H.234,1832). Secondly when Sir
Kingsley accused Mr Kinley of making libellous
statements when the latter asked for an inquiry on
the number of dying patients (H.235,1343).
The Minister (Mr Greenwood) and his secretary
(Miss S. A. Lawrence) provided factual information
when available. All too often the information
requested was not collected and the Minister showed
marked reluctance to ask for new statistical
categories to be introduced for collection
(H.246,1422). Criticism of the Board of Control or
the Ministry's activities were handled mainly by
evasion or denial. For example, the Minister opted
not to react at all in the matter of the inquiry on
the number of dying patients (H.233,1621-2).
Likewise requests for further changes in
legislation were answered at the technical level -
e.g. when asked to enable an ex-patient to file a
case court against a doctor, the answer was that
the principle was debated at the time in the House
of Lords and therefore nothing could be done about
it (H.239,2399). Night-long debates were another of
the measures used by the Minister in the name of
expediency, (H.235,2579; 278,1824) as was giving in
to the Lords (H.240,741-8). Selecting which of the
proposed amendments should be debated was the
prerogative of the Speaker of the House, who
declined to give reasons for his choices
(H.237,2527-9). The Speaker was no doubt directed
by the Parliamentary Secretary and thus the choice
reflected her preferences. Introducing amendments
to the Bill was often employed as a major strategy
to ensure change in the desired direction
(H.237,2529; 237,2535-8).

4.c.Issues of Concern.

The topics raised in the debates and Question Time
differed considerably in terms of frequency and
intensity. Only the issues that received a high
degree of attention in the House of Commons will be
outlined below. Sympathy with the families of the
mentally ill and with the patients was often
expressed. The plight of the mentally distressed
was thus portrayed as: "I do not think there can be
any worse human tragedy than that of the man or
woman wandering in no-man's land between sanity and
insanity"(H.235,957).

Suffering from the brunt of the stigma attached by the public to both patients and relatives was perceived as a major contributing factor. According to MPs the stigma consisted of fear and prejudice based on the belief that mental illness was caused through hereditary factors (H.237,2540; 235,pp.974-5). Without exception all MPs addressing the issue condemned the public's approach and saw it as a mistaken belief that needed to be corrected (H.237,972). "There is in the mind of the public great horror and shame about the name lunacy which is not confined to those who may be afflicted, but applies even more to the relatives, the wife or the husband and particularly to the children" (H.234,2529).

The politicians viewed mental illness "like a physical illness" (H.227,1564; 235,958) and therefore usually not incurable. The public was urged to adhere to this concept of mental illness on the assumption that such an acceptance would minimize or eliminate the stigma. Thus the optimistic view of the fate of the mentally ill was clearly anchored within the understanding of mental distress provided by the clinical-somatic approach. The advances made in medicine in regard to physical illness and reliance on the physician as the provider of new cures were keystones in the beliefs on mental distress held by MPs.

Apart from putting the blame on the Board of Control for mishandling the mentally ill and their relatives and thus causing the public to mistrust the professionals in charge there was virtually no discussion as to what might have led the public into such mistaken notions or how the change in opinion was to be introduced. Instead speakers were preaching to the public time and again from the pulpit of Parliament that it should change its "shameful" views (H.237,2529). The focus was on an ideological change which hopefully would lead to a basic change in attitudes towards hospitalization. MPs were anxious to let the "ignorant" public benefit from their "superior" level of knowledge. One of the most basic rules of attitudinal change was therefore never kept, namely that the road to voluntary change does not lie in instilling inferiority feelings among the subjects but through pointing out their possible positive contribution(4).

MPs were actively encouraging early hospitalization as a secure means for early recovery. More than once it was acknowledged in the

House that the rate of recovery from mental illness was not as satisfactory as was expected. The figure given officially by Mr Chamberlain in 1929 was 30% (H.227,1564-5) - a rate that matched the figures mentioned by Leeper in 1931(5) but was at odds with the much higher rates given by specific hospitals (H.235,961;247,2108-9). The Minister did not attach a figure to the rate of recovery, a wise policy in the light of the known discrepancies and variation in the statistics available and the widespread feeling of dissatisfaction with the existing system. MPs were aware that the public rejected the optimistic figures of recovery. (H.235,970; 238,1751). Thus the politicians were in a dilemma. On the one hand they wanted to convince the public that the prevailing situation was not so bad and had the potential for further improvement - i.e. that the public's gloom was unjustified. On the other hand MPs were equally aware of their own misgivings concerning the available services and which they were denouncing openly in the House. However, no doubts were brought up by MPs as to the value of medical knowledge, even though its level of performance was statistically a long way away from the optimism expressed in Parliament. It will be therefore repeatedly asked why in a situation fraught with a low level of recovery and criticism, psychiatry received whole-hearted support from MPs and the Ministry.

A member of the public listening to the debates would receive a highly ambiguous message on the quality of the services which he/she was to trust when seeking help for a mental health difficulty. For example, Chamberlain's major speech in 1927 on mental illness stated the progress which took place and the optimistic outcome produced for the mentally ill as compared with the mentally handicapped. At the same time he expressed the dissatisfaction with the rate of recovery and the fate of the mentally ill.

Another example was provided by Mr Greenwood. In his opening speech on the Mental Treatment Act he stated his belief in the ability of the voluntary patient to recognize his state and ask for help. The rest of the same page however is devoted to measures by which such a patient entered the category of temporary patienthood (H.227,1564-5; 235,962). "The public" was hardly ever defined and usually it is impossible to deduce who were the people the MPs were addressing. Only once did Mr Greenwood say explicitly that the fear of asylums was greater than that of the Poor Law institutions for the working class (H.235,961-2). Therefore it can only be speculated that MPs assumed that the better educated shared their view while the uneducated majority continued to perceive it as a fateful affliction. Thus a class connotation was implicity introduced to the discussion of the public's attitudes towards the mentally ill.

Being aware of class connotation and stigma led to a more positive conclusion too. The Minister and the majority of MPs stressed that the new legislation was aimed at severing any links between the Poor Law and being mentally ill. This emphasis served to accentuate the wish to eliminate the stigma of mental illness by dissociating the mentally ill from any other stigmatizing connections and connotations.

"A person shall not be in receipt of poor relief or be deprived of any right or privilege or be subjected to any disability by reason only that he or a member of his family is being maintained under the provisions of this principle of this Act in any place as a rate-aided patient." (H.235,969)

MPs seemed to be very concerned with the attachment of the stigma to family members and to people described as suffering from temporary crisis (H.235,961, 970) (e.g. women suffering from post-partum psychosis).

It was felt that it was totally unjustifiable to attribute the stigma to people who were seen as not deserving it. Thus a division was created between "the deserving" and "the undeserving". A number of MPs pressed strongly for the establishment of separate institutions for the two types of people in need of psychiatric intervention on the grounds that being with the certified group was sufficient to make people crazy (H.235,19, 2538).

MPs' preoccupation was with the sane suspected of mental disturbance rather than with the insane. This interest presented itself in several ways:

1.The concern mentioned above with the attachment of the stigma to relatives, specially to the children of a patient (H.2351,934).

2.The unhappiness with the negative attitude towards the neurotic patient or the sufferer from a temporary relapse (H.235,961, 983).

3.Expressed fears of wrongful certification, i.e of some people perceived mistakenly as insane by

the professionals (H.238,1747-8, 1751, 2585-6).
4.Stated suspicion of relatives assumed to have engineered the detention of a family member as a means of getting rid of the latter (H.237,990-1). While sympathy towards those suffering from mental illness 'proper' was expressed the explicit concern with this group was less frequent and more focused on providing the basic minimum of standards of physical care (H.247,1631). This attitude indicates perhaps that MPs shared - implicitly at least - the public's view of the hopeless state and future of this category of patients.

The lengthy discussion focusing on the category of voluntary patients illustrates the points mentioned above: MPs unanimously supported the creation of this classification (H.235,972,983,988,1003,1006). The reasons given for their preference included:

1.The wish to encourage early entry to hospital as a step towards early recovery by preventing the deterioration of the patient, and through applying the appropriate type of intervention (H.235,958, 961).

2.Protecting the patient's rights as a citizen :a voluntary patient not only had the right to decide on entry to hospital but could in principle decide on termination of hospitalization too. (The snag here was provided by the ease of transferring a patient's status from that of voluntary to a temporary one and in having to wait at least 72 hours after giving notice of intention to leave) (H.235,960).

3.By demonstrating that it would be realistically possible to leave a mental hospital it was hoped to reduce the fear of hospitalization (H.225,2537). In addition, voluntary admission was perceived as a means of improving the image of doctors hitherto seen as primarily interested in keeping people inside the asylums (H.226,1149, 1286; 235,975).

It should be remembered that the politicians' positive stand towards voluntary admission and discharge was in contrast to the suspicious reaction this idea received mainly from the general public. The hostile reactions were based partly on fear from the dangers of "raging lunatics roaming freely around" (H.235,971-2). The very few professionals who objected maintained that a lay person could not decide in any way his own degree of sanity/insanity. This type of judgement should be left entirely in the hands of the experts(6).

Thus the Ministry and Parliament were ready to adopt a revolutionary measure in the period's terms in regard to the voluntary patient. Apart from the reasons stated above it would seem that this eagerness was related to the impact of the relative success of treating war neurosis and similar disturbances during the 20s, mentioned in chapter 3. The belief in the preference of professionalism over lay methods of intervention was a contributory factor, as were the following:

1.A more humanitarian approach to the mentally ill (especially the less severley distressed).

2.An attempt to endorse citizens' rights whenever possible as part of the campaign to ensure such rights to the bulk of the working class. The discussion centred on the details of the voluntary admission and discharge and rightly so, as these seemingly technical details determined whether voluntarism would be genuinely implemented or not.

The details included: a.The definition of the category (H.235,250-3). b.Procedural steps to be undertaken by the patient (H.235,960, 2583). c.Whether magistrates should be involved in the process or only doctors (H.235,998; 237,972). d.The length of time required between a self-discharge notice and the actual discharge (H.235,960). e.The conditions under which a voluntary patient could be certified (H.235,960-2).

There was a broad consensus that only doctors should be a party to the admission process rather than magistrates. The latter were described in the House as ignorant of relevant knowledge, as unlikely to object to a doctor's opinion and as frightening people off hospitalization by stamping the stigma of criminal procedures on hospital admission (H.235,975,980). The few voices defending the retention of JPs' services were of those who claimed that magistrates represented the lay person. This argument could not have had the support of the majority of Labour MPs who were only too well aware of the class origin of magistrates. The issue at stake was whether the status of JP could be retained as an equal one to that of the professional doctor. For the majority in Parliament the preference of the professional's judgement over that of the lay person was taken for granted. The fact that this consensus marked a dramatic change from the English tradition of regarding JPs' decisions as the main safeguard of the lay person was hardly mentioned. The move towards leaning on experts and towards being content to leave major decisions to professionals who operate from a completely different set of assumptions to that of magistrates was fully endorsed.

The debate on procedures of admission and discharge reflected the existence of two camps. Those concerned with protecting the civil rights of potential patients and those primarily interested in easing access to intervention at the price of extending professional control over the mentally ill. The first camp successfully attempted to stall informality and imposed instead the requirement to prove volition and to delay discharge by 72 hours after giving notice (H.237,150,1739). The second group tried to ensure as informal procedure as possible especially for discharge (H.237,1741-42). In retrospect the reasoning behind the request that the intended patient should prove volition for the purpose of entering a mental hospital seems counter-productive. On the surface it would concur with the wish to secure that the potential patients were not forced into the hospital against their will. Yet the need to prove actively volition made the process of voluntary admission cumbersome. In a milieu primarily suspicious of the possibility of voluntary patienthood the awkwardness of the process was defeating the purpose for which it was created - i.e. to secure easy and dignified access to mental health provisions. The relative success of the first group and the related failure of the second are likely to be connected to the unease and covert suspicion taken on from the environment which the MPS were so set to change.

The category of voluntary patient remained ambiguous. It concurrently negated and reaffirmed the status and existence of mental illness and the qualities conferred on the person by that status. The debate in Parliament on the voluntary patient raised a number of crucial questions which were not debated directly: is easy access to services a citizen's primary right as compared to the right to be defended from being pushed into hospitalization? Can both rights be protected at the same level or are they incompatible in essence? These dilemmas are with us today as they were in the 20s. Their very existence is a further indication of the ambiguity inherent in the category of voluntary patient and in the position taken by MPs about it.

Conditions within the mental hospital.
MPs expressed often concern over the unsatisfactory

state of the asylum which were under the supervision of the board of control. The conditions criticized were mainly physical but highly relevant to the issue of dignified treatment:
1.Overcrowding (H.233,292; 235,1342).
2.Lack of adequate sleeping arrangements (H.232,292; 246,1495).
3.The nutritional quality of the food provided (H.249,1815).
4.Quality of clothing (H.233,1621; 250,570-8).
5.Lack of protection of personal belongings (H.246,1429, 249,585).
6.Treatment of physical diseases within the hospital.
7.Composition of age groups and mental illness categories within the hospital (H.250,507-8;233, 1621).
8.The size of institutions (H.234,2072).
9.Delays in building extensions to hospitals due to the Board's incompetence (H.935,343).

At times other provisions were questioned; such as lack of women's visitors in women's wards and the availability of chaplains (H.245,1422).

Criticism of the Board of Control's activities and attitudes was implied in each of the instances listed above. This highly negative evaluation of the Board got its best expression in an attempt to make the Ministry responsible for the new category of patients, rather than leave it to the Board. As the ministry was not interested in undertaking this responsibility the amendment was defeated (H.237, 2563-68).

Most of the psychological and social needs of patients and their families, so crucial in mental illness/health, got at best only a fleeting comment but never received the attention reserved for physical conditions. This omission is related to the fact that explanations and interventions were not discussed by MPs (see paragraph on Missing Issues).

Patients' and relatives' rights vis-a-vis the hospital were debated in conjunction with several related areas such as the status of the voluntary patient and conditions of hospitalization mentioned above. Implicitly it was assumed by the majority of MPs that patients have the right to be treated with respect (H.249,1811-9). The definition of what constitutes such an approach was never made explicit: to do so would require coming to terms with the ambiguity and ambivalence inherent in the notions concerning the mentally ill in the

twentieth century - namely of someone who is ill;
in need of care; unable to protect himself to the
point of applying for the right type of care; may
be endangering others and himself. Tellingly it was
never indicated by any MP that patients should not
be stripped of the basic citizens' rights in a
social democracy - such as property ownership,
voting, change of civil status. The level of rights
emphasized was much more elementary in the sense of
focusing on: 1.Not to harm patients (H.249,1817-9).
2.To deprive them as little as was deemed necessary
for intervention purposes (e.g. freedom to be out
of an institution, but not the freedom to refuse
intervention) (H.249,1811-9). The indignation
expressed by the MP who complained about selling
patients' personal clothes when a family was unable
to meet the hospitalization bill is an example of
what is meant by a rudimentary level of rights
(H.249,585). In the context of the period where the
majority wished to continue the segregation of the
mentally ill, including professionals, it does
honour to the MPs involved that for them the
mentally ill person was perceived as a human being
deserving respect and not just as an object of pity
and fear. The seemingly meaningless request for
statistics on the number of married patients in
long term hospitalization (H.233,997) reflected the
wish to review their prospects in the light of
their right to lead a married life. A much more
explicit and specific effort to ensure the
relatives' and patients' rights within the
institution was expressed by the attempt to force
the Board to display a statement of rights on the
walls of every ward (H.209,1485;235,1343). Such
rights included visitation, post censored and
uncensored (e.g. to one's MP), the right to appeal
to the Board for complaints and appeals against an
institution. A number of MPs have repeatedly asked
for it and got the Minister to nearly promising its
execution (H.235,2408-9). However, the latter
retracted at the last minute by saying that the
Board objected to the display of rights on
"therapeutic grounds" and the possible "misuse" by
relatives, friends or patients (H.274,1917-8).
Instead the superintendent of each institution,
already bogged down by so many duties, would have
the added responsibility of informing patients and
relatives. This suggestion amounted to shelving off
the idea. The reasons for the Minister's retreat
will be looked at in the paragraph on the
government's positon.

A different battle for patients' civil rights was fought by the few MPs who wanted to retain the right to sue doctors for wrongful hospitalization during an unlimited period of time (H.237.1834). It was one of the few instances where mental illness attracted sensational attention.

Several cases have been brought up before the House of Commons and at least two were heard by the House of Lords in its function as court of appeals (H.195,16). In all of these cases people who recovered from mental illness and who already left the hospital were suing the superintendent in charge of the institution for alleged unjustified and hence illegal detention in hospital. It should be remembered that to be able to file such a law suit was a privilege open only to the financially well-to-do minority, but not the majority of the patient population. In one of the most famous cases of the period - Harnett versus Fisher - the ex-patient filed the petition twelve years after certification took place because she was discharged only then (H.207,2039;235,978;239,2399). The right to petition was rejected in principle by the House of Lords on the grounds that because of the time lag it became impossible to investigate any such accusation in a satisfactory manner. The Lords' decision is understandable at the commonsense level because no detailed examination of interpretative data - such as psychiatric diagnosis consists of - can take place after such a lapse of time. Reliance on written records, even when they are available, will at best produce a partial picture. In addition it is unreasonable to expect a doctor to be able to have a detailed memory of twelve years' duration. Putting the onus of justifying past decisions on the doctor may expose the latter to unjustifiable tension during a lengthy court process and damage his reputation in an irreparable way.

The argument put forward by the patient's advocates claimed basic civil rights for the recovered person. Every citizen should be able to sue anybody in the kingdom, especially a person deprived of his/her freedom for so long and exposed to a high degree of suffering as a result of detention in a mental hospital. The fact that such hardship was caused by the rightful use or misuse of professional authority should not lead to further deprivation of the right to file a law suit. The issues at stake were those of civil vs. professional rights. They were made worse by the basic inequality in power relations. While one party suffered for a prolonged period from being in an inferior status to that of an ordinary citizen the other party was enjoying the status of being more than an ordinary person. The dilemmas involved in this case were related to the issue of magistrates vs. doctors, and patients vs. doctors and the judiciary. MPs were consistent in the position they took; the minority adhering to the ex-patient's side and the majority to that of the doctor's decisions and actions. Yet again, the absence of sufficient evidence and explanation to prove that psychiatry worked effectively for the majority of hospitalized patients did not deter the politicians from relying on it and rallying to its support.

The dilemmas put forward above do not lend themselves to clear cut satisfactory solutions. Yet it is of interest to note that no attempts were made to offer a more flexible mode of operation. For example conditions which would justify the reopening of a case at any time at the discretion of a judge could have been easily assimilated into a judiciary system that opted repeatedly for the flexibility of using precedents rather than having a written constitution.

Aftercare and out-patient clinics: Implementation of stated policy.
A radical and major principle of the Mental Treatment Act was the duty of local authorities to provide aftercare and out-patient facilities for the mentally ill. The idea was hailed as a breakthrough in public readiness to move from segregation to community based services (H.235,958; 237,1833-5, 1858). MPs unanyimously supported it. However when the bill came to the phrasing stage it became clear that the government would have the clause stand only as permissive legislation (H.235,964). The implications were clear: central government was not going to allocate specific financial support for aftercare services. Therefore local authorities would not have to provide these services. In the prevailing economic situation it was unlikely that the majority of local authorities would even attempt to establish the beginnings of a community based system. MPs were aware of these implications (H.235,964-6). Those who participated actively in the debate made it clear that the government was betraying the principle of community care. Through suggested amendments they tried to "sneak" the mandatory aspect into this piece of

legislation, but to no avail: the Minister refused
to budge (H.235,965-6).

Attitudes to non-psychiatric professionals.
Although doctors dominated the professional scene
in the eyes of MPs, some of them were concerned
with the condition of nurses' work. Nurses were the
largest workforce in the asylum system. Unlike
medicine nursing was not a socially prestigious
occupation. As mentioned above in chapter 2 and 3
there was no shortage of unemployed people ready to
take up a nursing job during the economic slump of
the late 20s and early 30S. The majority of nurses
were often untrained, more so in psychiatric work
than in the general hospital, and worked in
difficult conditions (H.232,1644; 233,980). Thus
taking up nurses' working conditions was
essentially taking up a trade union matter. It is
therefore not surprising the Labour Left MPs
brought it up in Parliament. Social workers and
pyschologists were not mentioned in the debates.

4.d.Case Descriptions.

Individual cases were described at times either in
an attempt to help the person to solve a particular
problem or to illustrate a point the speaker was
making. It seems to be useful to look at some of
the descriptions in order to share MPs' impressions
of patients, the latters' characteristics and those
of the situations. Dr E. Bentham provided four
vignettes in one speech, of which two appear below.
"I knew a case, a good many years ago now, of a man
who had been discharged from a lunatic asylum. On
the second morning after his discharge a lady
calling on his wife went into his house. It was in
one of those northern towns where the doors are
always on the latch, and she walked in just in time
to prevent him cutting his throat. She had the
presence of mind to say, 'Not there, man, not
there; come over to the sink. Think what a mess you
will make!' That saved him. Only two days before
that man had been discharged from an asylum,
supposed to be cured."
　　　"Then there was the case of a pauper patient,
an old man who was found wandering in the streets
of London and was taken to the reception ward by
the police. After he had been there two days the
time arrived for the bi-weekly visitation of the

114

justices who certify. During the time he had been there he had not spoken, and the medical certificate referred to him as being silent, morose and unable to give an account of himself and evidently needing treatment. Something, I do not know what, suggested to me that I should speak to him in French, and then he gave a very good account of himself." (H.235,989-91).

The amount of details in each case is minimal as they were described for the sake of making a point. Yet the message is quite clear: patients have to be protected: from themselves, from family members and from the insensitivity of the personnel. Patients are portrayed as helpless and weak, even when aggressive. Practical help and sensitivity is the type of support required. Mental illness may be a recurring pattern and its dangers do not stop at the point of discharge.

Dr Bentham was a Labour MP, an experienced physician as well as a JP. Yet she was more critical of doctors and the Board than the majority of MPs were. This stand was perhaps related to her evaluation that the available knowledge was far from sufficient for understanding mental illness. She believed also that magistrates may have a useful role to play in certain instances of certification - a position held by only a minority of MPs.

Mr Gould, another Labour MP, provided details of another case: (H.239,2399): "Mr Gould asked the Minister of Health if he was aware that a lady (MH) was placed in Camberwell House on the petition of her husband in December 1903, but is debarred from taking legal action against the doctors who certified her owing to the statute of limitations, which requires such action to be taken within six years of certification; and whether he will introduce legislation to prevent persons in such cases being deprived of redress on such grounds." Mr Greenwood's reply was: "I cannot properly comment upon an individual case, but I can understand that the effect of a decision in the House of Lords is as stated by honor. Friend. I cannot, however, undertake at present to introduce legislation on the point."

The person portrayed by Mr Gould differs considerably from those described by Dr Bentham. To start with she is an ex-patient, she wants justice and not pity or protection, though she quite likely needed both during the twenty-six years of hospitalization. It does credit to the lady that

115

she came out of such an ordeal with the ability to contact her MP and discuss suing the doctors. Though it has been suggested that her husband put her away, Mr Gould was careful not to imply that the doctors colluded with him or misused their professional authority in any way.

In all of the case descriptions crucial data on the past life of the patient/ex-patient is usually missing: patienthood has become a master status which erases all previous ones. MPs were stereotyping no less than others even when the intention was to help the patient.

To summarize, it is important to remember that only a minority of MPs participated in the debates on mental illness and the mentally ill. Among those interested the majority were of Labour-Left conviction for whom the mentally ill were a special case of exploitation, both inside and outside the class system. The group was dedicated sufficiently to the issues at stake to come back to them time and again but did not act as an organized lobby. Because of the focus on exploitation the major part of the debate was given to issues of patients' elementary rights. As there was no basic disagreement with the Ministry over the direction of the new legislation and modes of intervention the criticisms put forward were aimed at the level of implementation rather than at the level of principles. Despite the ideological preference of the MPs involved the analysis of mental illness and the conditions of the mentally ill was not carried out within the same ideological framework - i.e. socialism. Instead the assumptions and solutions were totally coloured by the preference for professionalism, which can fit a socialist approach but is far from using or incorporating the many more components of analysis available within such an approach. For example, the opportunity to look at the contribution of social factors and life experience to the mental breakdown of a person was not taken up in a systematic way.

As already commented by moving mental illness fully into the sphere of professionalism its divorce from being perceived as a basic moral issue was enacted. Yet the approach of MPs concerned with the mentally ill was primarily grounded within their moral judgement of the issue as a humanitarian issue. Despite the shared approach the debates were marked by ambiguities and contradictions which on the whole were neither acknowledged nor discussed.

4.e.The Ministry's Position: "Politics is the Art of the Possible".

Formally the two Houses had to ratify the Mental Treatment Act. In effect it was the Ministry that drafted the bill, took the final decisions and had the final say. It is therefore of great relevance to know the Ministry's stand towards the major issues raised above, its reactions to and its methods of handling suggested changes. Whenever an amendment was suggested the silent majority voted following ministerial wishes, despite the fact it was a minority government. The two individuals mainly involved were Mr A. Greenwood, the Minister, and Miss Lawrence, his parliamentary secretary. The junior position of the Ministry of Health implied that its leverage among the collective of cabinet members would have to depend greatly on the personal impact and connections of the Minister himself. In this sense Mr Greenwood was a very good person for the post, being well connected to the Labour parliamentary party as well as to the trade unions.

At the risk of repeating the obvious it should be remembered that the Ministry was operating within the framework of a minority government on the path to an economic and political collapse. The tendency was to avoid allocating financial resources to any programme; a very strong politically attractive argument was necessary to achieve a more positive policy.

The image emerging from the debates on the Mental Treatment Act is of a Minister aware of the moral and political issues at stake (H.235,961,969) but not well versed with the field and with relevant information (H.235,1582;244,1851). Thus a considerable part of his opening speech was devoted to the "plight of the mentally ill"; the assumed progress in intervention and to the attempt to provide equal and universal service across class boundaries (H.235, 957-970). The last point was exemplified by the declaration of severing the links between the Poor Laws and eligibility for mental health services. In effect, the Minister was claiming that the stigma which emanated from the Poor Law was spilling over to mental illness - i.e. from class membership to one's mental state. Interestingly he did not attempt to say that the opposite might happen - namely that becoming mentally ill would lead to downward social mobility. The Minister was also careful not to mention the statistical fact that the majority of hospitalized patients were of working-class origin. This omission is important because to mention this finding would have sounded as stigmatizing the mentally ill and/or the working class if seen outside the context of a socio-psychological explanation of mental illness. For an adherent to the medical approach this data implied evidence for genetic defects of working-class families(7), an explanation which Mr Greenwood had had to reject as a socialist.

It is unclear whether Mr Greenwood accepted fully the clinical-somatic model and its explanation of the aetiology of mental illness. But in the debates he consistently and relentlessly was on the side of doctors as the principal professional figures on the scene (H.235,963-4). He appeared to be totally unaware of the potential contradiction between his socialist beliefs and a clinical-somatic explanation. Likewise Mr Greenwood did not attempt to provide or look for a sociological approach to mental illness.

On moral grounds it was felt that mental illness should not be stigmatizing. According to Mr Greenwood the best way to reach this aim was through redressing the balance of powers in the field by three steps:
1.Eliminating the intervention of the magistrates in certification (H.935,962-4).
2.Giving more power to the professional authority which was perceived as neutral and has having counter-stigmatizing effects (H.235,963-4,969).
3.Giving more citizens' rights to the newly created category of voluntary patients (H.235,961).
4.Caring for the mentally ill in the community rather than in the hospital (H.235,969).

It was in line with the Labour Party's manifesto and beliefs to attempt to equalize and provide services for the poor and working-class people. To curtail the powers of the old middle class (e.g. the magistrates) in favour of the new one (e.g. the doctors) which was based on individually achieved meritocracy certainly followed Labour preference too (see ref. no.2). Thus Mr Greenwood's position was very much within mainstream ideology of the Labour movement in the 20s. At the same time no provisions were made for the transfer of those mentally ill hospitalized in

Poor Law institutions to county hospitals. Likewise the government refused to make compulsory local authorities' duties to provide community-based services. Mr Greenwood did neither acknowledge nor apologize for the discrepancy between the rhetoric and the practice. Therefore it would seem that while the Minister might have been sincere in his wish for equality of care he was not sufficiently committed to the two principles to the point of fighting for their implementation.

The only step taken towards moving away from Poor Law stigmatization was to change the term 'pauper' to that of 'rate-aided' (H.236,2150, 248,2272). While the new term was not rooted in the history of the Poor Law and therefore did not carry with it the same stigma it nevertheless maintained the difference between one type of patients (unaided) and another (the aided). The need to retain distinct categories by virtue of level of income and necessity for public fundings for intervention implies that the ideological change required for the move away from the Poor Law was at best only at its beginning.

If Mr Greenwood was unaware of the criticism of the Board of Control activities he was made acutely aware of them during the debates (H.235,939, 237,2536-40,2560). While acknowledging some of the glaring malpractices he consistently attempted to minimize the significance and scope of the criticism (H.233,1621;234,2072). The suggestion of several MPs to abolish the board was not even considered. Instead the ministry opted for a reorganization of the Board that implied an expansion of its authority and executive powers (H.235,967-8). In doing so the Minister demonstrated contradictory orientations. On the one hand he was against giving powers to amateur middle-class lay people (the magistrates). On the other hand he was ready to do so by investing more power in the hands of the Boards' commissioners, only two of whom were doctors.

The wish to justify the prevailing conditions and activities turned at times into a farce: replying to a question why do mentally ill patients sleep on the floor at a hospital, Miss Lawrence said that this practice was due to medical reasons (235.967-8, 249,1631). The Ministry did not appear to be open to the very few new ideas on intervention expressed in the House. For example, hostels (viewed today as a modern innovatory device) were twice suggested by MPs, only to be

119

dismissed as impractical.

The question begs itself as to why did the Minister prefer a public body in charge of the asylums system to bringing it under the direct control of the Ministry. In the absence of an open debate on this issue only speculations and tentative answers can be attempted. The Ministry of Health was established only in 1919. In 1929 it was still struggling for its position vis-a-vis other Ministries. This fact on its own would have equally led either to wishes for expansion or for maintaining the status quo. The national political and economic situation during 1929-31 warranted against any expansion that required further allocation of scarce financial resources. Incorporating the Board of Control would neither have required a substantial sum of money nor would it add any visible political gains. Therefore such a move would have been hard to justify at the time. Such a change was likely to create some headache to the civil servants in charge and they might have therefore stolen this move from the beginning. The defensive position in regard to the Board was also at the root of the Minister's backtracking from the display of relations' and patients' rights, mentioned above. To appear to be reforming the field and perhaps to be genuinely convinced that the new Act would contribute to a reform at no further cost was desirable for the reputation of the ministry, provided it did not go beyond this boundary.

The lack of political confidence of the government and the Ministry revealed itself on several occasions. For example the House of Lords did not accept an amendment agreed to in the Commons, which postulated the right of the Board to inquire into the financial affairs of a private nursing home, while such a right was part of its duties in regard to public institutions (H.246,1450). The Minister and his secretary recommended to the Commons to accept the Lords' decision in the name of expediency (H.240,741-8). The fact that this amendment negated the principle of equality of service and encouraged the profit motive which existed in the private sector was left unmentioned by Mr Greenwood, a self-professed socialist.

To summarize, the Ministry's position is characterized by a marked tendency to defend the existing system of services while at the same time attempting to reform it. The specific stands taken reflected often contradictory positions and readiness to give in for the sake of expediency. On the whole the basic approach of the Ministry was in line with Labour ideology on the one hand and with the wishes of the BMA and the Medico-Psychological Association on the other hand. Because of the support by the uninterested and silent majority of MPs the Minister could do as he pleased. Thus he was not considering seriously the critique put forward by the minority of interested MPs, most of whom belonged to Mr Greenwood's party.

The Minister stressed from the beginning of the debates that a non-controversial Bill was aimed at. To have a bi-partisan piece of legislation amidst growing difficulties in sustaining Labour in power must have been a relief for a Labour minister. Thus the Mental Treatment Act was brought before Parliament and passed by it partly because of its unifying component.

4.f.The Missing Issues.

To suggest that certain topics should have been discussed may be viewed as an imposition of the author's biases onto the parliamentary debates of MPs. Yet there are specific issues which are likely to be included in any major debate by virtue of the characteristics of mental illness and its significance to any audience. Elsewhere(8), and in the introduction it was suggested that the questions in regard to mental illness would differ firstly in accordance to degree of personal involvement. Secondly, the focus will depend on the function a person/a group have in relation to the mentally ill. Thirdly, the function of a group such as politicians in office is related closely to their role vis-a-vis the general public (H.235,988). The combination of these positions and what is taken for granted by participants in a debate will determine which issues will be overtly focused on and which issues would be likely to remain unmentioned.

1.Curiosity and a critical approach to explanatory models.
While a full scale conceptual discussion is not expected on any issue in Parliament it is inevitable that components of the explanatory and value preferences systems will crop up in a major

debate. Several aetiological explanations were mentioned in the 1930 debate. They range from mystery and Fate through physiological disease, (H.235,977) to poverty and escape from unemployment (H.237,1098;235,958,1006). Although raised they were never discussed. It seemed as if it was tacitly agreed that explanations of mental illness were shared by MPs. More specifically it was assumed that viewing mental illness as a physical illness was accepted by everyone, (H.235,959) including its implications for explanation and intervention. Perhaps because of this taken for granted supposition MPs did not express any doubts on the validity of the clinical-somatic model or any interest in any other approach, despite their knowledge of the insufficiency and inadequacy of this orientation in practice.

Alternatively MPs might have felt that explanations for mental illness have become a matter only for professional judgement and therefore excluded from the range of issues they need to be concerned with.

2.Lack of a manifested interest in and a critical approach to intervention methods.
Though a number of MPs made critical comments on the physical conditions of care only five times during 1927-32 was any psychiatric method questioned (H.247,1851). This marked reticence to look at intervention stands therefore in contrast to the expressed interest in the patients' welfare. It probably relates to perceiving intervention as a purely "clinical" (i.e. professional) matter which is outside the comprehension and judgement of a lay person. Thus while the politicians saw themselves as capable of legislating for the mentally ill they were ready to let the qualified physician have the only say on intervention. MPs were aware of cases of malpractice. More importantly, they knew the degree of inadequacy of the available services as reflected in the statistics on the patients' population, from the individual case histories and from their visits to hospitals. In fact MPs approached the main clauses of the new Bill as the vehicle of change in the stagnating situation (notably the creation of the category of voluntary patients). Not the slightest shade of doubt was cast on existing modes of intervention. The belief in medicine was strong enough to persuade them to leave it all in the hands of the doctor and to relinquish their duty as watchdogs for the public.

3.Lack of proposals how to ensure that the Poor Law will have no bearing on the mentally ill.
This issue was commented upon above in regard to the Minister of Health, Mr Greenwood (see the section on the Ministry's position). It merits to be raised in relation to all MPs, especially the socialists among them, since the same position was shared by all. MPs knew that a quarter of the mentally ill patients were in Poor Law institutions, where they and their relatives suffered from the effects of the combined stigma of being poor and incarcerated. They were also aware of the fact that by merely stating that "hitherto all relations between the Poor Law and mental illness were severed" (H.235,969) nothing was going to change for those hospitalized in the Poor Law asylums or for those likely to fall in this category in the near future. Yet no one brought forward any plans how it would have been achieved. In principle it could have been done by the amalgamation of county and Poor Law hospitals (which is how it eventually happened). Although in practice such a move would still allow for the majority of institutions to stay relatively unchanged for some time it would have paved the way for gradual changes with every new admission and certainly would have been a token of change. Scrapping terminological distinction between "aided" and "unaided" patients would have been at least a token in this direction.
    As none of these proposals were mentioned in the debate it is impossible to know whether they were discussed in private either in the Ministry or in MPs' circles. Their absence is astonishing for a Labour government and Labour Left MPs and can be explained only by the dread of the imminent fall of the government and the reflection of the depressed economic situation leading to the disbelief in implementing any large scale changes or imposing central government's wish on local government.

4.Changing the attitudes of the general public.
As was mentioned above, the general public was required to change its stigmatizing approach to the mentally ill without any suggestion how to implement such a drastic move. Certainly the topic could be approached as yet another example of politicians' love for rhetoric. The assumption that MPs would normally leave details of legislation and its implementation to the civil service is refuted

123

on numerous occasions in the debates, where MPs outlined minor suggestions for change (H.235,990, 1081-96). Therefore the question why desired changes in public opinion were not followed by contingency plans is not a rhetorical one. The tentative answer lies in the same realm as the answer to the previous issue of lack of suggestions for implementing the decision to severe ties between the Poor Laws and mental illness: namely the atmosphere of despondency over the possibility of carrying out any real change, as distinct from cosmetic ones. In addition it might have been realized that such a change in public attitudes depended on the outcome of the new legislation and/or was a difficult area to tackle in a systematic way and expect success in the short run.

5.Protecting the public from the mentally ill.
The issue was hardly ever raised. In the majority of previous parliamentary debates on mental illness this area was a crucial one(9). Ministers and politicians have had to satisfy themselves and others that the public's needs were looked after adequately. Instead, the 1930 debate was concentrated on the need to protect patients, family members and doctors, but not the public.

The focus on changing the public's attitudes towards the mentally ill commented upon earlier might have led to altering the traditional angle into a more radical one. In addition the ministry and MPs were likely to believe that the public's interests vis-a-vis the mentally ill were well protected by the main changes introduced in the Mental Treatment Act: 1.Changing the classification system and encouraging a voluntary status. 2. Treating mental illness as physical illness. 3.Severing links between the Poor Law status and that of mental illness.

The importance of listing and discussing the "missing" issues lies in realizing what were the possible dimensions of the debate as compared to its actual ones.

By omitting fundamental areas such as explanation and intervention the debate turned necessarily into a shallow discussion of anything that was not overtly related to civil rights. Without wishing to undermine the importance of patients' rights even those become quite limited when discussed outside the context of the meaning of mental illness and professional intervention. Throughout the debates and the 1927-32 period one observes radical steps contemplated side by side with retreating from implementing them.

Overtly, the political and economic background was casting its shadow on the mentally ill and the politicians alike. Covertly the value preference for a particular professional solution to issues with a much broader connotation was casting a much wider net on MPs' understanding and ability to act on behalf of the mentally ill.

The main innovations of the period came either from psychoanalysts or psychologists open to the impact of psychodynamic thinking but not from mainstream psychiatry, as chapter 3 demonstrated.

However this evidence was ignored and its significance left unrecognised for several reasons, some of which have been presented above. Firstly there was a genuine belief in the promise which medicine held and therefore readiness to wait for it to materialize. This belief was shared by all MPs. It facilitated the inclusion of psychiatry under the umbrella of medicine and prevented the consideration of the role played by social and psychological factors in mental illness.

Secondly, lack of deep interest in the field of mental illness led not only to indifference by the majority of the politicians. It also accounts for a certain degree of shallowness and readiness to follow existing solutions by those who expressed their interest.

MPs and the Ministry demonstrated an enthusiastic acceptance for the model of mental illness promoted by the mainstream of British psychiatry. Any other available view, such as psychoanalysis, was neither recognized nor considered. Similarly any other organizational structure of the psychiatric services not put forward by established psychiatry was not contemplated, even when it was not opposed as was the case with the setting up of child guidance clinics.

The politicians have opted for strengthening the domination of mainstream psychiatry in two of the main measures of the 1930 Mental Treatment Act: the rejection of a role for magistrates in voluntary admission and the creation of the status of voluntary patienthood inside the hospital enhanced the power of psychiatrists.

The commitment to the clinical-somatic view was reaffirmed at a time when the contribution of the protagonists of this approach to the theory and practice of psychiatry was unsatisfactory by its own standards.

Thirdly the measures adopted seemed to be in the direction of giving more dignity to patients than before and therefore welcomed as a liberalizing means.

Fourthly no professional group attempted to provide Parliament with an alternative policy, including those who preferred to see outpatients' clinics becoming the major organizational setting of psychiatric activity. Neither Parliament nor government can tolerate a vacuum to take place in an area sensitive from the social control perspective.

Lastly given the reasons just listed and the position of the Labour minority government the implicit wish would be not to rock any existing boats for the sake of largely unknown ones.

References

1.Who is Who (1932, 1937) A. S. Black, London
2.Pimlott, B. (1977) Labour and the Left in the 1930's, Cambridge University Press, Cambridge.
3.Miliband, R. (1973) Parliamentary Socialism, Merlin Press, London, p.13
4.For example, see the experiment conducted by Abelson, R. A., Miller, J. (1967) Negative Persuasion Via Personal Insult, Journal of Experimental and Social Psychology, 3, pp.321-33.
5.Leeper, R. R. (1931) Some Reflection on the Progress of Psychiatry, Journal of Mental Science, 77, pp.683-91.
6.British Medical Journal (1920), 2, p.695.
7.See Dr Carswell's speech in The Lancet, 1924, 2, p.613.
8.Ramon, S. (1978) The Meaning Attached: Attitudes towards the Mentally Ill, Journal of Mental Health and Society, 34, pp.164-182.
9.Parry-Jones, W. (1972) The Trade in Lunacy, Routledge and Kegan Paul, London, Ch. 2.

5 Mental Distress in the Social Context of the Fifties

5.a.The Social Context.

The considerable social, political and economic changes which took place in Britain between 1930 (when the Mental Treatment Act was passed) and 1959 (when the Mental Health Act was legislated) have been amply documented(1). Britain ceased to be an empire; the financial reserves from the colonies that it could draw on previously did not exist any more. Economic dependency on the U.S. was expected and feared at the end of the war. Nevertheless the wish for a radical improvement of the quality of life was apparent throughout the war period. This expressed wish led to the move towards a welfare state and the nationalization of major industries. This change was primarily implemented by the postwar Labour government.

The introduction of the National Health Service (the NHS)(2) was a major feature in providing universalistic welfare services. The care of the mentally ill became an integral part of the NHS, though not without doubts. A short reply was given to a question by Mr. Sorenson, MP, on April 15, 1943, whether the mental health services would be included in the proposed National Health Service: "The answer to the second question is No, Sir"(3). Yet the 1944 White Paper (Cmnd 6052) included mental hospitals in the scheme and reaffirmed the 1930 stand that mental illness should be treated like physical illness. It is assumed that the Ministry changed its mind from excluding mental health services to including them as a result of pressure from the BMA (4) but no references are made as to the evidence of such a pressure.

127

In terms of daily practice it meant that people did not have to pay directly any more for the services and had to be referred by their GP to the psychiatric service. The Poor Law was finally repealed; the 1948 NHS Act put an end to any use of means test in regard to health services. Thus the stigma attached to being poor and hence less deserving was reduced significantly in the use of health facilities. As eligibility became universal the quality of the service was to be equalized too. Though in operation from 1948 the NHS Act became statutory for the mental health sector only with the 1959 legislation. Little else changed in 1948 for the ordinary user of the service who was not interested in the administrative reorganization of the services that took place(5).

Mentally distressed people benefited also from the 1948 National Assistance law by becoming eligible for financial support regardless of whether they paid/did not pay insurance previously.It is relevant to our discussion to remember that the NHS structure gave greater responsibilities than before to the local level. Small hospitals became part of a hospital group with the advantages and disadvantages of such a merger. Though a large number of lay people became involved in hospital management committeees and in local authority management, few of them were likely to represent consumers of the psychiatric services.

Another cornerstone of welfare policies was the emphasis on the family as the primary social unit. Although ambivalent in its expression and serving at times contradictory purposes the focus on the family was maintained throughout the 50s(6).

When the Conservatives came to power in 1951 (and stayed until 1964) it was feared that they might limit or even abolish the welfare services established by the Labour government during 1946-51. As we know, this prediction proved wrong for the 50s. In one area of welfare - housing - the Conservatives did more than their predecessors in terms of the number of houses built, though the aim was to encourage private ownership(7). Most of the social welfare legislation passed during the fifties consolidated the legislation introduced by the postwar Labour government.

The major differences and political battles between the two leading parties seemed to have diminished during the 50s with the exception of the Suez campaign(8). The Conservative government accepted in principle not only the welfare system but also the Keynesian approach to economics. The internal division between the left and the right inside the Labour party deepened during that period. The right wing seemed to be winning towards the end of the period(9).

The cold war between the Eastern and Western blocks was reigning during the fifties in Britain too. In contrast to the US, it did not culminate in a witch hunt of the McCarthy type. With the exception of the Suez Campaign Britain's foreign policy was mostly played alongside that of the US, even more so after the campaign. The decision not to enter the European Common Market was taken and reconfirmed several times during the decade.

The Campaign against Nuclear Disarmament (CND) protest movement became prominent during the period. At its height it represented the dissatisfaction with the use of scientific achievements by politicians. Although a minority in the population, it was a large and vocal one, dominated by middle-class young people of socialist, pacifist and Christian beliefs. Towards the end of the decade CND had a considerable impact on the life of the Labour Party(10).

The notion of economic affluence was taken for granted from the mid 50s and onwards, expressed in the slogan "You've never had it so good"(11). In relative terms it was so for the majority of working and middle-classes in terms of increase in income and standard of living(12). Full employment seemed a realistic target.

On re-reading the statistics on standards of living in the 50s, Townsend suggested that the tendency towards levelling inequality changed in the mid-50s towards one of increased inequality(13).

The felt need for a larger unskilled workforce led to the beginning of encouraging emigration from the Indian sub-continent and the West Indies to the UK.

Although the economy was growing at a healthy rate, Britain went from one monetary crisis to another between 1955 and 1961, accompanied by a constant increase in the rate of inflation. The huge deficit in the balance of payments left by the Labour government in 1951 was put down to the effects of the war. The even larger deficit left by the Conservatives in 1964 could not be explained in the same way(14).

Disenchantment with the affluent society was already expressed by some middle-class young people - e.g. the "angry young men" as the very diverse group was called(15).

Both middle and working-class youth preferred new types of music (Rock'n'Roll) and styles of clothes. The "Teddy Boys" image was largely born out of an attempt by working class boys to be different; an attempt perceived by the British establishment as deviant and the teenagers being treated as such(16), perhaps indicating that the overall level of tolerating non-conformity was low.

The emphasis on youth, typical of the 60s, developed gradually in the 50s: it was expressed in legislation(17), in mass culture and in coaching young people to become conscious consumers(18). The characteristics of a full scale consumers' society unfolded in the 50s. The use of television as a common leisure occupation by the majority of the population contributed to the development of consumerism. The positive and the negative impact of television need not be spelled out here(19). Suffice it to indicate that the development of today's mass media and mass culture is rooted in the fifties.

By the end of the fifties the wish for radical social changes has been tamed into the wish for a higher standard of living and for stability. The mental distress scene, and in particular the 1959 Mental Health Act, have to be looked at in the light of this prevailing public attitude.

5.b.The Mental Distress Scene.

In the years between 1945 and 1960 a considerable increase occurred in the number of clients, type of activities run and monitored by the psychiatric services and the number of units and personnel(20). The expansion was seen as more dramatic in the field of out-patient facilities than in the in-patient sector. As only few out-patient units existed before the war any increase in this section expressed an expansion. However the largest share of investment in the service went to its hospital sector.

The reasons for the expansion of the services are multiple, of which demand could have been only one. It might well be that the impact of both the medicalization and the psychologization of mental distress (looked at in chapter 6), the very fact that people started to come out of hospitals

130

instead of staying there indefinitely, led to diminishing fears of psychiatric intervention and readiness to ask for it. As it is unlikely that demand on its own would convince the government to invest in the psychiatric services, the reasons for the involvement of the latter lie elsewhere. The creation of the NHS boosted the expansion of all of its branches, including psychiatry. The voluntary sector expanded too. Mind was established in 1946, as the national organization to which most voluntary associations became affiliated. In the fifties Mind played a major role in campaigning for policy and legislation changes within the parameters of established British psychiatry.

J. Busfield had argued convincingly(21) that the abolition of the Poor Law created a vacuum to be filled in terms of placing the categories of deviants catered for by the Poor Law. The responsibility for caring for and controlling some of these "misfits" has been transferred to psychiatry instead. The establishment of a health system based on universalistic principles and the use of the facilities by middle-class people have also contributed to the expansion of the facilities aimed at this group, e.g. out-patient psychotherapy oriented clinics and special units for mildly disturbed people.

The number of hospital admissions was 105,000 in 1959, with a total number of in-patient population of 139,000, while the general population size reached 45 millions(22). The admission figures were four times more than the 1930 numbers, though the general population growth was only 13% during the same period. The number of discharged patients was 94,000(23). These statistics indicate a high degree of movement within the in-patient population and a much smaller degree of chronicity, as well as pointing out that the magnitude of the problem has not diminished. Further details on in-patient numbers from 1951 onward appear in table 2, appendix 1(24).

The table portrays a large increase in admission for males and a smaller one for females. It pinpoints the dramatic increase in the rate of discharge for both sexes, especially for females. What this table does not demonstrate is a significant decrease in the overall total in-patient population size: at its peak in 1954 the number was 147,080 and at its ebb in 1959 it was 139,770 - i.e. a difference of less than 7,000 patients (if the number of deaths in 1959 is taken into account).

Rate of recovery for all but statutory patients was reported to be 71% while that of the latter category was only 16%(25). Sidebottom and Jones(26) pointed to the lack of positive correlation between categorizing a patient as recovered and his/her chances of returning to the hospital. It is suggested therefore to consider these high rates of recovery with an equally high degree of caution. By 1957 about 75% of the in-patients were there on a voluntary basis(27). Out-patient numbers were estimated as one milion with 145,000 new out-patients per year(28).

The increase in admission was put down to the combination of several factors:

1. Availability of services free of charge.
2. Increase of the probability of becoming mentally ill with the increase of longevity.
3. Greater public tolerance towards the mentally distressed.
4. Earlier discharge and readmission patterns.
5. The difficulties entailed for families in containing a mentally ill member within the family, given the tendency to live in small, nuclear households.
6. Changes in psychiatric definitions(29).

The reasons for the high rate of discharge will be looked at in the section on intervention methods below.

The cost of maintaining in-patients in hospital was £7.12.8d. per week compared to £10.18.7d. for the physically chronic patient and £25.16.7d. for the acute physically ill(30).

Whatever the reasons for the increase in admissions and discharge the size of the in-patient and out-patient populations meant that mental illness could be felt as a social problem in terms of awareness of its negative ramifications(31). For example the number of lost working days was estimated to be 80 million in 1957 by the chairman of the Board of Control(32). The cost of hospital services was put down to £80 millions(33). These variables do not include the expressed need for more staff, better facilities or the subjective component of suffering and its impact - all of which have to be considered.

Hospitals were inherited from the Victorian era in terms of unsuitable accommodation, type of building and large numbers of inmates(34). The new purpose-built units for neurotic patients looked brighter and offered more in terms of intervention methods and facilities to the residents(35). Thus a division between "long stay" and "short stay" wards emerged, corresponding roughly to demarcation lines between psychotics/neurotics, chronic/acute, and elderly/young. Only a few private and voluntary hospitals still existed(36). The majority of the hospitals were financed by local and central government and inspected by the Board of Control. The latter's performance was often criticized as inefficient and inappropriate by the press and MPs(37). Sidebottom and Jones (see ref. 26), Clark(38) and Barton(39) provide us with descriptions of the variations within the hospital system during the fifties.

The differences in size between one hospital and another seem to account for the degree of personal attention patients received as well as innovation in intervention methods: the larger the hospital the less the individualized attention given. Larger hospitals provided better facilities for physical treatment and research and were more likely to be run as independent units. Shortages of accommodation and staff, the tendency towards highly regimented and impersonal lives for residents were the target of criticism by professionals and lay people, MPs, the press and Mind(40).

Did mental illness become recognized as a social problem - i.e. not only by those involved with it but by public opinion? "Public opinion" is an elsuive concept. There is little doubt that usually the expression of such opinion does not represent the general population but reflects the views of a powerful and vocal minority (e.g. the media, politicians). Yet an impressive number of examples exists to provide evidence for the claim of the impact that public opinion has in Britain(41). It had been argued that public opinion is just one component of the ruling elites trying to influence another part of these circles(42). While this may be the case it still broadens the notion of the ruling class as open to contradictory interests and to influences from outside the elite groups(43).

Mental illness, the type of care patients were receiving, the Royal Commission report in 1957 and the debate on the 1959 Act became topics worthy of sporadic attention by newspapers such as the Times (e.g. October 15th, 1957); the Daily

Telegraph (e.g. July 5th, 1957); the News Chronicle
(e.g. November 8th, 1957). In all of these articles
a sympathetic approach was taken towards the
mentally distressed. They differed in the attitudes
towards professional activity, especially by
psychiatrists. While the Daily Telegraph was
praising their efforts, the News Chronicle
criticized the same activities.

The claim that public opinion became more
tolerant of the mentally ill is corroborated to an
extent by the articles mentioned above. Whether the
majority of the general public adhered to this
tolerance or became aware of changes in
intervention in regard to mental illness is much
more difficult to assess.

In the only available study during the 50s on
lay people's attitudes towards the issue, Carstairs
and Wing(44) analysed the 25,000 letters sent to
the BBC in 1957 as a reaction to a series of five
programmes on mental illness - "The Hurt Mind". The
impressive number of letters indicates best that
mental distress has become an issue of concern.
Relatives of patients were "over represented" in
this group (i.e. more than their percentage in the
general population), but many letters came from
people who did not describe themselves as
personally involved. The letters were biased
positively towards the distressed people themselves
and negatively towards the professionals,
especially GPs. Though the analysis of the results
merely categorized the responses, the findings were
sufficient to indicate the writers' readiness for
greater understanding and involvement with the
mentally ill.

The collection of patients' reports edited
and published by two MPs(45) indicates how
committed some MPs were to this cause as well as
the existence of a readership for such a book. This
publication was seen as sufficiently important to
lead to a reply by professionals in a book called
"Bridging the Gap"(46).

The following are two typical extracts from
the many which appeared in the first book. They
speak for themselves: one by one, patients' reports
give the firm message of disrespect towards them,
psychiatrists, duly authorized officiers and nurses
are accused of a dehumanizing approach, use of
coercion, neglect of basic citizens' rights, lack
of concern for patients' feelings and lack of
attempts at genuine communication. In short,
according to the patients' account what went on was

134

a far cry from being therapeutic. Even given the oversensitivity of patients and the likelihood of distortion of experiences the book as a document proved difficult to dismiss or ignore.

(a)   It was during the evening of Sunday, 15th July, that I was called to see the ward doctor, and I gladly left my bed to do so. I found later that he had consultant status. First he gave me a reasonably careful physical examination. Then he turned to the ward sister and said: "She will need to be looked after all her life." I stared at the doctor in horror. Then I asked him whether he found something wrong with my chest, and said, if so, I would rather be told. He answered: "Oh no, it was your mental condition I was referring to. I'm afraid you will have to get used to the idea of staying here for good. It is quite comfortable. There are plenty of entertainments on Saturdays. You can go to the pictures. You will settle down, but you will never be fit to earn your own living again."
       "But", I said, "less than a week ago I was earning my own living. How can you make that out? You have had no contact with my employers. You cannot have any reason to say what you have said. All you have done is to destroy my employment without enquiry there."
       He smiled his indulgent smile: "You see, you have no insight into your illness. You do not know how ill you are. You think you are fit to earn your living, but you are not. It is a permanent condition. It is irreversible. You will need to live in the shelter of a mental hospital for the rest of your life. You will have nothing to worry about. Your needs will be provided for. There is nothing I can do about it."
(b)   I asked for a report from my own doctor, who was at that period attending me. The psychiatrist said that it was quite needless. But then I requested her to telephone news of my whereabouts to my solicitor; and this request was also refused. Would they please telephone my employers and tell them that I could not go to work? No, they would not. If they had been trying to provoke me to some act of violence they could not have done better. But I behaved myself. However, there I was, spirited away by night by two men, locked up in a hospital miles away from my home, unable to notify anyone of my address, out of reach of any form of moral support, isolated from every means of help,

and being kept in solitary confinement. And this
was in England , during the Festival of Britain.
Next day was Friday, 13th July. I was brought
before a magistrate and stood before him between
two nurses, with two more behind me. The magistrate
coldly informed me that the medical certificate
stated that I was ill, and that he was therefore
going to send me away to a hospital "for a long
time". I answered that I perfectly understood him
and I asked to be allowed to go to hospital as a
voluntary patient. He refused my request, without
stating any reason.(47)

While the book covers loyally patients'
impressions it does not offer suggestions as to
desirable changes. This weakness will be taken up
in chapter 7.
The massive increase in the number of
voluntary patients mentioned above may indicate
that individuals, families and communities were
less afraid of what may happen to them in a
psychiatric hospital and of the impact of
hospitalization on the family's reputation.

Methods of Intervention.
The change in methods of treatment from those
available in the 20s was considerable. Insulin and
ECT emerged as the established new methods of
psychiatric treatment. A substantial growth in
out-patient clinics, experiments with therapeutic
communities inside the hospitals and a greater use
of occupational therapy were in evidence. The open
door policy and the psychotropic drugs were the
most recent additions(48).
More psychiatric wards were established
inside the general hospital. This development was
perceived as part of psychiatric community care and
as leading to the increase in stigma attached to
psychiatric patients and their hospitals. In fact,
these wards symbolize the greater tie between
psychiatry and general medicine(49). Within
medicine itself the move towards thinking in terms
of social medicine continued(50). This orientation
was prevalent in public health and epidemiology.
While it influenced the practice of public health
not much of the daily face-to-face intervention had
changed up to 1959.
As chapter 4 demonstrated, ideas on care of
patients in the community - rather than in hospital
- were expressed in the 1930 debate and in the
Mental Treatment Act, but were left largely

unimplemented by successive governments for reasons discussed in the section on the government's position and in chapter 3. Nevertheless, more out-patient clinics and child guidance centres were established. They were financed by voluntary organizations and some local authorities. The spread of the child guidance clinics was in part due to the impact of psychanalysis in Britain(51). This growth led to the employment of more psychiatric social workers and clinical/educational psychologists. However psychotherapy was rarely practised with in-patients or in adult out-patient clinics.

As in the twenties, the majority of in-patients were of working-class origin(52). The middle-classs population was more prevalent in the out-patient sector.

Therapeutic communities inside hospitals were tried successfully in several experiments(53). The model had been rejected by the majority of hospital staff throughout the country, as is pointed in chapter 6.

Today's unsuspecting reader of professional psychiatric literature and lay newspapers of the 50s is struck by the schism between the writings at the beginning and at the end of the decade on the open door policy and the psychotropic drugs. Contrary to the impression given from the late 50s and onward(54), it emerges that the decrease in in-patients' numbers has taken place wherever the open door policy was adopted, dating from 1942. By 1954 the Lancet(55) mentions the following large hospitals and districts as places where the open door was implemented: Warlingham Park(1942), Belmont(1944), Mapperly(1945), Dingleton(1947), Crichton Royal(1950), De la Pole(1951), Whitechurch, Oldham(1954). Repeatedly we find in all of these cases an impressive decrease in the number of in-patients, paralleled by a considerable increase in admission and discharge rates, and longer periods of stay outside the hospitals.

Like the psychotropic drugs, the open door policy did not require large numbers of qualified personnel. Unlike the drugs, however, it was not costly. At the time the side-effects of both interventions were not of interest to the majority of professionals or lay people. The open door policy's main side-effects are the effects of being discharged into an unreceptive and unprepared environment. High discharge rate seemed to become the main goal. Thus while meeting the same target, the open door policy was the least expensive option, yet the one which received less attention.

The psychiatrists' enthusiasm to experiment with the new drugs is easily understandable. The governments's apparent readiness to follow suit can be understood only if the latter was content to see the purchase and use of the drugs as a purely clinical decision. Indeed, the general attitude of the Ministry of Health towards prescriptions did endorse overspending; an attitude exploited by the pharmaceutical companies(56). Yet this explanation still leaves unresolved the reasons for the reconstruction of the almost omnipotent role allocated to the psychotropic drugs vs. the minor one given to the open door policy.

The sudden disappearnace of symptoms following taking the psychotropic drugs gave them the halo of a miracle not unlike that of penicillin, ECT and insulin, but without the risks involved in the last two types of treatment. No such spectacular changes could be linked with the open door policy - it demanded an ideological change from its initiators and the public. The likely reasons for the ideological shift that led to the open door policy and the rewriting of the history of intervention methods will be presented in chapter 6.

"Community care" became the key term in Britain with which to describe the direction of innovation in intervention. Some of the first community mental health services(57) and therapeutic communities(58) have originated in the UK. However, the theoretical development of this approach took place mainly in the US, under the name Community Mental Health(CMH). The following is an outline of the CMH main assumptions and conclusions up to 1960. The description is necessary to enable a comparison with the image of community care in the British press as a representative of the general public; the comparison with the British professional viewpoint will be attempted in chapter 6.

The roots of the CMH model date back to the moral approach and to the 19th century social medicine movement(59). Developments in public health during the 19th and 20th centuries and the readiness to accredit social factors the status of causal leads were an additional dimension. Neo-Freudian theory, the experience of brief psychotherapy and crisis intervention during the Second World War and after reinforced rethinking about traditional psychiatry and psychotherapy. Sociological studies of psychiatry influenced it too(60).

Its main assumptions and proposals were:

1.Mental illness can be caused by several factors, external to the person as well as internal. They can be social and/or biological and psychological, due to tensions in the family or the wider social content (e.g. emigration).

2.The person becomes more vulnerable and prone to become mentally distressed at crisis stages in his life. Most of these crisis are part of ordinary developmental phases(61). At the crisis situation the person is ready to receive help and - with support - can act at a higher level of competence than before, after the initial panic. The outcome of going through a crisis could therefore be a growth in the person's emotional, intellectual and social capacities(62).

3.The model of the person implicitly endorsed within the CMH framework is the one outlined by the Ego Psychology school(63). The ability for conscious and creative acivity - rather than defensive behaviour - is stressed. Although the power of the unconscious and the impact of childhood experiences is recognized, the focus is on the adult rather than on the child. The adult is more of a social than a biological being, capable of overcoming conflicts, of sustaining interpersonal relationsips, interested in the world outside the family circle and in acquiring new competence.

4.A number of background factors which may lead to mental illness can be identified and dealt with at the level of the general population at the preventive level (e.g. pre-natal and post-natal services). The application of the concept of a developmental crisis and social structure factors allows the early identification of groups at risk. These groups can then be offered appropriate services prior to the development of acute mental illness (unemployed people, youth in a disintegrating community, children of parents going through divorce).

5.Thus three levels of intervention are recognized: primary, secondary and tertiary(64). The acceptance of these levels implies a pyramid with a universal base of services (e.g. GPs firms) which become more and more selective towards the top. Examples of "the top" would be a special small unit for severly distressed people or a permanent home for the minority likely to stay socially disabled.

6.Cultural relativity is recognized and schemes of CMH should vary in accordance with cultural preference. But each of these should include a component of lay people working with the community at large on mental health issues. Thus an attempt to make mental distress into a community issue is suggested, as well as democratization of the system of carers. Consumers-patients were seen as participants in therapeutic communities. However, they were not considered in terms of their positive potential contribution throughout the care system.

7.Each profession has its own unique contribution to make. Some functions may be fulfilled by more than one profession (e.g. counselling). The contribution of each profession is of equal importance. The recognition of such equality should be expressed in the authority and decision making structure.

8.Professional people at all levels should be prepared to work outside their office, including domiciliary visits as part of ordinary practice. This requirement is part of the meaning attached to working in the community as well as an attempt to equalize the input of different professionals.

9.CMH does not oppose the use of chemotherapy and medical diagnostic tools as long as: i.it is judged to be relevant for an individual case; ii.its contribution does not imply discarding the contributions of social and psychological approaches.

The approach thus combines an explanatory and an intervention framework.

CMH does not reject the existing social order of Western parliamentary democracies. In fact, it is attempting to secure its perpetuation through the prevention and containment of mental distress. The model sees the mentally ill as sick, and does not blame their society for it, despite the recognition of the contribution of social factors. Therefore in principle it does not differ from the clinical-somatic model in accepting the social control brief allocated to psychiatry or in seeing the mentally distressed as deviants. The difference is one of degree and location of the causes for the deviant behaviour. For example, the CMH approach recognized the role of the public in treating the ex-mentally ill as sick through the stigma attached to this group and found itself attempting to change public opinion(65). Such an attempt could not have even been conceived as relevant within the clinical-somatic approach. On the range of intervention models the CMH orientation is closer to the communal end of the spectrum than to the clinical side.

The acceptance of the existing social order and the optimistic belief in the capacity to change elements of it on their own reflect on the notions of planned liberalism in the US and the UK during the 50s. The internal inconsistency in the CMH model is indicated by: 1.The assumption that a radical change in the existing structure of psychiatric care can take place without any change in the prevailing social control system of the mentally ill. 2.Even when social factors have been identified as causal factors, the person is "ill", yet his society is not asked to change structurally in order to prevent the illness.

The approach does not provide a systematic appraisal of professional activities or the psychiatric system. This deficiency is in part due to the fact that the approach borrowed liberally concepts and methods from different schools of thought and did not make explicit its value preferences.

It has been criticized as too vague, idealistic, unrealistic and overinclusive. The critique from the right disagreed with the emphasis on a comprehensive service and the need for continuous public investment. The proposed equal place given to social causality and the need to change public attitudes did not endear the CMH to this camp. The critique from the left viewed the CMH as a tool in the service of expanding the use of soft social control and of providing the rationale for decarceration which was used primarily for economic ends(66).

Most of the criticisms date from the seventies onwards, after a decade of experimenting with the approach in the US.

As mentioned above the CMH and the clinical-somatic approaches share the view that the patient is ill and not his society. This similarity has important implications as to the right of society to intervene in the case of the mentally ill for the sake of both care and control.

The similarity between these approaches ends here, because even the conclusion in regard to social responsibility as a principle for providing services differs between the two models:

Conceptually, social responsibility has no place in the clinical-somatic approach.

It should be clear by now to the reader that the two models are incompatible in regard to:
1.Aetiology of mental distress.
2.Intervention methods.
3.The place of the different professions involved in the service system.
4.The role of society.
5.The place of non-professionals within the service system.

This incompatibility was never acknowledged by British professionals, Mind, the press and the politicians. It is argued here that the lack of awareness concerning the incompatibility was a major component in arresting the development of community services for the mentally distressed by extending the clinical-somatic approach to the community rather than changing the spirit and the practice of the service. An analysis of this argument will be provided in chapters 6 and 7. The version of CMH with which the public was presented prevented it from becoming aware of the incompatibility, let alone accepting or rejecting its implications.

The following is based on newspapers' coverage of the Royal Commission report (July 1957) and the debate on the Mental Health Act in both Houses (May-June 1959). The newspapers looked at were the Times, the News Chronicle and the Daily Telegraph. Usually mental distress items came in the columns on parliamentary and ministerial activity. On some occasions specific innovating projects were described by the psychiatrist in charge. At times the source of information was outside the professional circle - e.g. the Provost of Sheffield University (Times, October 15, 1957), but it was never a patient, a family member or a professional who was not a psychiatrist. Rarely were comments added by the reporter. Community care was portrayed as a mixture of activities: domiciliary visits, GPs in charge of out-patient clinics, psychiatric wards in general hospitals, social clubs for patients and ex-patients, emphasis on early entry to hospital as well as early discharge. Viewed as a positive development the underlying assumptions for community care were:
1.It is better for the mentally ill to stay in their family home than in the hospital.
2.Community care costs considerably less than hospitalization.

3.It was acknowledged that the implementation of community care will require time, the goodwill of local authorities and the public and more social workers.

The image emerging was closely related to that of secondary and tertiary preventive medicine aimed at redressing the prevalent negative image of psychiatry into a more positive one.

The place allocated to other professionals than psychiatrists was left vague: social workers were described either as doctors' aides or as the core of the new system. Nurses, occupational therapists and psychologists were not mentioned. The parliamentary debate was reported loyally, including the crucial issue of whether local authorities' duties should be made mandatory or not. Yet no attempt was made at an independent evaluation of the issues involved or at a coherent description of the content of community care. Likewise, no critical comments were expressed: community care was described as the best available solution to which everybody was assumed to be a willing partner. Alternatives were never described or debated, even in newspapers which consistently criticized psychiatric practice (e.g. the News Chronicle).

As portrayed in the press the concept of community care reflected some of the CMH principles such as the emphasis on early intervention and preference for community based services to hospital facilities.

However, the reflection stopped short of any of the other basic elements of the CMH, such as:

1.The view of mental illness not as yet another physical illness but as linked to developmental crisis.

2.The principle by which medicine is relegated from the top of the profesional hierarchy to an equal position vis-a-vis other professional groups. At no point is the possibility of incompatibility between the clinical-somatic model and the CMH approach hinted at.

The press was quoting directly either psychiatrists or politicians. The various newspapers seemed content not to have an independent view on the subject matter, presumably because of the combination of confidence in psychiatrists' opinions and indifference.

The Royal Commission appointed in 1954 (the Royal Commission on the Law related to Mental Illness (Cmnd 169)) included MPs, physicians, psychiatrists, lawyers, social workers, representatives of the nursing profession and of the volunatry sector. It did not have patients or family members represented. The committee was established in response to expressed criticism by MPs, the press and psychiatrists on the physical conditions in hospitals, the cumbersome procedure for voluntary admission and unease concerning institutionalization. The options before the committee were:

1.To let the existing system - based mainly on traditional psychiatry with pockets of community care - stay unchanged.
2.To adopt the community care model.
3.To adopt the community mental health approach.

During the 50s the legalistic approach was in existence in so far as the emphasis on patients' citizens rights and the right to be treated in a dignified way was often expressed(69). Overtly such an approach was not disputed by any of those involved in the mental distress scene. However, it was by then taken for granted that the legalistic approach could at best be no more than an appendix to other interventions.

The main recommendations of the Royal Commission were:

1.To add psychopathy as a mental disorder category.
2.To minimize the formality in the admission procedure of voluntary patients.
3.To broaden the legal possibilities of compulsory admission.
4.To abolish the Board of Control while transferring its duties to the Ministry of Health.
5.To establish independent tribunals of appeal.
6.The Commission suggested an expansion of the existing psychiatric services in the community and called for the community care option to become the primary mental health policy.
7.Community care was to be implemented as a mandatory duty by local authorities and to be supported by a special grant from central government.
8.Hospitals were to become "de-designated" i.e. would be able to accept any patients they wanted or to refuse to do so.

The recommendations on psychopathy, the de-designation of hospitals, the establishment of tribunals and the request for central government's special grant for community care were radical. All

of the other suggestions followed closely the pattern of practice already established in the field. For example, the Board of Control suggested its own abolition to the Royal Commission.
The Commission's recommendations are a curious combination of potentially conflicting components. On the one hand the Royal Commission wanted to strengthen local authorities' position in the attempt to achieve an adequate level of services in the community. On the other hand a greater measure of autonomy was given to hospitals, thus making local authorities even more dependent on the goodwill of specific hospitals and area health authorities. Simultaneously the Commission offered more freedom to voluntary patients, yet widened the scope of possibilities under which they could become easily certified(67). While the Commission refused to define psychopathy and mental illness, it did not hesitate to add the clinically doubtful category of psychopathy as a main category of mental disorders(68). The decision to do so signifies the completion of the process of medicalization and psychologization of mental distress in regard to anti-social behaviour, as B. Wootton pointed out at the time(69). The place appropriated to the positive impact of the psychotropic drugs and other physical methods of intervention must have played a major role in convincing the Commission's members of the achievements of psychiatry as a branch of medicine. The 1945-57 commission had much more evidence in favour of medical psychiatry than its predecessor in 1927. Equally, however, the 50s commission had more evidence for the CMH approach than existed in the 20s.
The recommendation to have tribunals is an exception to the general trend described above: tribunals were to be set as a legal safeguard for patients' rights and to consist of lay people as well as psychiatrists. It is however questionable whether the same weight would be given in the informal proceedings of a tribunal to the opinions of psychiatrists and those of lay peole. Tellingly, only psychiatrists were mentioned as eligibile members of the professions to sit on a tribunal - and not nurses, social workers or psychologists.
It is not surprising that the Commission did not adopt the CMH model: as demonstrated above, and in chapter 6, the knowlede of the CMH as a distinct approach and the awareness of its incompatibility with the clinical-somatic model were not made known

to the British non-professional public.
The Mental Health Act, 1959, implemented all of the main recommendations of the commission with one exception: local authorities' duties in regard to community service (but not in regard to hospitalization) were to remain permissive, as in 1930. Yet again, as in 1930, local authorities would not be given a special grant from central government towards meeting their obligations in regard to community care. Thus in contrast to the commission, the Ministry was much less committed to the idea of community services for the mentally distressed. The likely reasons for the government's stand will be looked at in chapter 7.
To conclude, the 1959 Mental Health Act was a step forward in getting rid of terminology and legislation from 1890 which became outdated and cumbersome a long time before 1959. It cemented the social decision to incorporate mental distress firmly into medicine by extending the clinical-somatic approach into the community. The Act could be read as an encouragement for the development of community services for this group of people. Yet this support was weakened considerably by the absence of positive governmental action about it.
The CMH approach existed as an alternative policy in the fifties while such an alternative did not exist in the twenties. As was pointed out it did not question the right of society to control its mentally ill members and therefore did not pose a threat to the government. Nevertheless a public debate of the various alternatives did not take place. The decision on the character of psychiatric policies and legislation was taken on the basis of an implicit, majority shared, preference for the medicalization of mental distress.

References
1.Gilbert, B. (1967) Britain Since 1918, Batsford, London.
Williams, R. (1961) The Long Revolution, Penguin, Harmondsworth.
2.Eckstein, H. (1959) The English Health Service, Harvard University Press, Cambridge, Mass.
3.Hansard, vol.388, p.1401.
4.Jones, K., Sidebottom, A. (1962) The Mental Hospital at Work, Routledge and Kegan Paul, London. p.148.
5.Abel-Smith, B. (1978) The National Health Service, the First Thirty Years, HMSO, London.

6.Hall, P., Land, H., Parker, R., Webb,A. (1975) Change, Choice and Conflict in Social Policy, Heinemann, London. chapter 9.
7.Macmillan, H. (1969) Tides of Fortunes, Macmillan, London.
8.Pinto-Duchinsky, M. (1970) Bread and Circus: The Conservatives in Office. In: Bogdanor, V., Skidelsky, R. (ed) The Age of Affluence 1951-1964, Macmillan, London.
9.Bogdanor, V. (1970) The Labour Party in Opposition, Ibid, pp.78-116.
10.Taylor, R. (1970) Campaign for Nuclear Disarmament, Ibid, pp.221-253.
11.Lewis, P. (1978) The Fifties, Heinemann, London.
12.Halsey, A. E. (1972) Trends in British Society since 1900, Macmillan, London.
13.Townsend, P. (1979) Poverty in the United Kingdom, Penguin, Harmondsworth.
14.Britten, S. (1969) Steering the Economy, Macmillan, London.
15.Allsop, K. (1958) The Angry Decade, Macmillan, London.
16.Fyvel, T. R. (1961) Insecure Offenders, Chatto and Windus, London.
Cohen, S. (1970) The Teddy Boys. See ref. 8, pp.288-320.
17.Packman, J. (1967) Child Care, Need and Numbers, Allen and Unwin, London.
18.Bedarida, F. (1979) A Social History of England, 1851-1975, Methuen, London, pp.262-269.
19.Himmelweit, H. (1958) Television and the Child, Oxford University Press, London.
20.The Registrar General's Statistical Review of England and Wales, 1959. Supplement on Mental Health, table M.1. HMSO, London.
21.Busfield, J. (1982) The Historical antecedents of Decarceration: The Mentally Ill. Paper given at the conference on the History of British Psychiatry, 15th May, London School of Economics.
22.Ibid.
23.See ref. 20 and table 2 in appendix 1.
24.See ref. 20, note (a) to table M.1.
26.See ref. 4.
27.Jones, K. (1972) A History of the Mental Health Services, Routledge and Kegan Paul, London. p.361.
28.Ibid, p.364.
29.Baldwin, J. A. (1971) The Mental Hospital in the Psychiatric Service, Oxford University Press, London.
30.See ref. 27.

31.Becker, H. (1966) _Social Problems_, Wiley, New York.
Parton, N. (1979) The Natural History of Child Abuse: A Study in Social Problem Definition, _British Journal of Social Work_, 9,4, pp.431-451.
32.Armer, F. Report in the _Lancet_, May 18th, 1957.
33._Ibid_.
34.Barton, R. (1959) _Institutional Neurosis_, Wright, Bristol.
35.See ref. 4.
36.Parry-Jones, W. (1972) _The Trade in Lunacy_, Routledge and Kegan Paul, London.
37._Hansard_, vol. 560, p.14.
Johnson, D.M., Dodds, N. (1958) (ed,) _The Plea for the Silent_, C. Johnson, London.
38.Clark, D. (1964) _Administrative Therapy_, Tavistock, London.
39.See ref. 34.
40._Hansard_, vol. 651, p.53; vol. 600, p.41.
41.See for example the _Sunday Times_ campaign on Thalidomide in the 70s.
42.Milliband R. (1969) _The State in Capitalist Society_, Weidenfeld and Nicolson, London.
43.Gough, I. (1979) _The Political Economy of the Welfare State_, Macmillan, London.
44.Carstairs, G. M., Wing, J. K. (1958) Attitudes of the General Public to Mental Illness, _British Medical Journal_, 2, pp.584-598.
45.See ref. 37.
46.Tredgold, R. F. (ed) _Bridging the Gap_. C. Johnson, London.
47.See ref. 37, pp.94-95 and pp.97-97.
48.Swazey, J. (1974) _Chlorpromazine in Psychiatry: A Study of Therapeutic Innovation,_ MIT Press, Boston.
49.Baruch, J., Treacher, A. (1978) _Psychiatry Observed_, Routledge and Kegan Paul, London.
50.Frazer, W. M. (1950) _The History of English Public Health_, Bailliere, London.
51.Bowlby, J. (1951) _Maternal Care and Mental Health_, World Health Organization, Geneva.
Robertson, H. (1959) _Young Children in Hospital,_ Tavistock, London.
Jones, M. (1952) _Social Psychiatry_, Tavistock, London.
52.Hare, E. H. (1955) Mental Illness and Social Class in Bristol, _British Journal of Preventive Social Medicine_. pp.191-195.
53.See ref. 51.
54.Unlocked Doors. Editorial, _Lancet_ (1954), 2, p.953.

Freedom in Mental Hospitals: The End and the Means,
Editorial, Lancet (1954), 2, p.954.
55.See ref. 48, pp.160-161.
56.See Dr. Good's letter to the Lancet. Lancet,
(1954), 2, p.1130.
57.Macmillan, D. (1956) An Integrated Mental Health
Service, Lancet, 1, pp.94-95.
58.See ref. 53.
59.Rosen G. (1976) From Medical Police to Social
Medicine, Science History Publications, New York.
Dunham, W., Faris, R. (1939) Mental Disorder in
Urban Areas, University of Chicago Press, Chicago.
60.Hollingshead, H., Redlich, F. (1958) Social
Class and Mental Illness, The Free Press, New York.
61.Erickson, E. (1951) Childhood and Society, Basic
Books, New York.
62.Caplan, G. (1959) Concepts of Mental Health and
Consultation, Children's Bureau Publications, no.
373, New York.
63.Hartman, H. (1951) Ego Psychology and the
Problem of Adaptation. In: Rapapport, D. (ed)
Organization and Pathology of Thought, Columbia
University Press, New York.
Sullivan, H. S. (1955) The Interpersonal Theory of
Psychiatry, Tavistock, London.
64.See ref. 62.
65.Cummings, J., Cummings, E. (1957) Closed Ranks,
Basic Books, New York.
66.Castel, R., Castel, F., Lovell, A. (1982) The
Psychiatric Society, Columbia University Press, New
York.
67.Ewins, D. (1974) The Origins of the Compulsory
Commitment Provisions of the Mental Health Act
(1959). Unpublished M.A. thesis, University of
Sheffield.
68.See ref. 49.
69.Wootton, B. (1959) Social Science and Social
Pathology, Allen and Unwin, London.

6 Professionals' Theories and Value Preferences in the Fifties

6.a.Overview: Major Developments in the Field of Psychiatry during the 1945-1960 period

The two trends which emerged in the twenties have become more dominant during the fifties: 1.Securing a physical treatment for the psychoses and severe neuroses inside the hospital. 2.Treating sufferers of mild neuroses in outpatients and child guidance settings (e.g. in 1935 there were 19 child guidance clinics, while in 1937 there were already 46 such units(1)).

The search for a physical, medicine-like, intervention was best exemplified in the use of insulin shock, convulsive therapy and psychosurgery which were successively fasionable since the 30s. The protagonists of these forms of intervention shared not only a focus on physical means but also the readiness to obtain knowledge on a trial and error basis without an equal investment in the explanatory component. Consequently information about frequencies of effectiveness per diagnostic condition accumulated without a similar growth in recognizing and understanding either side-effects or causes.

Thus insulin gave way to ECT largely on an empirically established lower risk for patients and a need for a smaller team rather than on the basis of proof of greater effectiveness of the new measure(2). The controversy concerning the efficacy and irreversibility of side effects in psychosurgery and ECT is more vocal today than it was in the period under discussion. Cautious optimism was expressed on psychosurgery while unlimited enthusiasm welcomed the introduction of ECT(3). The psychotropic drugs were relatively unknown until the very end of the 50s when they were hailed as a revolution(4), a point to which we will come back later in this chapter.

The child guidance setting and those outpatients clinics based outside a hospital continued to developed along psychoanalytic lines and within the voluntary sector. There they were far removed - conceptually, methodologically and administratively - from the hospital sector. They shared in common with the main sector the clinical approach to the consumer, the explicit disregard for social factors and the belief that theirs was "the" scientific and value free discipline.

The main components of the 1930 legislation were largely unimplemented in the interim wars period: the number of voluntary admissions increased but very slowly; the links to the Poor Laws were not severed before 1948. Apart from the growth of the child guidance sector there was no sign of introducing psychiatric care facilities in the community. The number of inpatients was growing steadily(5).

The Second World War period
This period led to change and opening up of new possibilities in psychiatry. During the war a multidisciplinary state psychiatric service was created, preceding the creation of the NHS. It was aimed at supporting the civilian population in such tasks as evacuating and living under bombing. These emergency medical services treated also soldiers who suffered from neurosis. Members of all of the professions in the field of psychiatry were engaged in working with a population which could not be labelled as mentally ill and where the reasons for intervention lay way beyond individual factors. At the same time less time was spent by psychiatrists in the mental hospitals, some of which were evacuated of their occupants to free the space for the war casualities. This move too went down with neither a public cry nor a reported increase in violence which is often expected of the mentally ill.

Simultaneously more professional time was given to soldiers at two levels. Firstly psychological screening of soldiers was introduced during the war, checking of abilities, personality features and manifested psychiatric symptoms(6). Psychiatrists and psychologists became involved in training officers. Secondly psychiatric units were established at the front and at the rear which

151

treated soldiers suffering from a variety of reactions to the war experience. The method of work with the soldiers took on from the direction outlined in the First World War (see chapter 3). Proportionally more psychiatrists were drafted during the Second World War than in the first, greater attention was paid to diagnosis and soldiers with psychotic symptoms were separated from those with neurotic or psychopathic signs(7). The death penalty for desertion meted in the first war was abolished, without an increase in the rate of desertion(8). Considerable efforts were made to ensure that only a small proportion of soldiers with psychotic symptoms would receive war pensions and that none of those with neurotic symptoms would get such a pension(9). At the same time neurosis stopped to be a sufficient reason for military discharge and transfer to suitable occupation within the army took place instead.

Psychiatrists and psychologists who worked in the army came into contact with people who broke down under unusual circumstances and who often demonstrated a high degree of bravery and endurance. Partly as a result of this experience the process of normalizing the neurotic took off together with the abnormalization of people who showed anti-social behaviour and psychoses. The reinterpretation of neurotic and psychopathic behaviour was primarily due to the accumulation of the impact of psychoanalytic thought to which we will come later.

The emphasis on group morale so typical of war periods was influenced by pre-war American experiments in milieu therapy(10). In Britain the Northwick Park unit became a hothouse for attempts to use psychoanalytic groupwork and therapeutic community structure which will be looked at below(11). At this stage it is important to remember that the therapeutic community approach liberalized considerably the day to day regime inside the special units, encouraged emotional expression and a greater degree of independence for residents. These aims were closely related to the national war effort and to the attempt to prevent soldiers' chronicity while enhancing an early return to their role as soldiers.

To summarize, the war experience led to:
1.More co-operation among the different disciplines albeit under the leadership of psychiatrists.
2.More contacts between professionals and the

general population in a national crisis situation.

3.Liberalization of approach towards soldiers who broke down under the war strain yet securing the economic interest of the state on account of its soldiers.

4.Emergence of interest in small groups.

5.The realization of the negative impact of the hospital as a social institution.

As already mentioned in chapter 5 the readiness at the end of the war for social change led to the provision of universalistic welfare services in Britain. However at no point was a radical restructuring of the psychiatric system envisaged during the war. The emphasis was on unstigmatized access to existing services and the liberalization of internal hierarchical regimes inside the hospital.

The post-war period: 1945-1960

At the beginning of this period the NHS was established as the system to ensure unstigmatized access to the health services. It brought on also the expansion of the whole health sector, including psychiatry. Strengthening consultants at the expense of the medical superintendents yet increasing the autonomy of hospitals and of all professionals were equally crucial features of the new system. The NHS did not attempt to introduce specialized health care in the community. To the contrary, on the whole it encouraged the provision of this type of intervention inside the hospital, whether intentionally or as a result of giving in to the medical profession's pressure. The strengthening of the consultant's autonomy encouraged the entry of a younger generation into hospital psychiatry, while before some of the best psychiatrists tended to work outside it. The high degree of autonomy allowed also for a higher measure of variability in style of management of different units within the same institution and thus permitted internal experimentation more than before.

The expansion of the health sector led also to an increase in the number of social workers and to the introduction of psychologists and occupational therapists in sufficient numbers to become professional groupings.

As part of the legacy of the war experience the emphasis on work with the non-chronic inpatient population was expressed in the establishment of units for neurotics, psychopaths and short-stay residents(12).

The Open Door Policy.
Day hospitals became possible mainly with the introduction of the open door policy during the 1945-1954 period. The open door policy accepted the assumption that the impact of the mental hospital becomes negative if prolonged beyond the crisis point. Its protagonists also could see no reason why the majority of the in-patients could not live outside an institution given the right type of support in the community(13).

This policy merits our attention not only because contrary to the post 50s mythology it preceded the introduction of the psychotropic drugs as already mentioned in chapter 5. It primarily deserves our interest as a case of change of attitudes which took place without a preceding change in mode of intervention or organization within the psychiatric system. Insulin shock treatment, ECT and psychosurgery had been employed for some time before the open door policy started to be practised in several hospitals in Britain around 1950(14). Where a therapeutic community was introduced it usually coincided with an open door policy. However there were more institutions which adopted the open door policy without creating therapeutic communities.

We should ask therefore what made hospitals' directors contemplate such a move. The demand did not come from the outside (i.e. the government, the general public, politicians) or from the inside (the inpatients population or other professions). It was engineered by psychiatrists inside the hospitals who had to struggle with the rest of the staff and often with the local community too to get it going and to let the doors stay open(15).

It is important to remember that though the unlocking occurred in an unco-ordinated way we are not looking at isolated cases but at a group's approach to the issue(16). This point is best illustrated by the fact that the first hospital to open was the Littlemore in Oxford which did so in 1922, but had to lock its doors anew since it was an isolated case(17).

Scull(18) claimed that decarceration was engineered by governments interested in reducing public spending on unproductive components of the population. While this motive might have been dear to the heart of the Ministry of Health the

154

documentation indicates that the Ministry followed the professional outlook rather than pioneered it. There is also little to support this claim for the period under discussion in Britain which undoubtedly has been one of expansion of the health sector.

It is therefore necessary to locate the reasons for this change inside psychiatry. Hospitals were systematically criticized for overcrowding and their management knew how well justified this criticism was. Yet the response to overcrowding could have equally been to press for more hospital beds and to keep the pressure up by not discharging people earlier than before as much as choosing to open the doors. Naturally the wish to reduce overcrowding and to secure more attention to a smaller number of inpatients were contributing factors, but they were not the prime mover reason.

In the absence of research information it is speculated here that the total war experience led to a reduced fear of the largely imaginary violence of the mentally ill when compared to the aggression and brutality exhibited during the war by sane people. As with overcrowding this element on its own did not suggest a specific course of action. The readiness to accept a psychological basis to mental illness was the single most important factor that led to the open door ideology. It followed from and fed back into the psychologization of everyday life which took place from the 20s onward. Under the influence of both psychoanalysis and behaviourism psychologization emerged as the solution to the pre-First World War crumbling explanatory system of motivation for human behaviour.

The unprecedented cruelty against European populations by the Nazi regime had to be explained or else the whole world view of parliamentary democracy would collapse. Psychologization and individualization of the motivation for the atrocities came instead. The only other attractive social alternative - socialism - was discredited in the late 30s and especially at the post war period. Stalin's behaviour - like Hitler's - was explained on a psychological basis. Conceptualization of the German or Russian national character became fashionable(19). Similarly ambitions for psychology as a tool for bringing peace were voiced by some of the more creative people in the psychiatric system(20).

As in all monolithic beliefs when one

component of a rather complex reality is overemphasized it tends to repress the due recognition of other, and equally important, elements. Yet the monopoly serves precisely because it prevents the recognition of factors which may lead to discomfort with the type of legitimation offered by the new perspective. In the use of psychologization the realization that every regime might commit atrocities under certain structural circumstances was the discomforting feature which had to be masked. The fight against Fascism and later Communism was made easier for the ruling groups and the general population if the opponents were assumed to be suffering from psychological problems which rendered them too as victims of forces outside their control.

In relation to mental illness psychologization had an undeniable liberalizing impact, not least because psychological factors do indeed operate as aetiological, precipitating and maintaining factors. However, the subjection of the psychological perspective to a clinical-somatic view of the person and the further exclusion of social structure factors from being considered as aetiological components reintroduced a distorting dimension.

The psychological approaches which fitted in particular the function of such an explanation and legitimation were ego psychology and crisis intervention on the one hand and behaviourism on the other hand(21). All three were more developed in the US rather than in Britain (with some notable exceptions, such as the writings of Eysenck, looked at in the section on psychologists). They were also all linked to the functionalist-structuralist model of society(22), which in the 50s accepted the psychodynamic view on socialization. This approach to society tends to minimize the role of conflict and to maximize the function of solidarity, conformity and rationality in any social structure.

In Britain the child guidance clinics have been the carriers of psychoanalytic ideas on everyday life from the 20s onwards. The major single British contribution to the psychologization of everyday life was the research project on child rearing practices undertaken by Bowlby and his co-workers(23). The research used ethology as its main method and thus offered a bridge to natural science on the one hand and to anthropology on the other. The main findings indicated the existence of critical periods of development in which the impact of psychological crisis may be irreversible. It emphasized the importance of stable mother-child relationships and the possible harm of separation in early childhood. Although the group never concluded that only the natural mother should look after her child this interpretation was the one adopted by the professionals and the public(24). In addition while the findings did not imply that only one person should look after a small child this assumption was adopted too. The social outcome of this research was that it became an important tool in the prevention of institutionalization and hospitalization of young children and in allowing parents to stay with their children in hospital. Equally it led to the revival of the pre-war view that mothers should stay at home to look after their children and that no sharing of this task could be justified.

This spontaneous use of the research findings became the perfect explanation as to why all nurseries were closed after the war and women who were mothers were literally forced to retreat to their homes. Such an answer fitted well the desire to ensure employment for veterans and the conservative atmosphere of the 50s based on relative affluence and the Cold War climate. The selective use of the research findings is further illustrated by the fact that Bowlby's call for increasing financial benefits paid to poor families was ignored.

The greater degree of public tolerance and the greater measure of interest in mental illness and health is exemplified by the creation of the national organization for mental health (Mind) in 1946.

Another strand which dates from the war period was the attention paid to the systematic understanding of large scale organizations which came from industrial psychology and sociology(25).

For the open door policy adherent the anti-institutionalization message from the Tavistock research and from the theory of organizations was crucial in terms of re-evaluating the impact of the mental hospital.

Most British psychiatrists were largely uninformed regarding the psychological sociological approaches mentioned above, though as middle-class citizens they might have been exposed to these influences in their private lives. The content of intervention with the bulk of hospitalized patients remained unchanged and - with the exception of the open door policy - also largely unchallenged.

In contrast to psychoanalysis which operated mainly outside the hospital sector, it was more difficult to dismiss the protagonists of the open door policy who were well known superintendents and held the most senior posts in the army during the war (e.g. Dr. Rees of Warlingham Park was the chief army psychiatrist).

Unlocking the wards became also a potentially useful tactic in the battle between superintendents and consultants. Here was a task which if completed successfully re-established the authority of the superintendent, thus making the risk taken worthwhile for him.

As already mentioned the challenge posed by the open door policy was the questioning of the usefulness of hospitalization after the initial crisis period. Finding itself in a quandary, psychiatry sorted it out by employing a time-honoured device (which it used before in the 19th century and World War 1): it joined in and ensured the rewards of the change for itself. At this conjuncture its inherent pragmatism was helpful. However the joining in did not imply a move from the preference for somatic explanations and means of intervention, as will be demonstrated below.

The majority of the leading figures of the open door policy pursued also the establishment of a domiciliary visits system and district based services, usually using the local hospital as headquarters. Inside the hospital they favoured the creation of rehabilitation wards. Thus the open door policy did not offer a detailed alternative to the clinical-somatic approach to psychiatry.

It is therefore understandable that with the spreading use of the psychotropic drugs from 1957 onward the temporary capitulation of traditional psychiatry ended by a triumphant reinterpretation of the events of the 50s as due to the effectiveness of the drugs(26).

The new group of drugs filled in a major conceptual and practical gap. From the end of the fifties there was no need to rethink further the effectiveness of what was on offer or to ponder on the meaning of community mental health.

Psychiatric wards in general hospitals
Although psychiatric wards in general hospitals existed since the twenties they became fashionable in the fifties, renamed as district general

hospital units (DGH). They were seen as an innovation aimed at the minimization of stigma and at convincing the public that mental illness was like a physical disease.

Is it indeed the case that people who suffer from physical illness are not stigmatized? Research findings on reaction to people who suffer from cancer or a visible physical disability demonstrate a whole range of negative reactions by the general public and the professionals(27). Stigma is attached in proportion to the felt threat to taken for granted assumptions on health and illness, sanity and insanity, life and death, cross cutting the boundaries of physical and mental perspectives. We have no evidence on social mixing between physically and mentally ill people in general hospital.

A spontaneous segregation seems to continue unabated inside the general hospital. Staying in the general hospital may help the relatives who wish to fend off stigmatization in their neighbourhood. But this fending off is based on hiding the real reason for hospitalization rather than a diminished stigma on mental illness.

Psychiatric wards have been instrumental in shortening periods of hospitalization(28), because the atmosphere in a general hospital and its structure are geared towards short stay of people suffering from an acute illness. The population in the psychiatric ward tends therefore to consist of crisis cases, short stay and relatively mildly disturbed, non aggressive, clientele.

The shift of a number of psychiatric patients to the general hospital also made it possible to demonstrate a reduction in the number of inpatients in the psychiatric hospitals. However, even today only a quarter of people hospitalized for psychiatric reasons enter a DGH unit.(See Personal and Health Statistics, 1982, Table 4.3, DHSS. The percentage is calculated by subtracting the figure on average daily occupancy for mental illness from the number which occupies psychiatric hospitals.)

The preference for physical means of treatment in these wards is self explanatory as it modelled itself on the treatment of physical illness.

Therapeutic Communities

A minority among the protagonists of the open door policy attempted to create therapeutic communities inside the hospital(29). The approach was based on the realization of the negative impact of institutionalization in an hierarchical regime. Therapeutic communities were attempts to democratize the hospital's regime, to give more say to non-medical staff and residents and to create a community of shared interests inside a ward. It was believed that such a regime would decrease passivity, dependency and isolation and would prepare inpatients better for life outside the hospital.

All of the therapeutic communities continued to use the traditional psychiatric dianostic system and the available physical intervention methods. In all of them a psychiatrist was the official leader. At the same time a decrease in the use of physical means and an increase in the use of psychological methods was noticeable in therapeutic communities. Thus while this experiment was not one of de-medicalization it was aimed at reducing the hegemony of the clinical-somatic model in favour of a psychosocial approach. This alternative model provided a new perspective with which to understand staff-inpatients and staff internal relationships. The shift of emphasis from the individual patient to the care givers led to more interest in intersubjective aspects of living and functioning in a closed environment.

Concerning soldiers, the therapeutic community approach was an attempt to prevent total dependency and to promote a quicker pace of recovery.

For the first time a sociological model was employed in British psychiatry, namely the functionalist-structuralist approach, with an emphasis on the analysis of small groups(30). As already mentioned it is a model which stresses social harmony and solidarity and demotes the place of conflict in social relationships. For both soldiers and civilians the emphasis on the small group prevented an investigation and recognition of the social structural dimension and links between individual psychiatric problems, the psychiatric system and the wider social context.

The therapeutic communities seem to have had a more dramatic effect on the staff than on the patients as they put into doubt the validity of the staff's training and beliefs. More often than not the head figures were the pioneering and most enthusiastic personnel, with the nursing staff the more unhappy group with the changes. The changes were considerable in terms of informality, degree of criticism and emotional expression encouraged and a less rigid daily routine. It was a much more demanding regime from both the staff and the residents, precisely because the demands could not be always neatly phrased. Given the encouragement to express feelings openly after years of repressing such an expression, and the nature of mental distress it is not surprising that negative feelings were expressed in abundance compared to positive sentiments. This feature was another difficult element for the staff to contain. The achievements of the therapeutic community were on the whole unspectacular in nature since they were focused on the quality of life rather than on its quantitative aspects. They were also difficult to measure by any natural science methodology.

All of these features led to the isolation of therapeutic communities into pockets of one ward or a small hospital and ensured that it was not adopted by the majority of British psychiatrists and nurses. It was too uncomfortable and at its base incompatible with the clinical-somatic approach. The isolation became a rejection whenever the pioneering consultant left, resulting in abandoning the approach.

Psychopathy
The majority of inpatients were diagnosed as suffering from schizophrenia, while those seen in outpatients clinics as suffering from neurosis. The category of psychopathy was reactivated during the war period in relation to soldiers whose a-social behaviour was regarded as psychopathic(31). Usually people diagnosed as having a psychopathic disturbance were to be found in the newly created units for neurosis, in prisons or in units specializing in treating psychopathy. Psychiatric wards in general hospitals would not have them on grounds of fear of aggressive behaviour. Most psychiatric hospitals preferred not to admit them on grounds of being unable to offer suitable intervention for this group.

As already discussed in chapter 5, the Royal Commission Report, published in 1957, suggested the inclusion of psychopathy as a specified mental illness category. This proposal led to the debate in professional circles which focused on the inability to define precisely psychopathy and on what psychiatry had to offer people diagnosed as suffering from psychopathy. The points raised in this debate will be looked at in the section on psychiatric journals below. At this stage it is important to remember that the inclusion of psychopathy under the brief of psychiatry implied a redefinition of some forms of deviant, at times criminal, activity in a way which fitted the already mentioned growing psychologization of everyday life.

More research was carried out in psychiatry during the late forties and the fifties than before. In part this fact was the result of the lean interim wars and war years, in part the outcome of growing interest in psychiatry by professionals and the public. Most of the research was devoted to the clinical-somatic aspects, but some research on the newly developed programs - such as therapeutic communities and rehabilitation units - was conducted too(32). With the exception of Bowlby's group the majority of the research projects focused on the analysis of outcomes rather than on causes. However, research funds were given less generously to psychiatry than to the study of physical illness, as already mentioned in chapter 5.

To summarize, the 1945-1960 period was one of introducing some innovative measures in psychiatry. By the end of the decade, under the impact of criticism on institutionalization, the psychiatric hospitals were split into two relatively clear cut sections: the first, for chronic patients, was characterized by the total passivity of the residents and nearly total reliance on physical means of intervention. The population in these wards tended to be elderly and long stay. The second section concentrated on patients with more acute and recent history of disturbance who also tended to be younger than the first group. The regime in these wards was more flexible and it did not rely solely on physical means but also on psychosocial ones (e.g. grup meetings, industrial workshops, rehabilitation units).

Although the rate of discharge increased considerably and the rate of first admission diminished somewhat the rate of readmission did not change. In part the reduction was influenced by the admission of acute cases to DGH units.

Such a situation implied that the bottleneck was to be located equally in the services outside the hospital for those who left it only to return often. The rate of readmission summarizes also the limit of the open door policy to change the system.

The major changes were due to changes in

attitude by top psychiatrists which were tolerated by the general public.

By the end of the fifties however the recent history of British psychiatry was largely reinterpreted and the changes were put down to the introduction of the psychoactive drugs. This rewriting was possible because the explanatory and value systems of British psychiatry remained largely unchanged. If anything the halo effect of the psychotropic drugs reinforced the belief in the "faulty machine" model of the person, already mentioned in chapter 1.

At the same time two powerful psychological approaches to mental disturbance came to the fore and started to compete for cultural and professional hegemony - i.e. psychoanalysis and behaviour modification (this development will be discussed in the section on psychologists).

A component of sociology entered psychiatric theory and practice in the form of the attention paid to small groups and the hospital as an organization. In both instances only the functionalist-structuralist view was utilized. However the acceptance of this US-exported model into British psychiatry was limited to those few who engaged in group therapy. Even this acceptance was further limited, as the less comforting componetns of this model were omitted from consideration. The list of what was omitted is rather long. It includes the relevance of social class to psychiatric problems and intervention, the role of alienation in leading to mental illness, the need to create multi-disciplinary community mental health centres as distinct from outpatients clinics and the need to work with non-professionals. The reasons for this inattention lie in the resistance to any major rethinking of the psychiatric system, typical of the majority of British psychiatrists, which prevented the minority from going further in reconsidering psychiatry.

6.a.i.Psychiatric Textbooks in the Fifties

Henderson and Gillespie's "A Textbook of Psychiatry" appeared for the eighth time in 1956. Although this edition came out two years after the second textbook to be reviewed below, this book will be looked at first because of its links to its 1927 edition commented upon in chapter 4.

Nearly all of the 1927 text has been reproduced in the 1956 edition. It has been updated to an extent in terms of references to research published after 1927, but the majority of such references date from the 30s and the early 40s. The same case descriptions are reproduced and therefore we are at a loss to know whether there have been changes in the prevalence of symptomatology; preference for specific diagnostic categories or a different approach to understanding mental illness. The considerable social change which took place between the 20s and the 50s is hardly represented in the book. The fact that the NHS is never mentioned in the text is perhaps indicative of the emphasis on locating psychiatry outside the social context, despite the stated aim to relate it to everyday life.

The introduction confirms that for the authors the future of psychiatric knowledge lay in neurology and genetics and not in sociological or psychological understanding. The latter two were dismissed as imprecise and insufficient compared to the scientific standing of neurological and genetical knowledge. At the same time it was stated that the psychiatrist has become acknowledged by the general public as an expert on social problems.

It was advocated that the way forward for psychiatry is the return to bedside medicine, clinical observation and proper diagnostic procedures. We are warned that "an excessive preoccupation with individuals is heuristically sterile" (p.5).

The few omissions and additions in the 1956 edition deserve our attention since they point out which of the relevant changes which occurred inside and outside psychiatry managed to penetrate established psychiatry as exemplified by Henderson and Gillespie. The 1956 edition is the first in which the section on eugenics has been amended and the paragraph on the German laws on sterilization has been taken out. The German laws come under a heavy attack in the second textbook, justified in the light of the murder of several thousand mentally ill and mentally handicapped Germans by the Nazi regime for eugenic reasons. Not a word about this use of the law appears in this textbook. In the 1950 edition the German law is still discussed as dogmatic but clearer than the British one (1950, p.50). Thus eleven years after the end of the second World War were required to convince the authors of the need to take out the reference to the German law.

However most of the section on eugenics is

164

reproduced, divided into two parts on negative and positive eugenics. No doubt was left as to the writers' belief in the need for social control of reproduction.

Early childhood experiences, in particular family relationships, were given a more prominent place than before as likely reasons for adults' disturbances, for delinquency and psychopathy. In fact childhood experiences came to stand as "the environment". It is at this context that the Tavistock group's work on maternal deprivation is considered (p.73) It was concluded that a broken home was a contributing factor but one of less importance than heredity to future psychiatric disturbances (p.75).

Unemployment, loneliness and the impact of modernization were mentioned as factors which may lead to mental distress (pp.76-78) and then were ignored throughout the book. The preponderance of women over men in the inpatient population was ascribed to their prolonged longevity and was left unconnected to their social role and its psychological significance.

Figures on admission in the 50s were presented, the tendency for an increase was recognized as likely to continue, yet no reason was given for this trend and no worry was expressed about it (p.31).

In terms of aetiology the belief in heredity was reaffirmed, though the possibility of contributing psychological factors was accepted. The impact of the psychologization process described above is reflected in the attribution of psychological reasoning to and intervention methods for people with neurotic symptoms and children with psychiatric problems. The type of psychology adhered to was psychoanalytic in regard to children and essentially behaviouristic concerning adults. However behaviour therapy is not presented in the same systematic way that psychoanalysis is. This fact is surprising in view of the growing number of publications during the 50s on behaviour modification. The omission may be related to the above mentioned lack of incorporation of professional literature of the 50s and to the superficial treatment of non-organic theories in the book as a whole.

Pride of place in terms of intervention methods was given to Special Methods of Physical Treatment (Ch. XIII) which include insulin therapy, convulsion, leucotomy, continuous narcosis and nacro-analysis. The last two methods were dismissed as unuseful. The benefit of insulin was not really doubted despite mentioning a research which demonstrated that the effects of insulin could be put down to the impact of the hospital's environment (p.413). But insulin was dropped in favour of ECT primarily because of ease of administration of the latter, lower level of risks to patients, less need for qualified staff.

Leucotomy was treated as an innovation which deserved an enthusiastic reception, even if not hasty use. It is advocated as suitable for diagnostic categories including the psychoneuroses, after other physical means of intervention have been tried unsuccessfully (p.425). It was claimed that the risk involved was nearly nil and that the improvement rate was around 70% (p.426). The state of mind of the post-leucotomy person, his quality of life and the irreversibility of the intervention were ignored.

The psychotropic drugs were mentioned just once when Largactil (of the Chloropromoazine group) was suggested as a useful device in the reduction of excitement in manic states (p.276). Thus the "drug revolution" has definitely not registered by Henderson and Gillespie as late as 1956.

Psychopathy
The senior author - Prof. Henderson - was a recognized authority on this category. His classification of psychopathy formed the basis of the definition used in the 1959 Mental Health Act. Prof. Henderson said: "We include under this title people who have been from childhood or early youth habitually abnormal in their emotional reactions and conduct, but who do not reach, except episodically, a degree of abnormality amounting to certifiable insanity; they show no intellect defect ... and therefore cannot be classifed in terms of the Mental Deficiency Act; and they do not benefit under prison treatment. They are not sufficiently well balanced mentally to be at large, nor yet are they sufficiently involved as to be suitable for mental hospital care" (p.384).

The definition assumes abnormality in terms of emotional instability and social unfitness. However both of these indicators are prevalent in any psychiatric disturbance and any mental distress. Therefore the justification for designating this behaviour as a specific psychiatric diagnosis remains unclear. For example

166

people who exhibit neurotic symptoms usually demonstrate asocial behaviour in some aspects of their lives. However, on the whole they are not seen as socially unfit. It is therefore the aggressive anti-social conduct of psychopaths rather than their emotional instability which singled them out as a diagnostic group. Prof. Henderson, however, did not spell it out for us and seemed to be unaware of the logical difficulties which arise from his definition. We are not offered criteria or a range on which to measure either emotional instability or social unfitness. Two additional clues are provided; namely the unimpaired intellect yet the inability to learn from experience. Again, these two features are typical of neurotic clients whose intellect remains unimpaired and who have not learned from experience that their fears are unfounded in objective reality. Hence the reference pertaining to psychopaths becomes relevant only when related to a particular type of inability to learn - i.e. the lack of internalization of the preference for conforming behaviour. The repetition of non-conforming behaviour without apparent guilt feelings leading often to being punished (and hence self-defeating) is the main feature which distinguishes most clearly between psychopaths and neurotics. Yet again Prof. Henderson does not explain it to be so; it can be only inferred from the case descriptions presented in the book. Aetiologically this state seems to be the outcome of a configuration of heredity, personality traits and environmental conditions, most of which remain unspecified. Prognosis is poor and no specific intervention is suggested. Instead we are told that treating psychopaths is a challenge not only to the profession but also to society and civilization (p.400). However, this intriguing comment is left undeveloped. While a hospital environment was not seen as desirable for intervention and observation the authors had no doubt that "they are desperately in need of help, of guidance, of encouragement, and the psychiatrist should be better qualified to assist them than anyone else" (p.384).

M. Jones' work with psychopaths and the Danish experiments are mentioned positively, but no conclusions are drawn from these experiments for psychiatric intervention in Britain. Instead, the hope for successful intervention with psychopathy was located within preventive genetical engineering (pp.401).

On the one hand the authors were promoting the idea of psychiatrists' responsibility over psychopathy. On the other hand they seemed unable to suggest any specific psychiatric method and doubted the value of hospitalization for this group (p.384). This doubt is all the more unusual in a textbook which recommends early hospitalization for the majority of illness categories.

We are therefore left with a degree of unease felt by established psychiatry towards treating these patients and with a question mark as to why British psychiatry would wish to expand its control in the direction of psychopathy. No unhappiness was expressed about the possible value bias underlying the definition and approach towards psychopathy. It did not occur to the authors that psychiatrists are agents of social control, a role they seemed to relish as a way of proving the worth of psychiatry in the eyes of lawyers (p.401). This professional rivalry might have been a key motivation, because the legalistic viewpoint was a persuasive alternative method of dealing with psychopathy. The threat of being taken over by psychoanalytic explanations - i.e. the maternal deprivation hypothesis - might have been another reason for the readiness of psychiatrists to incorporate psychopathy as a mental disorder category. B. Wootton has accused social workers and analysts of creating the myth of psychological reasons for psychopathic behaviour (see ref. 143). Interestingly she neither disapproved of psychiatrists' activities in this field nor posed the question of the legitimacy and rationale behind the annexation of psychopathy not to psychology but to psychiatry. In fact the case of psychopathy is another example of how psychological thinking has been used by psychiatry for its own benefit and without necessarily even accepting it.

The chapter on psychopathy was included in the textbook only since the Second World War, confirming the re-emergence of psychopathy as a central theme in British psychiatry as an offshoot of the war experience and the impact of psychologization.

The meaning of Community Care
Four periods of shifting emphasis in psychiatry since the 18th century are listed:
1.Human reform
2.No restraints
3.The hospital period

4.Social or community psychiatry period

The fifties are described as part of the last period. As already mentioned the authors claimed to adhere to social psychiatry. Nevertheless we are left guessing what are the "social" or "community" oriented elements in British psychiatry as presented in this book. We are not provided with a definition, dimensions or description of community psychiatry. The open door policy is not mentioned, together with the day hospital or social clubs for ex-patients. However it is suggested that DGH units demonstrate the move towards community psychiatry. Therapeutic communities are mentioned only in regard to psychopathy. Child guidance clinics are referred to only to express a preference that they should be under a medical authority. Neither the Dutch, American or British community mental health projects nor the literature on this approach are reported. It is unlikely that the authors were uninformed of these experiences which were presented in the Lancet and the British Medical Journal. Anti-Americanism too could not have been the case in a book dedicated to A. Meyer, an American psychiatrist active in the 20s.

With ignorance and anti-Americanism ruled out, we are left with the rejection of the validity of psychological and sociological knowledge, mentioned at the beginning of this section. To anyone coming from a social science perspective, including psychology, there is very little of the spirit and practice of social or community psychiatry in this textbook. But perhaps for those who adopt an almost exclusive medical and natural science perspective - as Henderson and Gillespie did - any mention or psychology and sociological knowledge seems like the introduction of a social perspective.

The biased perspective goes even further: it is stated that the introduction of social medicine into general medicine is a follow-up on an already existing practice with psychiatry (p.13). Thus psychiatry has had nothing new to learn from social medicine. Since for the authors medicine offered the only legitimate perspective for change, there was no place for any rethink within psychiatry.

With two exceptions, little has changed for the authors between 1927 and 1956. The two exceptions concern the rediscovery of psychopathy and the coming to the foreground of ECT and leucotomy. The first signifies the way psychiatry has used the impact of psychologization to further its hegemony when it patently had little to offer. Equally it indicates the readiness to serve as agents of social control. The second, together with the preference of psychiatric wards in general hospitals, points to the ever present wish to be an integral part of medicine and to continue to treat human beings as clinical entities.

Consequently the value preferences system, images of patients and restoration have remained the same as in the 1927 edition and need not be repeated here.

Mayer-Gross, Slater and Roth's "Clinical Psychiatry" appeared for the first time in 1954. Its authors state that they aim to incorporate research findings from the 30s and the war period which have not yet been applied to clinical practice. They are unhappy about presenting case descriptions which they see as "likely either to confirm to daily practice or to offer curiosities which, however interesting, cannot be adequately discussed and evaluated in a book in which general principles ... have to be emphasized" (p.xv). They also criticize other textbooks for being one sided and claim to present a multidimensional model. However, it is concluded that even if the theoretical framework differs the practice does not because: "They share a community of experience" (p.xvi). The inherent contradiction in the last two statements is missed by the authors, perhaps because the preference for pragmatism is taken for granted.

The nature of the multi-dimensionality becomes apparent in the introduction: "This book is based on the conviction of the authors that the foundations of psychiatry have to be laid on the ground of the natural sciences" (p.1). This position is defended on the ground of lack of precision of sociological and psychological data. "It seems far-fetched to maintain that sociology, or cultural anthropology, occupies such a basic position in relation to psychiatry, as does neurology ... our knowledge of neurology is detailed, precise, and capable of clear definition" (p.3). The relevance of sociology is seen in providing background information (p.10). It is claimed that the relationships between psychiatry and psychology are closer than those between sociology and psychiatry (p.10). Nevertheless we are assured that "It would be absurd to maintain that psychology can be to psychiatry what physiology has been to medicine, not only because the claim would be exaggerated, but also because it implies that psychiatry and medicine are mere cousin sciences" (p.11). According to the authors, as academic psychology has been inadequate psychiatrists had to provide their own psychology. "Psychoanalysis is a striking example of what a neurologist could do in evolving a theory of normal psychology, a mechanistic mythology which is far behind what contemporary psychology has to offer" (p.11). Throughout the book, however, neither psychoanalysis nor any other type of psychology - inclusive of behaviourism - are described and considered in relation to psychiatric disturbances.

Eight pages of the introduction - out of the 600 pages of text - are given to psychoanalysis, two of them devoted to criticism of the following type: "It is difficult to see how the theory can either become a part of the main body of scientific knowledge or itself develop in a fruitful way, without a fundamental reorientation" (p.23)... "It is, therefore, something of a paradox that psychoanalysis continues to grow in popularity, especially among psychiatrists of the American schools ... The theory provides certainties for those who cannot bear to be alone in the dark. The psychoanalytic approach fits in extremely well with dominant American biases. It is of a mechanistic and deterministic type which suits well a society based on the exploitation of the machine ... Lastly, in the relative significance it gives to mother and to father, it fits American upbringing as well as, or even better than, the home of the child in an Austrian Jewish family, which was its starting point" (p.24). This blatant anti-Americanism may come as a shock to the reader who assumed naively that he was looking at a scientific text. Under the heading "The multidimensional approach" we are told that a general conceptual framework on psychiatry is required and that it should include the following dimensions:
1.The functional-organic scale
2.The physiogenic-psychogenic scale
It is further suggested that "just as genetical causes influencing development may be single and gross or multitudinous and slight, so also may environmental causes" (p.27). The list of environmental causes, however, relates either to physical factors (e.g. poisoning, nutrition) or psychological habit-formation factors (trust, suspicion, aggressiveness). The social components

171

of every environment are simply ignored - yet another surprise for the reader who thinks that environments are essentially part of a social context and structure.

The introduction gives us also a clue as to what worries the authors about the state of psychiatry in the 50s. Their main concern is the move away from the focus on diagnosis and from treating people as clinical entities (pp.3, 8). They envisage with trepidation the possibility of approaching people as persons in a social context who suffer from distress. Instead they are "searching for a quantitative relationship" and see diagnostic knowledge as the key in "judgement of causation" (p.6). The fear behind neglecting the diagnostic side relates also to the threat of being removed from medicine which is often expressed in the introduction.

Following a chapter on psychiatric examination chapters on specific diagnostic categories are presented. Each of them includes sections on definition, incidence, aetiology and pathology, psychopathology, clinical picture, course, prognosis and diagnosis, treatment. The largest part of each chapter is thus given to a description of symptoms and relatively little to intervention and aetiology.

An interesting innovation in the book is a chapter on ageing and mental diseases of the aged (chapter xi). This chapter acknowledges the social problem perspective of ageing and the impact of the social role prescribed to elderly people in leading to mental disturbances. However the authors reiterate their organic position by stating that there are no new neuroses in old age but only endogenous or organic diseases which cannot be explained by psychological or social factors (p.452).

Psychopathic states are grouped together with neurotic reasons, a grouping which makes sense on the basis of level of dysfunctioning.

Aetiology is largely dealt with from an organic perspective. Although the role of psychological factors in neurotic reactions is not denied even there they are not given the primary aetiological place, but only a secondary one after genetic predisposition (chapter iv). The following exemplifies best the authors' approach to the issue of aetiology: concerning schizophrenia the text says: "Summing up our present knowledge of physical aetiology and pathology, one cannot point to any striking or universal factor responsible for schizophrenia or certain forms of it. Many minor findings pointing to the organic nature of the disease have, however, been reliably reported and A. Meyer's refusal to accept an organic aetiology because it has not been supported by adequate factual material can hardly be upheld ... it seems impossible that a severe mental illness could be psychogenically determined, even if a strong genetic predisposition is assumed" (p.228).

This judgement is passed without an attempt to present any of the psychological explanation of schizophrenia, let alone any sociological approach. Only the organic possibilities are discussed.

The chapter on childhood psychiatry emphasizes the importance of approaching the child as a totality where one symptom should not be overrated. The child-parents relationships are regarded as important because the child is assumed to respond more than the adult to his emotional environment (p.513), an assumption which no school of psychology would support. The likelihood of preventing mental disturbances in adulthood by treatment in childhood is dismissed as baseless. This outright rejection of the relationships between experiences in childhood and adulthood is perfectly justified within a purely organic approach.

Child guidance clinics are mentioned. Interestingly their development is traced to the US movement and not to the Tavistock Clinic which is left unmentioned. Likewise the British psychoanalytic contribution to understanding and working with children is ignored. Since ignorance is highly unlikely to have been the reason for this omission ideological reasoning is more likely to be at the root of this highly selective approach to child psychiatry.

Methods of Intervention
As already mentioned, this section receives relatively less attention that the description of psychiatric disturbances. As can be expected, most of the intervention suggested comes under the heading of physical methods. ECT and insulin therapy are the methods which the authors see as the most promising. They view leucotomy as relevant for some of the severe conditions, such as schizophrenia and do not outrule its use for obsessive states. But they suggest caution in applying it and see this method as a last resort

(p.288). However, we are not told what are the reservations which lead the authors to such caution. Several drugs are mentioned, mainly bromides, but not the psychoactive group; yet another confirmation of the late arrival of this group during the 50s.

Psychological and social methods of intervention are mentioned too, even if less frequently. The authors prefer simple and short psychotherapy for clients with neurotic reactions and behaviour modification for alcoholics. Thus the only occasion on which behaviourism is discussed is in regard to alcoholism. While lack of acquaintance with behaviour modification might have been the case in the early 50s lack of knowledge of behaviourism could not. One wonders if the overwhelming preference for the organic approach prevented the serious consideration of any psychological approach, including those which would not contradict an organic model.

Reference to the social context
Unlike Henderson and Gillespie's text there is no chapter on the impact of the two wars, although there are some references to war traumas and to the assumed overuse of such a label for squeezing a pension out of the state. There is one page devoted to the administrative structure of the service which states the factual situation since the establishment of the NHS.

There is also a chapter on relevant legislation, which offers a comparison with European countries. The authors would like to see a change in the laws on diminished responsibility due to psychiatric impairment. According to the writers the law does not cover psychopathy and does not distinguish between doctors and legal advisers yet treats physicians as ordinary witnesses. The preferred status is one of a witness for the court rather than for either of the two sides. As already mentioned the German law on sterilization is severely attacked for its brutal use. The debate on this law is the closest reference in the book to the social reality in which psychiatry operates.

The writers come out against psychiatrists taking over the responsibility for the mentally ill offender because of the contradiction inherent in having the dual identity of a gaoler and a doctor. Logically it would follow from this statement that if asked the authors would oppose the responsibility for psychopaths who have offended

174

but not for those who did not commit an offence. The inevitable effects of prolonged institutionalization are briefly mentioned. In the case of chronic schizophrenia we are told that spontaneous recovery occurs as a result of environmental change (p.229). It is further stated that schizophrenics do better after leaving hospital if they live outside their families (p.281) but the reasons for this finding are not expanded upon.

However neither the possibilities of change inside the hospital nor outside it are discussed. Other professions are rarely mentioned. It is suggested that social workers should be "handmaiden of psychiatrists" in prisons in supplying information (p.580).

The impression thus gained is that apart from research into the organic side of psychiatry very little has changed in the world outside and inside psychiatry since the pre Second World War period. Such an impression is possible when psychiatry is perceived as only a branch of medicine.

The image of the patient is difficult to get hold of due to the lack of case descriptions. Only the symptoms are described, fully divorced from the totality of the person. We are told that in contrast to the patient suffering from a physical illness the one who suffers from mental illness does not have an insight into his condition (p.32). The psychiatrist is thus instructed to evaluate the form of the patient's message and not its content (p.33). In this way it is assured that the subjective meaning is neither listened to nor taken account of. Invalidation of the person's perception of his own experience takes place from the beginning. Instead the meaning is given by the psychiatrist as an objective observer. Information given by other people is usually considered as valid unless they are known to be very involved with the person - e.g. we are told not to accept the information given by the wives of alcoholics on the grounds of their collusion with the drinking habits of their husbands.

A demarcation line between mild and severe disturbances is suggested in terms of instances where the psychiatrist can understand and empathize with the client and those in which he cannot. This delineation follows a criterion proposed by Jaspers (p.93). However it is difficult to find in this textbook a sign of empathy with a patient, since the latter is presented only after being dissected into clinical symptoms.

Likewise the image of the restored patient can only be speculated from the section on outcome and prognosis. We are told that in principle there is no doubt that Western society influences socialization and hence individual personalities (p.104). However it is unclear whether it is possible to change the personality and only a genetic aetiology explains why a particular person in a family becomes mentally ill (p.105). Given the firm belief in heredity and unchangeability it would transpire that only minor modifications of the personality are possible. At best the physical means of psychiatric intervention and simple psychotherapy for the very mild neurosis would eliminate the symptoms. Thus the restored person is the one without overt symptomathology.

The relationships between the professional psychiatrist and the patient are characterized by professional distancing aimed at reaching objective evaluation. The preoccupation with the diagnostic process lends itself to imagining the psychiatrist as a fair and benevolent judge who does not want to be tainted with legal matters. The dynamics of the professional-patient relationships or the possibility of professional bias are not considered.

The issue of social control is acknowledged twice. Firstly in the case of the mentally ill offenders and secondly in the comments on the harsh use of the German laws on sterilization. The attention given to legal issues implies also a covert notion of a social interpretation of the power and abilities of psychiatry which the authors would like to see.

The meaning of Community Care

It should not come as a surprise that community care does not figure as a key concept in this textbook. The term is mentioned in regard to invervention with chronic schizophrenics in an insignificant way. The therapeutic communities, the open door policy, the day hospital, rehabilitation wards, occupational therapy and services in the community are not mentioned. This omission is fully understandable in a text which approaches psychiatry as independent of the social context and as a field which should follow solely the natural sciences.

Value preferences.

The following emerge:
1.Mental disturbances are illnesses and often diseases.
2.The primary causal factor is heredity.
3.The main functions of psychiatry are to diagnose the illness and intervene in order to minimize the impact of the symptoms.
4.Physical means of intervention are to be preferred whenever possible.
5.Psychiatry is universal.
6.Psychiatrists should be given a higher degree of autonomy as against the judiciary system.
7.Psychiatry is an integral part of medicine. Natural science methodology is the most promising path to be followed.
8.The patient's views have no internal validity, they only reflect the illness.
9.The patient too exists independently of a social system and only knowledge related to the symptoms is worthwhile pursuing.

The book is written from both a prescribing and a critical stance. The critical attitude divides into two. The first is kept for the type of knowledge the authors like in principle, where criticism means considering some of the findings which highlight a particular aspect in a slightly modified way from the previous mode. The second type of critique is high handed, abusive in style and does not present the other side's point of view. This form of approach is employed in regard to material which the authors disagree with in principle (the prime cases are psychoanalysis and the American psychosocial approach to psychiatry).

It should be remembered that this textbook was written as a new text for the fifties. On the basis of this book it can be suggested that British psychiatry has become more medicalized, more organic in its outlook than it was in the interim wars period.

A comparison of the two textbooks
The two texts differ considerably in their style. The first is more interested in the patients as people and in providing living material for the students of psychiatry. The second book prefers the presentation of research findings to that of cases.

The difference in style is a reflection of differences in beliefs about patients, the relationships between professionals and patients and the role of research in the practice of psychiatry. The two textbooks differ also in the degree of belief in the supremacy of natural science over psychological and sociological knowledge.

While Henderson and Gillespie took the position of preference for the first they gave a place for the second type too. The authors of Clinical Psychiatry express a belief in the absolute supremacy of natural science and in the exclusion of psychological and sociological knowledge from psychiatry. Both texts are not critical at all in regard to the principles of psychiatry. They do not point out gaps in knowledge in a way which will lead to further research. In this sense they continue to be books of prescription.

6.a.ii.Contributions to Psychiatric Journals

The following themes reappear in the journals during the fifties:
1.Mental hospitals: Problem aspects and alternatives within the hospital.
2.Alternatives outside the asylum.
3.Physical means of intervention.
4.The new mental health legislation: focus on psychopathy and superintendent-consultant relationships.
5.Needs of and services for children and the elderly.

Mental Hospitals

By the end of the 40s it was generally acknowledged that the psychiatric hospitals were overcrowded, lacked a sufficient number of beds, buildings, staff and adequate recreation facilities. From time to time during the fifties a scandal concerning the physical conditions of hospitalization would erupt and these shortages would be re-exposed. In 1954 an editorial in the Lancet(33) concerned with the suggestion to pay "danger money" to nurses stated that the difficulties lay not in patients' behaviour but in the objective conditions in the hospitals.

The overcrowding rate was estimated to be 14% for the 137,000 inpatient population. Complaints about overcrowding were repeated several times during that year and in 1959(34). Thus it was not accidentally the Royal Commission was set up in 1954, at the peak of the feeling of growing pressure inside the asylums.

178

Lack of staff is commented upon too, in particular of nurses and consultants(35). However the reasons for the shortage differed for the two groups. While there were not many established posts for consultant psychiatrists, those who moved in stayed in their posts. There was no shortage in established posts for nurses and not even so much of a shortage of new recruits. The rate of leaving while training was the bottleneck: it is claimed that 65-80% of entrants left(36). Poor financial rewards, work conditions and low status vis-a-vis general nursing were mentioned as the main reason for leaving(37). At a Royal College of Nursing conference in 1954 psychiatrists were the main contributors. Their analysis will be presented in the section on nurses. At this stage their main solution to this problem should be remembered, namely that psychiatric nursing should be amalgamated with general nursing(38).

Throughout the period under discussion it was acknowledged that while first admission numbers might be decreasing and the rate of discharge increasing, the rate of readmission was continuing to accelerate(39). In the attempt to explain this puzzling statistic several hypotheses were put forward. An editorial in the Lancet suggested that the difficulty may lie in the inability of families to look after their mentally ill members at home after discharge from the hospital(40). It also points to a misleading notion about intervention which the public entertained, namely that "treatment" has to do with high technology, biochemistry or the analyst's sofa (ibid, p.119).

It was realized that discharge rates were not synonymous with recovery rates(41). A high discharge rate unaccompanied by a high recovery rate implied that the symptoms have subsided but not the problems which led to their appearance in the first place. However, this suggestion was left unrelated to the then available findings which demonstrated that discharged schizophrenics not living with their families did better than those who went back to their families.

The third main problem to be acknowledged was the differential rate of discharge: while short stay patients discharge rate was high, for long stays it was not. Length of stay of chronic inpatients, quality of life inside the institution and reasons for not leaving after two years became issues of concern(42). Brown(43) indicated the magnitude of the problem by stating that 80% of the inpatients were long stays, of whom 70% were diagnosed as schizophrenics.

Dr. Bickford, a well known superintendent, outlined his view of the reasons for this depressing state of affairs. He blamed the low level of spending on psychiatric patients compared to the physically ill, impersonal relations inside the hospital, insufficient contact between psychiatrist and patient, lack of suitable employment outside and behavioural problems(44). Mayer-Gross(45) suggested that social isolation and not the psychiatric condition was the main reason why so many chronic patients remained inside the hospital.

The overall message therefore is that psychiatry has succeeded in stabilizing the psychiatric state of this population and in preparing them to leave the hospital. It is therefore largely the failure of the services outside the hospital which prevented a higher recovery rate. Such a view fends off the criticism laid at the door of the asylum. It is indicative that terms such as "institutionalization" hardly appear in the contributions to the journals and that every writer expressed how much the regime in his hospital actively discouraged chronicity (none of the writers was a woman). It could well have been the case that only those who already implemented a change in their hospitals wrote about these issues.

Alternatives within the hospital

Following from the problem aspects several solutions have been proposed for changes inside the hospitals. The proposals include the establishment of rehabilitation wards, unlocking wards, day hospitals, social clubs, industrial units, groupwork and therapeutic communities(46). Underlying these alternatives is the belief in the need for hospitalization; the wish to create a supportive atmosphere but one which is closer to the reality outside and in the necessity to activate more the inpatients. On the whole they did not challenge the established modes of psychiatric thought and practice. At most they express doubts about the benefit of practised psychiatrist-patient relationships and the passivity of life in a rigid environment.

Yet the common thread of activating inpatients away from the traditional passivity of institutional life provided an understated

challenge to the unstated philosophy of total
dependency of inpatients. Coming from the
protestant work ethic with a clear utilitarian
streak this line of reasoning implied also greater
respect towards patients and belief in their
capacity to become productive. Undoubtedly this
attitude echoed of the moral approach, as some of
the more sophisticated writers of the 50s were
aware(47). The majority was ignorant of this
connection and would not have wished to become
aware of it because of the belief that the then
current psychiatry was scientific and therefore
value free.

Of these alternatives only the therapeutic
community approach took account of the critique
posed in publications such as A Plea for the Silent
mentioned in chapter 5. There the high handed and
disrespectful approach to patients was exemplified.
Several reactions to this appeared in the journals
and in the collection of articles "Bridging the
Gap"(48). Most of the reactions were negative and
dismissive. It was claimed that the first book
overstated a case which belonged to the Victorian
era. In particular the publication was deplored for
damaging the case of the mentally ill by being
unrepresentative of current practice and seeking
sensationalism(49). In the absence of research it
is impossible to know which of the two sides was
more correct in its observation. The fact that the
publication was rejected outright would, however,
imply that the psychiatrists did not ask themselves
why so many inpatients seemed to be so bitter.

Alternatives outside the psychiatric hospital
The possibilities listed below are perceived as
either limiting or extending beyond the function of
the hospital. At no point were they seen as coming
instead of the hospital. The alternatives included
day hospitals outside the hospital's site, hostels,
psychiatric wards in general hospitals, domiciliary
visits and setting up district services(50). The
last option was the more comprehensive of the lot,
and several variations were proposed. Querido, the
psychiatrist who initiated Amsterdam's crisis
intervention service, visited London twice during
the fifties and was visited by British
psychiatrists. His scheme was commented upon in the
British Medical Journal and the Lancet(51). From
the Amsterdam service the British psychiatrists
picked up the idea of domiciliary visits. They left
out the 24-hours emergency service, the drop-in

centres and the crisis intervention conceptualization. Querido's service was criticized for not focusing enough on diagnosis. The underlying belief that the British system was the best resurfaced from time to time in reaction to the Dutch scheme(52).

Nottingham, Worthing and Bolton provided illustrations of district services. The psychiatric hospital continued to be the centre of the new system. Part of it was used as a day hospital, another part as rehabilitation wards or industrial units, and yet a third part as the outpatient clinic. Domiciliary visits were made at the requests of GPs for new clients mainly by social workers and nurses(53). The psychiatrists at the hospital offered consultation to their colleagues at the general hospital. Although district services tended to work closely with mental welfare officers employed by the local authorities the preference was to maintain the independence of the psychiatric service.

Physical means of intervention
Psychological and social methods of intervention were mentioned at times, but much less than physical methods. Although the reorganization inside and outside the psychiatric hospital was an implementation of social methods it was not recognized as such, perhaps because there was no fundamental change in the conceptualization of mental illness and the role of the psychiatrists.

Psychotherapy implied only psychoanalytically oriented psychotherapy. On the rare occasion when it was discussed the disagreement between those who were for it and against it remained as acute as before.

Insulin therapy, ECT, leucotomy and the psychotropic drugs were the physical interventions which preoccupied contributors to the journals during the fifties. Cautious yet enthusiastic reaction was given to all of these means. If British psychiatrists were aware - as they must have been - of the criticism about insulin and psychosurgery voiced at the time such an awareness was not reflected in their written communication.

Toward the end of the fifties small scale studies on the effectiveness of psychotropic drugs were published(54). At times each project claimed the opposite results from the previous study. None of the research carried out by psychiatrists searched for an explanation of why or even how these new drugs worked. Such questions were posed at times by psychologists(55). Effectiveness was defined in terms of the reduction of symptoms and length of hospitalization. Subjects were treated as clinical entities; none of their subjective reactions was recorded; no information on their social and personal background was given.

The meaning of Community Care
The notion of community care which emerges from contributions to journals is of finding a base in the community from which to continue to practise the clinical-somatic model of psychiatry in a less rigid way than inside the hospital.

Reactions to the new mental health legislation
Calls by psychiatrits to put right the existing laws on psychiatry were made from 1954 onward. In that year they focused on easing the process of voluntary admission. With the publication of the Royal Commission report in 1957 psychopathy became the centre of psychiatrists' reactions. Yet another shift in focus took place with the reading of the law in Parliament in 1959. The relationships between superintendents and consultants became the major bone of contention.

Psychopathy
The majority of contributors saw psychopathy as a psychological inability to adjust, caused by a brain defect. A minority suggested that the reason lay in early childhood deprivation(56).

Few dissenting comments were made from those who saw psychopaths as dangerous rather than as sick people. This group did not wish that the category of psychopathy should be included in the brief of psychiatrists. The debate concentrated on the diagnostic difficulties and intervention repertoire. The lack of clear-cut diagnostic criteria was acknowledged(57), yet the Lancet called the government's decision to adopt a definition "a courageous act"(58). Following the fashion in behaviourist psychology it was also suggested to sort out the diagnostic mess by applying a factorial analysis to data on psychopaths.

No physical means of intervention were proposed for psychopaths, a rather strange state of affairs in a system in which these means were favoured. The special units for psychopaths were the only innovation on offer, following from M.

183

Jones' work in the therapeutic community of Belmont(59). It was taken for granted that specialization was a good idea and that the expected aggressive behaviour of psychopaths would be contained within separated settings.

The issue of confounding social conformity with psychiatric disturbance did not surface at all in the internal debate within British psychiatry. Such a position befits a professional group which perceives it subject-matter to exist outside the social context. The lack of a thorough debate on psychopathy perhaps indicates the conceptual and practice poverty in regard to this category.

Prime of attention was given to the issue of the medical superintendent's status within the hospital hierarchy vs. that of the consultant. By giving effect to the NHS 1946 Act, the 1959 Mental Health Act promoted the role and stature of the consultant. Most of the published correspondence was pro-consultant and the pro-superintendent group was on the defensive(60). A high degree of bitterness was expressed in the letters. Comments such as "we are murdering our brother superintendent"(61) were unusual but leave the impression that only the tip of the iceberg of frustrations was glimpsed. The majority's position which favoured the consultants indicated a preference for a clinical expert rather than for an administrative authority. Although the issue of the consultant/superintendent covers some of the major structural obstacles in the hospital setting these obstacles were not debated.

On the whole the reaction to the Mental Health Act was favourable. It was seen as a law which upheld the psychiatrists' point of view, defended patients' rights and made progressive statements on intervention(62).

Needs of and Services for Children and the Elderly
These two groups received more focused attention than others during the fifties. The two groups have in common a greater degree of dependency on others based on physical and social vulnerability. In the period under discussion they were also demographically on the increase.

The interest in children has been traditionally re-sparked after major wars (e.g. the interest in children's physical health after the Boer war) when the realization of loss of lives dawned on the public and the politicians. The focus on child psychiatry was related to the impact of the Second World War as well as to the growing psychologization of childhood, discussed in the overview section.

The contributions concerning children fall into three categories: the first speaks about shortages in beds and units and simply assumes a continuation of a clinical-somatic model into child psychiatry(63). The second focuses on the continuation of the psychoanalytic framework in the field of child psychiatry. Scott(64) describes the Tavistock research group's work and one of its outcomes, namely the multidisciplinary welfare centres. The emphasis was on the mother-child relationships and how to enable reasonable emotional separation of the child from the mother. Another offshoot is a description of a hostel for adolescents with difficulties in their family relationships. The third strand is the effort to ensure a better understanding of children's emotional problems by GPs, paediatricians and psychiatrists. Winnicott(65) used a review of a book by Tizard on the role of the paediatrician in mental distress to state that psychiatrists' knowledge of childhood disturbance is found wanting. While the diagnostic process is complex paediatricians were not receiving any psychiatric training. Three letters to the editor followed(66); one of which supported the writer. The two others opposed the listening stance advocated by Winnicott and favoured direct advice giving.

The impression gained is that the mainstream of British psychiatry had little interest and little to offer to the field of child psychiatry.

The elderly were the latest new group to arrive on the psychiatric horizon in the sense of becoming aware that this group had different needs from the rest of the population. It was also the largest group among the long stay, chronic inpatients population (29% of the inpatients were 65+)(67). As such it deserved attention in the effort to unhook the mental hospital structure.

Physiological deterioration was taken for granted as the primary reason for psychoses in old age. Mortality rates among the elderly diagnosed as senile were quoted to be as high as 75%(68).

However an editorial in the British Medical Journal(69) proposed that senility was an incorrect explanation for the increase in hospitalization rate of this group. Instead it linked the mental state of the elderly to their social isolation, financial difficulties, loss of independence and

185

occupation. As a preventive measure it was proposed to create general advice centres for the elderly, an interesting idea which is yet to be followed.

A follow-up of two years of a group of discharged elderly patients demonstrated the ability to predict from within the hospital the ability to live outside it. Moreover, while inside the hospital ECT did relieve depression the same symptoms reoccurred outside. Only 29% of the sample did not need to be supported in the community. Lack of interest of GPs and insufficient services and manpower were mentioned too(70).

Summary

The expansion of psychiatry during the post-war years is reflected also in the number of publications and contributions by psychiatrists of that period. The innovative experience of psychiatry in the war period enabled the rethinking of the viability of prolonged hospitalization for mental distress. Together with American and Dutch influences it paved the way for the development of the British approach to the reorganization of the asylums from within and to the creation of community facilities for the discharged patients.

However only a minority in British psychiatry was keen to see the system change. The majority continued to believe in the overall validity of the clinical-somatic approach which does not link itself to either an organizational and/or a social context. This belief led to variations in the degree of rejection of psychological and sociological knowledge in favour of a liberal use of any new physical means of intervention. Many contributors demonstrate a caring approach towards the inpatients. However this attitude is accompanied with a reluctance to adopt a self-critical appraisal towards the theory and practice of psychiatry. Consequently doubts are not raised, questions are not asked and tentative solutions are not encouraged to be provided.

Despite its expansion the mainstream of British psychiatry became more insulated than before since it responded only superficially to the major changes in the British social context.

Its clinical language, prevalent in the textbooks, became even more devoid of any subjective and intersubjective meanings. Contributions to journals show more concern with the real life of patients and use a more ordinary language at times than the textbooks do. They

highlight some of the pressures to which
psychiatrists were exposed and some of the measures
employed to reduce these pressures.

As a professional group psychiatrists were
not so much concerned with the additional social
control aspects exemplified in the lack of this
dimension from the debate on psychopathy. Instead
they were preoccupied with one intra-professional
issue, e.g. the relationships between
superintendents and consultants.

In the twenties the psychoanalytical model
was the only alternative to the clinical-somatic
approach. In the fifties several such alternatives
existed, only to be ignored by mainstream British
psychiatry. Thus the professional literature as a
whole confirms the domination of the
clinical-somatic model.

The hegemony of this approach survived the
criticism laid at its doors at the beginning of the
fifties. By the end of the decade this hegemony was
reinforced in an unprecedented way with the
reception given to the psychoactive drugs. The
place allocated to psychiatry by society has been
extended by the inclusion of the responsibility for
those diagnosed as psychopaths, and by the mistaken
yet persuasive association of mainstream
psychiatric practice with the growing
psychologization of our lives.

6.b. Nurses' Theories and Value Preferences

Between the introduction of the NHS in 1948 and
1954 the number of psychiatric nurses increased by
15%. However, the number of trained nurses
increased by less than 8% and the number of student
nurses decreased by 30%. The main increases were in
the categories of nursing assistants and domestics
(by 26% and 20% respectively)(71).

With the establishment of the NHS salaries of
nurses in psychiatry were equalised to those of
nurses in general hospitals.

<u>Staffing and Training</u>
Given the undisputed overcrowding in psychiatric
hospitals and the increased rate of readmissions,
staffing and training preoccupied nurses'
publications throughout the fifties. A three-day
conference in 1954 on "Staffing problems in mental
nursing"(72) exemplified the concerns, explanations
and solutions the nurses had. The drop in number of

students preoccupied the participants. Some, like the representative of the Employment Ministry, saw it as part of a reduction in numbers of students throughout the spectrum of nursing and not as specific to psychiatry. The majority of the contributors concentrated on factors related to psychiatric nursing. Dame Russell-Smith, Under-Secretary to the Minister of Health, listed the following reasons for the decrease:
1.Family reasons. 2.Unsuitability. 3.Pay. 4. Conditions of work. 5.Teaching and training. The last three issues were the ones on which dissatisfaction centred. Concerning pay, men in mental health nursing earned less than the average male salary. Nurses in long stay institutions were earning less than nurses in hospitals. Mature students with families were earning less than single students.

Conditions of work which caused dissatisfaction included: overcrowing, lack of sufficient co-operation between doctors and nurses, the hierarchical structure of the nursing profession, using nurses as domestics, working with people viewed as incurable and not being rewarded appropriately. Given the magnitude of these indicators it is difficult not to feel that something was missing in the way the nurse's job was organized. From comments made it seems that the content and form of the training process too was found wanting(73). Out of a period of three years of official training 15 months were devoted to general nursing. Only a very short period was spent at the beginning in the school; relationshps between tutors responsible for training and sisters on the wards where students practised were strained; students felt they were exploited in having to carry out menial jobs.

The solutions offered at the conference focused primarily on the form of organization of the training. Much less attention was paid to the content and the satisfaction of those who survived the training process. The organizational alternatives included:
1.Reducing the age of entry to the profession while lifting the upper ceiling.
2.Employing more nursing assistants rather than students (a solution favoured by the ministries of employment and health).
3.Teaching in smaller groups.
4.Better co-ordination between tutors and sisters and between doctors and nurses.

5.Greater participation in case conferences and multidisciplinary meetings.
    Suggestions for improvement in content included an increase in the components of psychology and sociology on the curriculum; visiting settings outside the hospital; understanding the work of related professional groups(74). Each of these proposals had its protagonists and antagonists and the debate on training continued throughout the decade.

Professional status and role.
Although pay equality with general nursing was achieved the assumed professional inferiority of psychiatric nursing was taken for granted. Part of the debate on training was also about means for improving this status. For example, a high degree of dissatisfaction was related to the feeling of being employed inappropriately as domestics and not as nurses. Pointing out the technical skills of psychiatric nurses, such as performing ECT was one method of bolstering the image. Another means was to list the personal qualities and high level of maturity required from psychiatric nurses in establishing and maintaining the relationships with patients, in particular with those who needed special attention(75). Yet another mode of improving the image and status was to create a strong professional association. Miss Altchuler suggested in 1957(76) the unification of the existing four professional organizations, whose representatives were already meeting regularly together by that time. Interestingly 65% of psychiatric nurses belonged to a trade union compared with only 6% of general nurses(77). This fact is explained by the higher percentage of males in this branch of nursing. The feelings of inferiority and exploitation could have been another reason. However trade unions were not perceived as a professional association.
    A shift of emphasis from the twenties in the definition of the nurse's role is noticeable, both in style and content. More of the professional jargon is used and the nurse is portrayed as a professional person working in a team. The content given to the role reflected the growing division within psychiatric nursing between those who wanted nurses to be skilled doctors' aides and those who saw nurses primarily as social therapists(78). The image of the first group was of the nurse who understood well physical means of intervention and

189

was highly skilful in applying them. He/she was also more concerned with the smooth running of a ward, including the level of cleanliness. The approach of such nurses was to be characterized by objectivity and lack of overt emotionality(79). This portrait corresponds well to the self-image of mainstream British psychiatrists at the time. The images employed by the second group focused on the nurse as the key figure in the rebuilding of the relationship between the patient and the world. This role definition was exemplified in the description of nurses' performances in therapeutic communities, using the examples of Belmont and Claybury. There the nurses largely gave up the traditional professional distance between patient and nurse, the hierarchy among nurses themselves and the attention to cleanliness. All of these features were to be given up for the sake of encouraging patients to change their attitudes about themselves and the world. As already mentioned in the overview section the interaction in therapeutic communities permitted a greater measure of verbal and emotional aggression to be expressed than before. The staff group had to contain this burden, which fell in particular on nurses as the members of staff who had more frequent interaction with patients than other personnel.

As within psychiatry so too within psychiatric nursing the protagonists of the therapeutic community approach were in a minority.

The social role of the psychiatric nurse

Nurses saw themselves as intermediaries between the doctors and the patients, family members and doctors and as defenders of the patients against the prejudiced public(80). The custodial aspect was seldom mentioned. The introduction of the category of psychopathy was accepted as a fact which not necessitate a discussion.

In an interesting exchange of letters to the editor several nurses who suffered from a mental breakdown wrote mainly to protest against the negative attitudes they received from their colleagues while being patients and after recovery(81). Prejudice was thus located not only at the general public level but at the profession's too.

The delineation of the role was related only to the hospital setting. Nurses continued to be largely excluded from the out-patient sector. Yet

190

this exclusion was not seen by them as a problem.
The wish to improve the professional status did not include an attempt to branch out of the hospital. While visits to other health and social agencies were infrequently mentioned, no desire was expressed for a role outside the hospital boundaries.

Prevalent theoretical approaches

With the expansion of the hospital sector and the growing impact of psychologization a number of contributions appeared which offered a psychoanalytic perspective on the role of the nurse in the general hospital(82). Not surprisingly the majority of these articles were on "child care in the hospital" and the "psychological aspects of pregnancy and birth", i.e. areas in which the effect of psychologization was most noticeable. In addition there were several contributions on the psychological aspects of some physical diseases, e.g. psychosomatic complaints and pulmonary tuberculosis. However the number of psychoanalytic-oriented papers on psychiatry and psychiatric nursing was similar to the number in the twenties. This finding implies that the influence of psychoanalysis on mental nursing was not greater than it was for British psychiatry as a whole - i.e. very small within the hospital sector.
With one exception behaviour modification was not mentioned. The exception was a report on a rehabilitation ward which used a social habits approach only to discard it later as too rigid(83). In this respect too nurses were following mainstream British psychiatry.
The level of abstraction in the theoretical contributions was kept low and ample examples were given. Fear of abstraction was in fact expressed by some of those who opposed the inclusion of psychology and sociology in the training curriculum(84). Two important strands were missing from the theoretical debate: 1.A conceptual model of the professional activity, including its knowledge base. 2.A conceptual approach to the social context in which psychiatric nursing operated. For example, despite the attention paid to the long stay group of chronic patients none of the sociological approaches to institutionalization was considered.

Methods of intervention

Physical intervention techniques were often

mentioned and frequently described in detail(85).
They were evaluated as unproblematic and very
promising. The psychotropic drugs were rarely
mentioned, usually as part of the process of
administering ECT rather than as a therapy on its
own.

Mental health legislation
Little attention was paid to the Royal Commission
report when it appeared in 1957. But a conference
was organized on the 1959 Mental Health Act(86).
The speakers were only psychiatrists: no MPs,
nurses, no social workers and no representatives of
voluntary organizations. The psychiatrists were
those who pioneered the open door policy and
district legislation which was hailed as a
progressive step.

Attitudes towards other professions
Psychiatrists remained the most important
professional group for nurses and the only point of
reference. Titles of books on psychiatric nursing
were often about "psychiatrists' aides"(87), a term
which did not seem to distress the nurses. Given
the lack of a conceptual model of the profession
and lack of an attempt to have a coherent and
consistent body of knowledge, even if taken from
other disciplines, the dependency on psychiatry was
to be expected.
    However the occasional complaints of not
being consulted and of not being taken seriously by
doctors implied that some nurses were unhappy about
the type of relationships between psychiatrists and
nurses.
    Social workers were seldom referred to by
nurses. When not mentioned factually, only negative
attitudes were expressed which viewed social
workers' activities as very unsatisfactory(88).
One wonders whether this evaluation of social work
was linked to its psychosocial language or to its
relative autonomy in comparison to nursing.
    Occupational therapy was mentioned as a
useful activity in which nurses should
participate(89). There was not, however, a
recognition of occupational therapists as a
professional group.

Value preferences and patients' images
Both value preferences and the image of the patient
remained basically the same as in the twenties.
The only difference was a greater emphasis in the

192

fifties on the psychological aspects of childhood disturbances, neurotic symptoms and some physical conditions. It is difficult to judge how deep was the belief in the psychological dimension for the majority of nurses. This belief should be compared as against the firm belief in the somatic aetiology of psychoses and the impact of the training which followed closely the medical-somatic approach.

The meaning of Community Care
The concept of community care remained largely non-existent within psychiatric nursing. Nurses were not concerned with the term or its meanings as they did not see themselves working in the community. To the extent that the concept was given meaning it was simply synonymous to any non-psychiatric hospital facility. It therefore included psychiatric units in general hospitals.

To conclude, the development of British psychiatric nursing mirrored the development in British psychiatry. While enhancing the professional standing of nurses either as technical experts or as social therapists the profession did not manage to develop a coherent conceptual framework. Moreover, even attempts to produce such a framework are not apparent.

The lack of a social dimension continued and with it continued the inability to perceive a role for nurses outside the hospital. While individual nurses were becoming more autonomous in some places - e.g. in therapeutic communities - the profession as a whole became less autonomous than before. Psychiatric nursing became a more conservative group than it was in the twenties.

6.c.Psychologists' Theories and Value Preferences

The war period was a boom period for intelligence, personality and vocational testing, due to the relevance of testing to army selection. Clinical psychology established a monopoly in the field of personality tests and of screening defects in perception, with which it started to enter the psychiatric hospitals from the war onward. The second role of clinical psychologists was to provide psychotherapy in the settings which tolerated it, i.e. mainly child guidance, some adult out-patient clinics and in the few hospitals which followed psychodynamic lines (e.g. the Cassel, the Belmont).

Educational psychologists established themselves during 1920-1945 with the growth of the children's services. The third task of the two groups was the traditional one of research. In contrast to the dominancy of psychoanalysis in the field of non-academic clinical psychology during the 20s behaviourism emerged as an alternative theory and practice in the 50s.

The monopoly status in regard to testing was attractive in terms of securing professional power and uniqueness(90). It also had the halo of scientific work attached to it as tests are based on an attempt to standardize and objectivize a particular method of observation of behaviour, thought and emotions(91). Tests were there to describe, assess and predict the way the person functions. Such objectives necessarily have a wide range of assumptions on human beings as their background. Explicitly these assumptions were usually kept at best as a background and were often simply ignored. This attitude was the outcome of the belief that tests and testers were largely free from cultural biases.

The division within clinical and educational psychology between the pro-psychodynamic and the pro-behaviourist camp was reflected in testing too. The first group opted for projective techniques which were less standardized and depended more on the interpretation of the tester. These tests were aimed at investigating pre- and unconscious material. This group used tests less as it was less concerned with classical psychiatric diagnosis. The second group invested in preparing tests of the standardized and quantitative type.

The power of psychological tests - and hence of the psychologists - depended on the readiness of other professions to use them as a tool in their own diagnostic and intervention processes. In the clinical setting psychiatrists were the most dominant group and therefore their attitude to psychological tests was crucial. In the period under discussion psychiatrists were ready to use tests as a tool of secondary importance to their own. In addition tests were seen as an instrument of validation of psychiatric assessment and at times in psychiatric diagnosis and prognosis. It is hardly surprising that the majority of psychiatrists preferred the standardized and quantifying, behaviour-oriented tests over projective techniques. Though autonomous, psychologists were kept at a secondary place compared to psychiatrists.

British psychoanalysis in the fifties has achieved a position of cultural hegemony when psychology became equated with psychoanalysis in the mind of the general public. It also established an original British contribution in the form of the Object-Relations approach(92).

Briefly, the object-relations school differs from Freud's formulation in moving further away from a mechanistic model into one which emphasizes relationships. For some analysts the search for relationships replaces in importance the search for pleasure(93). It focuses much more on the first year of life and on the subjective interpretations of relationships in that period. It is assumed that the baby goes through several phases of development during the first year of life which mirror the major possible relationships and stances towards oneself later in life(94). The relationship to the mother, usually the most significant one in this period, is viewed as crucial for the development of self-identity because it forms a prototype for all future relationships. Although reality exists regardless of the person, what matters most is the interpretation it is given. The emphasis on building up the self is depicted often as a struggle between the id and the superego. The latter, represented initially by the mother, received more attention in the object-relations approach than in Freud's psychoanalysis. While the existence of the ego is accepted, this component of the personality is viewed as less conscious and less central by the British object-relations school than by the ego psychology US-based school. Although the sexual connotations of children's images are taken for granted they too are interested in the light of the relationships between the child and his parents.

While the components of the personality are believed to be innate the object-relations approach signifies a move away from a biological orientation further into a purely psychological position.

At its beginning this school concentrated on children and initiated play therapy. This interest was extended to ordinary children and mothers, as exemplified in particular by the work of Winnicott and Robertson(95). Thus the psychologization discussed in the overview section of this chapter was fed by the object-relations group as much as it fed back into the development and status of this group.

The Hampstead clinic, established by Anna Freud, followed more closely her father's line. At the same time Miss Freud developed further her own version of ego psychology(96). The clinic was involved in supporting evacuated children during the war(97).

Like the rest of psychoanalysis research methods employed by both the object-relations group and the Hampstead clinic were far removed from those of the natural sciences and focused instead on interpretation of events and subject experiences of clients in the light of the theoretical model. Some of the case studies presented are very detailed and cover a long time-span. However they are not verbatim reports and therefore do not allow the reader to draw his/her own conclusions from the material(98).

The views of these two groups led to a growing normalization of the child with psychiatric symptoms, as well as to searching for psychological problems in children without consistent symptomatology. The object-relations approach glorified motherhood(99). At the same time its writings and practice must have been alarming to many mothers as they indicate the likely damage due to insufficient mothering, whether intentional or not. Middle-class mothers were more directly affectd by the group's attitude by virtue of reading manuals on mothering and child development and by being more likely to consult professionals and stay in psychotherapy when difficulties were identified.

Although fathers were occasionally mentioned by the group, they were left out of the basic paradigm of relationships. At best they are portrayed as the supporting cast. This proposed division of labour was in sharp contrast to the place of men in our society. Though it supported the privatization of the family, it conflicted with the noramtive notion of the nuclear family by moving from a triangle as its basis to an inter-generational dyad which diminished the place of the peer dyad, i.e. the couple. The exclusion of the father/husband was portrayed as temporary, yet we are not informed of the process of change from this position. Although focused on relationships, these were devoided of their place in the internal and external system in which the family operates. All other relationships are perceived as variations of the basic set of relationships and ignore the social position of a family and its individual

196

members.
       While focusing on individuals, group therapy
was developed by this school in an innovative
way(100).
       A strong interest was professed in child
welfare policies, including financial benefits by
this group. Yet the group did not demonstrate such
an interest in adults, in the mentally distressed
as a client group and in the services provided for
them. No debate took place on community care,
hospital care or the 1959 legislation.
       The value preferences, patients' images and
the restored patient's image remained the same as
those of psychoanalysts in the twenties.
       Behaviour therapy developed from the
application of specific learning theories to
changing symptomatic behaviour. This application
was formed on both sides of the Atlantic. The
person to embody behaviourism in Britain was/is
Professor Eysenck, whose list of relevant
publications on behaviour therapy was up to 32
items in 1960(101). Eysenck's own interest and
investment in testing, experimental research in
physiology, cognitive psychology, intelligence,
personality traits, learning theory, drugs,
psychiatry and psychotherapy indicate the origins
and the scope of behaviour therapy, as well as its
limitations. From the beginning behaviour
modification saw itself as an applied science
modelled on the natural sciences methodology and
principles(102). The preference for natural science
as the only true model led to several consequences:
       1.Theories were seen as primarily aimed at
prediction and only secondarily at accounting for
existing phenomena(103).
       2.A positive emphasis was put on objectivity and
a negative one on subjectivity(104).
       3.Mathematization of experiences and
relationships became the preferred mode of
expression of knowledge(105). The preoccupation
with quantification has also led to the view that
"the" solution to theoretical problems lies in
the application of factorial analysis, i.e. to a
further reduction of the notion of theory(106).
       4.Although behaviour therapy concerned itself not
only with observable behaviour, change was
measured primarily at the level of behaviour and
much less at the level of motivation.
       5.The research instruments focused on behaviour
and statements on attitudes presumed to be given
at a conscious, rational and free from social

desirability level. No qualitative difference was acknowledged to exist between people and animals. Animal research served as the basis for building up the theoretical model.

6.The person is portrayed as a reward seeking, anxiety avoiding organism. The body-mind relationship is more stressed than in other psychological models.

In principle this organism can be taught everything provided the right type of training is given, since no qualitative difference is attached to different individuals, their traits, motives of behaviours (e.g. eye wink rates as equal to the ability to experience anxiety)(107).

The capacity for symbolization is acknowledged and used instrumentally, but not as a qualitative difference (e.g. between animals and human beings). Learning itself is viewed only from the perspective of conditioning. Not accidentally creativity and inquisitiveness are missing from the vocabulary of behaviourism.

Emotions too are recognized as a human trait, only to be divided into adaptive and maladaptive in conjunction with behavioural patterns. The force of emotions, their impact on the experiential and intellectual aspects of life is disregarded.

Suffering is an absent term, because it is rendered meaningless beyond the notion of adaptiveness.

Interpersonal relationships are either dismissed from consideration or given the status of a reinforcement, but are never taken up in their own right.

The basic disregard of relationships implies that even those behaviour therapists who acknowledge the role of relations in a therapeutic encounter discard it from systematic use and understanding.

Such an approach leads also to ignoring the role of relationships in creating and maintaining psychiatric disturbances.

Likewise value preferences are nothing more than another set of learned behaviour based on a hierarchy of rewards in which the preference for a particular reward is at best idiosyncratic and usually simply meaningless.

In this scheme of a physiological organism capable of learning, socialization is a key process of learning(108). Yet again it is a concept removed from its social and interpersonal context. The only variable which can influence it is the genetic capacity for conditioning and the type of learning employed.

An emphasis is put on inherited abilities for learning, conditioning, intelligence and personality traits such as extraversion and introversion(109). The focus on the innate components signifies that there are limitations which have to be considered as the baseline for learning. However we are assured that the existence of these trends does not imply inability to learn or change, but indicates the specific type and quantity of practice necessary for change to occur, a position which differs radically from some later stands taken by behaviourists on issues such as intelligence and personality(110).

Thus living is equated with behaviour in behaviour therapy. Behaviour is further equated with psychiatrically symptomatic and symptom-free patterns.

As part of the attention paid to the physiological aspects of the person, psychopharmacology was looked at and psychotropic drugs were used to facilitate behaviour therapy(111).

In contrast to psychiatrists, clinical psychologists were keen on understanding the reasons for and mode of operation of the drugs and not only in their effects. For one, Eysenck was very much aware of how unsatisfactory the explanations given by psychiatrists were(112). Instead he proposed that drugs worked on the excitation-inhibition dimension of the brain, especially on that of autonomic functioning(113). Individual differences in responding to drugs were then related to innate levels of excitation and inhibition which marked levels of tolerance of drugs. For example a person high on excitation was assumed to require a lower dosage of drugs to lead to a sedated state than a person high on the inhibition side of the range. As excitation and inhibition are related to personality traits as well as to psychiatric diagnostic categories (e.g. hysteria, psychopathy, obsession) it follows that individual dosage has to be adjusted in accordance to these traits.

Psychiatric diagnostic categories are theoretically linked to conditioning capacity on the one hand and to basic personality dimensions on the other hand(114). The method of establishing such classification, namely accumulated observation, is seen as another layer of validation of knowledge derived from experimental studies, testing and therapy situations. For example psychopaths are assumed to have an innate poor ability for conditioning and a high level of extraversion(115).

Behaviour therapy does not doubt the validity of psychiatric classification. In fact it lends support to psychiatry as a branch of medicine more than any other psychological approach to mental distress. Behaviour therapy does not oppose openly any of the tenets of traditional psychiatry or its intervention methods. At times sloppiness in psychiatric thinking is criticized, but not its principles (see ref. 112). However some of the case descriptions beg the question as to the motivation for not criticizing at least some aspects of traditional psychiatry. One such description(116) details 72 weeks of psychiatric intervention concerning a young woman who was hospitalized and given ECT. Although discharged several times, returned to the hospital and further given ECT without an apparent improvement, it was not before week 72 that she was referred to the psychologist. The latter started her on a very different procedure in which ECT had no place. The writer-therapist did not ask himself why was the patently unsuccessful psychiatric intervention allowed to continue for so long, whether it should have been the duty of the psychologist to initiate intervention in such cases, whether the psychologist should have questioned before week 72 the effectiveness and justification for the treatment the woman was receiving. Since ethical considerations are viewed as a distraction from the desired level of objectivity they are simply omitted from the debate. However as it is literally impossible to work with human beings and not to come across ethical considerations, behaviour therapy practice shows how its adherents have gone about these deliberations. On the whole efficacy justified indignities caused to people (e.g. aversion therapy). Professional autonomy comes out as a more respected principle than damage done unwittingly to a client. Suffering in the present was justified if it was believed to lead to a decrease in symptomatology in the future.

Although not stated as such, behaviour modification had/has a very different model of mental distress from that of traditional psychiatry. It does not view such distress as a disease or see people with psychiatric symptoms as

qualitatively different from others(117). Instead
it postulates that psychiatric symptoms are anxiety
avoidance reactions which have been maladaptive
through excessive or/and inappropriate use(118).
Thus symptoms exhibit faulty learning which needed
first to be undone and later to be replaced by
appropriate learning of new and more adaptive
responses.

The methods of unlearning and relearning are
taken from the various types of conditioning and
include variations in terms of quantity, spacing
and quality of conditioning. Stimuli to be used
have to be tailored to the particular person,
symptom and to be couched at the level of everyday
life. Very detailed attention is given to the
procedure of intervention which usually included a
considerable part to be played by the client for
himself(119). The client is given intensive support
at the beginning which is then gradually withdrawn.

Behaviour therapists believe in the value of
intensity and often opt for massed practice at the
beginning. The system of rewards and punishments
has to be worked out beforehand and be made clear
to the client. Thus consistency of approach was
strongly advocated.

Most of the work done in the 50s related to
the wide range of neurotic symptoms and
psychopathic states. The bulk of patients with
psychotic symptoms was hardly referred to, either
in theory or in the practice.

Concerning age groups a focus on children was
prevalent, though work with other age groups was
described too. Thus in regard to the emphasis on
the neuroses and children, behaviour modification
resembles psychoanalysis rather than traditional
psychiatry.

The Image of the Client
Case descriptions provide us usually with age, sex
and personal status, and at times with educational
and occupational background(120). The rest consists
of symptoms and the procedure of removing them.
The emerging profile is of an individual with some
specific innate abilities insufficiently developed.
In conjunction with unpleasant life events,
learning procedures and reward systems these
underdeveloped traits would manifest themselves in
maladaptive behaviours which would cause further
discomfort to the client. The person is therefore
stuck in a closed circuit and needs professional
intervention by experts in learning to unhook

himself from this vicious circle. While the patient could and should be encouraged to be fairly independent of others and to do things for himself, the authority of the professional expert should not be questioned. The patient is portrayed as a passive recipient who is flexible enough to be changed by following loyally professional advice. Although motivational roots to a symptom were recognized they were not seen as requiring change for the sake of symptom elimination(121). It was also assumed that once symptoms were removed the person would behave in a rational manner. Whether he/she would be content beyond the removal of the symptoms, active or goal-oriented was not asked, as such objectives are not part of the aims of behaviour modification.

The person's acceptance of his/her social position is taken for granted, as well as the acceptance of the existing social order in which he/she happens to live.

The difference between a patient and the restored person is located in the removal of the symptoms and the reinstatement of ordinary behaviour.

The subjectivity of the person is largely denied at the theoretical level. At best such focus would be replaced by attention to idiosyncractic preferences of rewards and interpretation of stimuli.

The clinical approach to the person-patient is retained as part of the taken for granted from medicine and natural sciences.

The following value preferences of behaviour therapists emerge:

1. Behaviour rather than inner and social experiences is the most important facet of human existence. Human motivation is considerably less central than behaviour to our lives, although the first influences the second. There is no qualitative difference between types of behaviour.

2. Mental distress is not a disease and people who show psychiatric symptoms do not differ basically from those free of such symptoms.

3. Symptoms are the outcome of faulty learning tied at times to specific genetic vulnerability.

4. Every behaviour is learned and therefore can be changed, including psychiatric symptomatology.

5. The main method of changing behaviour is to de-condition established experiences and re-condition positive reactions to anxiety

provoking situations.
6.Behaviour therapy is an applied science based
on the principles of natural sciences.
Consequently prediction, mathematization of
behaviour and an attempt to follow the
experimental method follow. The knowledge thus
gained is objective and universal.
7.Social structures have no structural
significance to human behaviour.
8.Only the individual organism counts as the
basic unit for study and intervention.
Interpersonal relationships and membership in a
society are largely irrelevant concepts.
9.Human beings will accept any personal or social
content, provided the form will utilise the
correct learning principles. Any social context
equals another, since the same rules of learning
operate and ethical considerations are
non-scientific, and therefore irrelevant.
10.Medical knowledge is assumed to be correct and
corroborates behaviour modification. Medical
intervention may be useful in facilitating
unlearning and new learning.
11.Psychologists are experts in the field of
human behaviour, at the levels of theory
formulation, research and behaviour modification.

Relationships with other professions
Only psychiatrists were discussed in this context.
They were approached as allies whose judgement was
not doubted. Given that their body of knowledge was
based primarily on clinical observations and not on
experimental research it was found wanting and in
need of validation as well as theorization(122). No
evaluative reference was made on psychiatrists'
intervention methods, some of which were used at
times by behaviour therapists (e.g. drugs).
Behaviour modification modelled itself on physical
means of intervention to the extent that
improvement of electronic instruments was
desired(123).
     Eysenck has posed the question of whether
psychologists should have a monopoly on
psychotherapy, or whether psychiatrists should be
trained in behaviour therapy and take over the
psychologist's role. He settled for the situation
as it was - i.e. with psychiatrists in charge but
preferably with an understanding of behaviour
therapy while letting psychologists get on with the
job of therapy(124). It is intriguing to speculate
on what made him so reluctant to confront

psychiatrists with their ignorance of psychological
theories and methods of intervention.

The fact that other professionals in the
field of psychiatry were of no importance to
behaviourists provides us with a clue as to where
their allegiance lay and with whom they identified
themselves in the pecking order of psychiatry. It
is particularly revealing that nurses were left
unmentioned since they were in a position to ensure
that patients followed the procedure suggested by
the psychologist. Perhaps the low status and the
lack of academic training prevented behaviourists
from considering seriously the therapeutic role of
the nurse.

The meaning of Community Care

No meaning was attributed to community care since
it was never discussed in publications by clinical
psychologists, either psychoanalysts or behaviour
therapists. This omission is hardly surprising in
the absence of attention to issues which were not
seen as part of direct intervention with an
individual who had a psychiatric symptom. The
service system, institutional setting, policies,
legislation, parliamentary debates on psychiatry,
society's attitudes towards the mentally ill,
relatives' views, the impact of social structure
factors on mental distress - all of these issues
were never mentioned.

The role of the intermediary

The absence of the social structure dimension
implied also that no attention was paid to the role
of the intermediary and to the social control
function of psychologists. From their writings it
can be inferred that behaviour therapists took for
granted a social control function as illustrated by
the emphasis on adaptive behaviour. Advocating an
a-social and a-moral position behaviour therapy
would be unlikely to accept a role as an
intermediary for itself explicitly.

As already mentioned in chapter 3, the
psychoanalytic position on social control was more
complex because it advocated liberation from
societal repression as well as accepting such
repression for the sake of living in a
civilization.

To summarize, clinical and educational
psychologists in the fifties have become socially
acceptable and respectable, their tasks were
relatively well defined around testing, research

and therapy.

The group was divided into two major groupings, those in favour of psychoanalysis and those who preferred behaviourism. The internal degree of cohesion with each group was as high as the animosity toward the other group. Examples of the hostility between the two groups are available in abundance and need not be reproduced here(125). The main arguments for and against psychoanalysis and behaviourism have been too amply discussed(126).

The sharp and clear language of the behaviourists, their affinity to the natural sciences and the focus on definite outcomes have made their approach attractive for those psychologists unhappy with the vagueness of psychoanalysis. Despite the attention paid to genetic qualities, behaviour therapy was more optimistic about the possibility of symptom removal for children and adults than psychoanalysis ever was. This feature must have won over for this school of psychology more professionals. The lack of an overt conflict with traditional psychiatry was an advantage too in enabling psychiatrists to approach behaviour therapy as an alternative to psychoanalysis. Like psychoanalysis behaviour therapy adopted the clinical approach to the person, thus invoking its own version of paternalism and distancing.

Behaviourism is both a theoretical model and an intervention method, as psychoanalysis is. Although most of its adherents would oppose that it offers a world view, some of them have been ready to acknowledge this aspect(127). Like psychoanalysis, behaviourism postulates a universal model of the person and his relationships to the environment.

Although still small in numbers in the fifties(128) clinical and educational psychologists secured a position of monopoly and authority much stronger than the one accredited to social workers and nurses. This position was due to the academic credibility of the discipline, its claim for and demonstration of uniqueness of knowledge and skills.

6.d.Social Workers' Theories and Value Preferences

During the war psychiatric social workers (psw) worked with evacuees, in particular children and their mothers. In the immediate post-war years work with veterans took place too(129). Thus although not employed by the army social workers branched into new areas as a result of the war experience. The work with children and mothers without identified psychiatric problems continued after the war, when some psw took posts in maternity services and child welfare centres.

With the growth of the hospital sector after the war, more psw students began to be trained in several psychiatric hospitals and some continued to work there. However the majority of social workers in hospitals and in the aftercare services remained unqualified.

The 1950-1960 period

This period can be justifiably described as the golden age of psychiatric social work. Compared with the rest of social work, psw had a stronger professional association, expressed a greater interest in professionalism and provided leadership outside their own brief.

The professional body - the association of psychiatric social workers - acted consistently as the gate keeper in allowing only university graduates of psychiatric social work courses to be recognised as psw and to join the association(130). Equally consistently it rejected the request of the Duly Authorized Officers Association for joint training programmes and joint organisation. One unintended outcome of this position was that in 1959 most psw could not become mental welfare officers (the term which replaced the duly authorized officer in the 1959 Act) under the new legislation because they were not usually in direct contact with the identified patient but more likely with his/her relatives.

The association opposed the Feversham Committee recommendations in 1940 to amalgamate all four aftercare voluntary organizations in the field of mental health and to have only one type of worker to be called mental health workers. In 1952 the association considered whether psw should be called "medical auxiliaries". This move was ultimately rejected due to opposition from the university courses, but not because of the wishes of the practitioners.

With the recommendations of the McIntosh Committee in 1953 that only university graduates qualified in psychiatric social work would be recognized as psw, the association won the battle for professional accreditation. The achievement was short lived in terms of its implications because both the McIntosh committee and the Younghusband committees in 1959 put the emphasis on the need for generic training in social work. It was yet again the London School of Economics, the first to start the psychiatric course in 1929, which opened in 1954 the first university course for a generic social work qualification.

The association was preoccupied with training standards of professional activities and ethics. The emphasis on training was limited only to its members, leaving the training of the duly authorized/mental welfare officers on a limb. The association did not put pressure on the government to ensure that only qualified social workers should participate in certification and/or that gradually all social workers in psychiatry should be qualified.

In the tradition of professional associations, less emphasis was put on work and pay conditions, but the association became affiliated to NALGO as early as 1955. Surprisingly, research, social policy or advocacy roles were not taken up by the association. The association did not concern itself with the form and content of the psychiatric system.

The number of psw grew steadily until the mid-50s, when the number of students on courses went down. The reasons for this trend are not clear, though Timms suggested that potential students became aware of the possible incorporation into mainstream social work(131). By the end of the decade the number of qualified psw reached 500(132). Proportionally, fewer social workers were added to the psychiatric services when compared to psychiatrists and psychologists(133).

The majority worked in child guidance clinics, a few in psychiatric hospitals and even fewer in the community mental health services (only 35 out of the 500 mentioned above)(134). Child guidance practice continued to follow psychoanalytic directions. Under this umbrella a range of approaches was practised. The social worker's role continued to be that of the team member in charge of taking social history, working with parents/relatives and with outside agencies.

The work done by psw in child care departments included more attention to the material aspects of living. It was also less in the mould of psychotherapy and more problem-oriented. Still psw

were criticized justly by other social workers for
their disdain at dealing with financial matters.

Attitudes towards work inside psychiatric
hospitals.
It was already mentioned that only a few of the
qualified psw took up posts in the hospitals. The
basically negative attitude towards working in a
mental hospital was due to: 1.Psychotherapeutic
work by psw was not encouraged in most hospitals.
2.Social workers were less autonomous in the
hospital than outside it. 3.The bulk of the work in
hospital had to do with sorting out financial and
other resources, a rather bottomless task. 4.The
pessimistic view of the likelihood of change in
adulthood derived from the psychoanalytic
perspective contributed to the lack of wish to work
in a hospital. 5.The majority of psw were reluctant
to become involved in certifying clients, viewed as
an act of overt social control agents.
     Towards the end of the decade, with the
publication of the Royal Commission report, the
debate on the last issue was rekindled. Those
against participation in certification stressed the
nature of the client-professional relationships
would alter if the element of coercion would come
into it(135). Implied was the notion that
involvement in compulsory admission is
counterproductive to securing clients' trust in
their social workers. Those psw who wanted to
become mental welfare officers argued that
certification was an unavoidable part of life for
some psychiatric patients who nevertheless continue
to require social work assistance(136).
Interestingly it was not claimed that the latter's
contribution would be unique or would mitigate the
circumstances of compulsory admission. Only one
paper(137), published in 1949, was concerned with
the suitability of the training given on the
specialised courses and the largely psychoanalytic
placements for the work required of duly authorized
officers in the hospitals. The article did not
create a stir and the debate it deserved did not
follow.
     The impact of psw was much wider than the
settings in which they were located. Every textbook
on social work and many contributions to journals
during this period demonstrate this influence,
which was part of the process of psychologization
of everyday life and of mental distress. The
emphasis on the impact of childhood events and

relationships has been the single most significant factor in terms of its lasting impact. It had implications for evaluating parents' child-rearing practices, judging whether children should/should not stay with their parents on the basis of emotional harm, encouraging mothers to stay at home rather than to work outside. This focus led also to a move away from placing children in institutions or at least to delaying such a placement as much as possible because of the importance attached to lasting relationships. The size of institutions and the quality of staff-children relationships there came also under scrutiny.

The belief in the largely irreversible impact of childhood on change in adults, especially those who were not undergoing psychotherapy led to pessimism. Since the majority of adults with identified psychiatric problems were not in psychotherapy it was felt that not much could be done for them or by them for themselves. While specific issues could be sorted out, these were believed to be either superficial or only indicative of deeper and unresolved intrapsychic motives(138).

Concerning methods of intervention, psychiatric social work followed most closely the casework method. That "casework" became synonymous with "social work" during the 1950-1970 period in Britain is yet another reflection of the impact of psw on the rest of social work(139). In its practice, social casework focused on the client-worker relationships, the emotional aspects of living, interpersonal relationships and intrapersonal conflicts. In contrast to psychoanalysis it was more geared to the present, more interested in the strengths of clients and more ready to mobilize environmental resources. From case descriptions it emerges that a problem-solving approach was more frequently used than admitted. The problem-solving direction relies more on ego psychology and crisis intervention than on orthodox psychoanalysis(140). It is also more akin to learning theorists' perspective and to commonsense understanding of sorting out specific problems rather than a totality.

B. Wootton's fierce attack on psw(141) exemplifies the wide impact of this small group of workers. Wootton is correct in treating this group as the spearhead of psychologization, but incorrect in not locating the source in psychoanalysis and the cultural-political climate of the post-war period. However, the majority of psw's writings of the decade do not reflect the grandiosity which Wootton ascribed to them; it is only at the level of underlying assumptions that an imperialistic desire existed. As already mentioned in section 6.a., Wootton's lack of criticism concerning psychiatrists' approach to psychopathy exhibits her own biases.

Attitudes towards professional autonomy

Given the background outlined above, it would have been logical to assume that this group of social workers would want to secure a high degree of professional autonomy. Such a level of autonomy would have been easier to achieve in an independent setting which British social work experienced during the war to a large extent. However the issue was rarely raised by psw. Those few who commented on such a possibility were firmly against it and could not envisage psw without a psychiatrist directing the service(142). It would seem that this highly qualified and prestigious group within social work internalized the image of itself as no more than "medical auxiliaries". Although psw adopted the clinical approach to clients, their practice and value preferences still differed considerably from those of mainstream British psychiatry. However this incompatibility was never raised or debated, as it should have been by a self-respecting professional group.

Professional knowledge

The knowledge base of psw was explicitly taken from psychology, psychiatry, sociology and social administration. The first two disciplines were considerably more in use. Psychiatric classification and assessment were accepted by psw without doubts. Likewise the possibility of organic causation was not rejected. However, the emphasis was put on psychological factors in the case of neuroses and childhood disturbances, with unsatisfactory mother-child relationships viewed as the core of the problem(143). The child was perceived primarily as a recipient in the relationships. At times relationships with the father, siblings and spouse would be focused upon too.

Co-existing environments - such as the school, the peer group and the work place - were acknowledged as relevant reinforcers in supporting change by providing a base in everyday life from

210

which to re-evaluate one's feelings. However these
environments were treated as secondary to the home,
both in terms of problem inducing and resolving.

Pertaining to adults a greater emphasis was
put on the present and current important
relationships. This focus meant a shift to ego
psychology and to a problem-oriented approach.

The most central debate in the 1947-50 period
was on the significance of "the social" in social
work. Walderon cited the case of group therapy as
an example for the insufficient attention paid to
the social dimension(144). She claimed that
although psw accepted the importance of groups it
was not incorporated into the practice. For her,
the person must be seen as part of his natural
environment rather than as a collection of
symptoms. Social work attitudes should be less
distancing, more focused on the present and less
psychiatrically and psychoanalytically oriented.
Instead they should be more geared toward ordinary
life styles. Walderon suggested that the social
work task should move from that of history taking.
In short, the writer was opposing the hegemony of
the clinical approach to clients. In replying to
this critique, Goldberg(145) emphasized that there
was sufficient recognition of "the social" within
social work, exemplified by the attention paid to
the writings of M. Mead and R. Benedict (both were
cultural anthropologists who combined the
functionalist-structuralist sociological school
with a psychodynamic view in their research).
Goldberg associated Walderon's approach with
unprofessionalism, which was described as not
integrating enough present knowledge with that of
the past. Likewise, Hunnybun(146) reiterated the
importance of a psychoanalytic approach and the
benefit of history taking for conducting further
work.

While Goldberg and Hunnybun were defending a
known territory, Walderon seemed less sure of her
ground. The article neither defined "the social"
nor specified what should be the new psw role.
This debate was reminiscent of the "reform vs.
therapy" debates in social work, typical of the
beginning of the century and the late 60s.

The attention to the social dimension in psw
was also reflected in the curriculum of psw
courses. According to Timms (147) less sociology
and more psychology were taught in the fifties than
in the interim wars period.

This important exchange reflected also on the

theoretical poverty of British psw, which stood in contrast to the relatively lively theoretical debate in American psw at the time. The British side was aware of its own deficiency, as exemplified in the first editorial to the British Journal of Psychiatric Social Work (BJPSW)(148). The editor apologized for the journal coming so late on the scene compared to the American journals. Timms(149) provided in 1960 the only attempt to break out of the total reliance on practice wisdom in his two papers on "theorizing about social work". However, at this stage no more than a critique of the American stand and a framework for a typology of theoretical approaches was presented. The intriguing issue why British psw did not develop a theoretical framework remained unanswered. In the absence of research, it is speculated here that the lack of theorization was related to several factors:

1.The tendency among British professionals - not only in social work - towards pragmatism and the preference of practice wisdom over conceptualization.

2.The preoccupation with the professional status led to a preference for borrowing "safe" theories, i.e. from more prestigious disciplines.

3.The dependency on psychoanalysis led to relying on it as a theoretical model and therefore to lowering the felt need for an independent model.

A related indication was the fact that research was not a subject taught on the curriculum of the psw courses. The opportunity to train people to think about social work from a conceptual perspective was either not recognised as worthwhile for it to be part of their training or else a narrow definition of preparing practitioners was overriding.

Often value preferences came instead of the theoretical component. For example, contributors wrote that it was the social workers' role to mediate between the client and his family and between the client and society. The role of the intermediary included being an interpreter for clients, their families and the community(150). This important belief could have become an assumption for a model of the person and society relationships as well as of social work vis-a-vis society. However such a model was not constructed and remained implicit.

As in the twenties psw professed their ethical commitment to respecting their clients, to refraining from a judgemental stance and to providing active support to the clients. Equally they continued to perceive of themselves as serving the community. The debate on their lack of readiness to participate in certification indicated that the service to society was ethically bound by professional values held in higher esteem than a pure social control function.

During the decade, contributions were predominantly devoted to descriptions of specific aspects of the practice, usually focusing on a particular client group. In contrast to psychiatry the elderly were not identified as a group worthy of psw attention. This omission reflected on the lack of work with and attention to the needs of the largest group of long stay patients in the mental hospital. It perhaps signified how far removed from the reality of psychiatric hospital psw was.

The significance of physical intervention methods in psychiatry for social work intervention received attention in a contribution by Crump in 1959(151). The author expressed her enthusiasm at the impact of the new drugs and at the hospital becoming a community. The absence of a serious debate on the psychiatric means of intervention was understandable in the light of the unquestioned acceptance of psychiatric authority by psw. Surprisingly however the role of social workers in therapeutic communities was hardly mentioned. Contributions on these communities appeared in the BJPSW, but they were written by psychiatrists. The open door policy too did not receive any specified consideration, despite its implication to the role of psw inside and outside the hospital.

The Royal Commission report and the proposed 1959 legislation received more coverage in the BJPSW than in any other professional group publications, with one issue devoted only to the Commission report(152), perhaps reflecting on the awareness of the social context in which psw operated. The editorial to this issue stressed the intermediary role of psw in cultivating social tolerance on the one hand and readiness to accept treatment by clients and families on the other hand. Possible expansion of the psw role was envisaged. Heap(153) pointed out that social work was likely to offer the only continuous contact between the client, the hospital and the community. Therefore psw could and should act as advisers to other professions, provided it acquainted itself with the needs of these professions. Other writers were unhappy about the implications of the new legislation. Thomas(154) was afraid of the separation of psychiatric treatment from social care by virtue of the separation between local authority and hospitals. She was also worried by a decrease in quality and quantity of the service if local authorities would become responsible for it. However Thomas did not ask herself why local authorities' services would have less resources at their disposal and what would be the advantages of having a psw service located in the local authority.

Concerning the report's recommendations on people diagnosed as psychopaths a number of qualifications were raised by psw. Myers(155) doubted the wisdom of accepting without question the psychiatrists' view on the matter and supported B. Wootton's request for a sociological study on psychopathy. The report emphasis on treatment was viewed as unrealistic and as wrong in not taking into account the fear of aggressive behaviour of psychopaths by hospital staff.

Lastly, the reluctance of psw to carry out the statutory duties of the duly authorized officer/mental welfare officer was severely criticized as professionally irresponsible(156). It was stressed that psw should see certification as part of their practical duties. Equally they should attempt to understand administrators instead of complaining that the latter do not understand social work. Thus some of the 70s and 80s central foci of tension between management and social workers and between professional and statutory duties were already expressed in the 50s.

The meaning of Community Care
Community care was attributed wide ranging meanings and functions in the psw literature. A combination of health and social services was envisaged which should have provided psychological, medicine, financial and social support to those in need. The role of the psw would be to work directly with clients as well as to offer consultation to other professions. Although wide, the meaning attached was not well defined and no program was worked out for the implementation of such a wide ranging service.

Attitudes towards other professions
Attitudes toward psychiatry were already mentioned. They were characterized by accepting a secondary

214

role for social work vis-a-vis psychiatrists.
Nurses, health visitors and administrators were the
groups to whom social workers could provide
advice(157). Interestingly psychologists were not
referred to in the literature in terms of a
professional group.

The image of the client.

The image of the patient for this group of social
workers was not any more that of the economically
deprived person of the twenties, but the person
with emotional difficulties. The person became
classless. Instead his/her role in the family was
stressed and the severity of the disturbances which
were causally related to family relationships.
Respect and basic acceptance of the person was
reflected in the writings of psw. At the same time
the vulnerability of clients was taken as a sign of
immaturity, even when the client was quite
successful in the world outside the clinic.

The restored patient was the person capable
of finding sublimating defences, of acting
rationally and not any more in need of psychiatric
symptoms as a way of repressing emotional
conflicts.

Given psw value preferences the right to have
emotional difficulties and psychoanalytic
intervention was not limited to the middle class.
Thus B. Wootton's criticism that psw attempted to
treat not only the poor was justified. However
instead of being a reflection of an imperialistic
wish it was equally the logical conclusion of the
universalistic mesage of psychoanalysis. In this
sense it was a liberating message rather than a
repressive one because it saw the poor and the
middle classes as equals in terms of their human
nature. As already mentioned the psychologization
of everyday life and the psychoanalytic version of
it legitimized the exclusion of social forces and
structures from being considered as causes and
maintaining factors of mental distress. Given the
acceptance of the role of the intermediary, this
role became one-sided in psw. The balance of
individual/society relationships was tilted with
the individual and his most significant
relationships being seen as the sole responsible
factors, putting aside the knowledge social work
had of the role society played in determining human
existence, including mental distress.

Summary

Several major developments took place during the 50s in the field of psychiatry.

Firstly, with the introduction of the NHS, psychiatric services became more available for the majority of the British people. The undeniable expansion of the psychiatric system was due to the expansion of the NHS as a whole as well as to the greater use of and demand for psychiatric facilities. All four groups benefited from this change, but perhaps the consultant psychiatrists were the group to benefit most in terms of power and rewards. Given the impact of psychologization psw and psychologists became more prestigious than before.

Secondly, important areas of everyday life as well as mental distress were attributed psychological significance on an unprecedented scale. The psychologization of motherhood, childhood, interpersonal relationships, reasons for war and national character could not but encourage the interest in psychiatric issues.

Thirdly, as a result of the first two factors and the continuation of the modernization trend in the post-war period a greater degree of professionalism was aspired and closely adhered to within the different professional groups in the field of psychiatry. This professionalism was expressed primarily in modes of professional organization and gate keeping of entry to professional activities.

Fourthly, for the first time since the decline of the moral approach there were several viable alternatives to the clinical-somatic model of mental distress and psychiatric practice. Psychoanalysis, behaviourism and community mental health were the three major alternatives. These three approaches differ in terms of content, coverage, level of analysis and proposed system of services. Nevertheless they have in common the move away from viewing mental distress as a medical issue. Instead mental distress is perceived as problem in living. Therapeutic communities, the open door policy, behaviour therapy, the child guidance movement and the anti-institutionalism stand were partial expressions of these models.

The majority of British psychiatrists rejected the message of psychological understanding and intervention. Yet the profession benefited from the readiness of the public to widen the scope of psychiatry by equating the latter with psychological approaches.

Nurses have come to accept the validity of psychological approaches side by side with the value given traditionally to the clinical-somatic viewpoint.

The attitude to the psychological dimension was reflected in the reactions to the alternative models: psychiatrists largely rejected the viability of such alternatives and at best saw them as additional techniques. Social workers and psychologists championed specific versions of these models.

Concerning professionalism the two groups with less social prestige, social workers and nurses, were more openly preoccupied with professionalism. Both groups debated frequently training programs, entry to the profession and types of professional organization. They paid less attention to role definition, uniqueness of theory and skills. The secondary position vis-a-vis psychiatrists was internalized by both nurses and social workers.

Pertaining to psychiatrists, interest in professionalism was reflected in the debate on the relationships between consultants and superintendents. The readiness to incorporate psychopathy within the brief of psychiatry indicated the wish for the expansion of professional authority and activity. The attacks on psychiatrists professing psychosocial views signified another focus of professionalism, as the critique was made out of fear of straying away from the right path for psychiatry (i.e. as a branch of medicine).

Psychologists manifested the least interest in professionalism, although at times the relationships with psychiatrists were discussed. Entry to the profession was well defined and guarded, as were the professional tasks. Perhaps the high degree of clarity and rigidity within a relatively narrow field of responsibility made a preoccupation with professionalism unnecessary.

Of the four groups the role of the social worker was the least well defined. The role of the nurse was the most comprehensive and thus difficult to be defined for the work done inside the hospital.

Theory Formation
In the fifties, as well as in the twenties, social workers and nurses did not succeed in building up their own theoretical framework. However, while psw

attempted to create a systematic framework based on borrowing from other disciplines nursing has not tried seriously to formulate a theoretical model.

The majority of British psychiatrists continued to rely on neurology and physiology as their conceptual base. To the extent that research done in these areas shed light on psychiatric issues, they gained. However the focus on outcomes and the opposition to any non-medical perspective prevented this majority from becoming knowledgeable of relevant explanations presented by psychologists and sociologists. The most striking example of such an a-priori rejection was the ignorance of and lack of interest in behaviour therapy, despite the fact that this approach was not hostile to psychiatry. The lack of interest in explanations contributed also to the readiness to use intervention methods without due attention to side effects.

Psychologists remained committed to an interest in conceptual frameworks. Albeit of a very different nature, both the object-relations approach and behaviour therapy created fuller theoretical schemes than was the case for mainstream psychiatry, psw or nursing.

All of the four groups did not incorporate a social structure dimension within their theoretical perspectives. Although psw continued to utilize environmental resources, less emphasis was put on the social dimension within psw than was the case in the twenties. Only in the case of social work a shift away from this component took place. All other groups did not have such a dimension either in the 20s or the 50s.

With the growth in professionalism and formal theorization, the subjectivity of clients was hardly allowed to be heard in professional publications. Interestingly some of the subjective experiences of nurses and social workers surfaced rather than those of their clients. Only nurses admitted to having mental breakdowns themselves.

With one exception, self-criticism was applied only by social workers. The exception was provided by those nurses who complained of negative attitudes towards them by other nurses following a period of mental breakdown. All other professions did not express self-criticism.

The absence of a social dimension was closely related to the type of meaning given to mental illness/health and the attention paid to social policy in this field. Different aspects of the 1957 Royal Commission report and the 1959 Mental Health

Act were debated by the different groups with the exceptions of psychologists. However even when such a discussion took place it never went as far as analysing the psychiatric system and/or proposing alternatives to the existing service. The impact of psychologization enabled a favourable response to community care. Social workers' ideas on community care were the nearest to the American and Dutch models of it. Yet the professional reactions were less enthusiastic than the public response and remained often at the level of slogans. Underneath the slogans each profession wished for a continuation of its own mode of operation outside the hospital sector, if need be. None of the professional groups had come up with either a conceptual model on community care or a worked out programme for its implementation.

No desire for change came from the majority of professional contributions. Consequently no pressure was put on the government by professionals to implement community care and no alternative programmes were presented by professional organizations.

Although the fifties have seen important developments in psychiatry, at the end of the period the status quo was more confirmed than at its beginning. This state of affairs ensured the continuation of viewing mental distress primarily through the clinical gaze, despite the innovations in other directions which took place during the 50s. Thus the hegemony of the clinical-somatic approach was secured at the very time when alternative approaches became available.

References
1.Timms, N.(1964) Psychiatric Social Work in Great Britain (1939-1962), Routledge and Kegan Paul, London, p.90.
2.Henderson, D. Gillespie, R. D. (1956) A Textbook of Psychiatry, Oxford University Press, London, pp.419-20.
3.Ibid.
4.This term appears in: Better Services for the Mentally Ill. Cmnd. 6233, 1975 and in: Jones, K. (1972) The History of the Mental Health Services, Routledge and Kegan Paul, London.
5.Busfield, J.(1980) The Historical Antecedents of Decarceration: The Mentally Ill. Unpublished paper, Dept. of Sociology, University of Essex.
6.Ahrenfeldt, R. H. (1958) Psychiatry in the British Army in the Second World War, Routledge and

Kegan Paul, London.
7. Ibid, p.6.
8. Ibid, p.117.
9. Ibid, pp.144,147.
10. Myerson, A. (1939) Theory and Principles of the Total Push Method in the Treatment of Chronic Schizophrenia, Americal Journal of Psychiatry, 95, pp.11-97.
Sullivan, H. S. (1962) Schizophrenia as a Human Process, Norton, New York.
11. Main, T. F. (1946) The Hospital as a Therapeutic Institution, Bulletin of the Meninger Clinic, 10, pp.66-70.
12. Bierer, J. (1948) The Day Hospital, Lewis, London.
Jones, M. (1952) Social Psychiatry, Tavistock, London.
Carstairs, G. M. et al. (1956) Organization of a Hospital Workshop for Chronic Psychotic Patients, British Journal of Preventive Social Medicine, 10, p.136.
13. Rees, R. (1954) Freedom in Mental Hospitals: the End and the Means, Lancet, 2, p.964.
14. Clark, D. H. (1964) Administrative Therapy, Tavistock, London, pp.5-7.
15. Ibid, Ch.4.
16. Lancet (1954), 2, p.953, (1954), 1, p.1117.
17. Lancet (1954), 2, p.1130 (letter to the editor by the son of Dr. S. Good.)
18. Scull, A. (1975) Decarceration, Prentice Hall, Englewood.
19. Erickson, E. (1951) Childhood and Society, Basic Books, New York.
20. Sullivan, H. S. (1957) The Fusion of Psychiatry and the Social Sciences, Norton, New York.
21. Hartman, H. (1951) Ego Psychology and the problem of Adaptation. In: Rapaport, D. (ed) Organization and Pathology of Thought, Columbia University Press, New York, pp.362-396.
Caplan, G. (1959) Concepts of Mental Health and Consultation, Children Bureau Publication, New York, No. 373.
Shoben, E. J. (1949) Psychotherapy as a problem in Learning Theory, Psychological Bulletin (US), 46, pp.366-392.
22. Parsons, T. (1951) The Social System, The Free Press, New York.
23. Bowlby, J. (1951) Maternal Care and Mental Health, World Health Federation, Geneva and: (1958) Can I Leave my Baby? National Association for Mental Health.

220

24.Pearson, G. (1976) The Deviant Imagination, Macmillan, London.
25.Caudill, W. (1958) The Psychiatric Hospital as a Small Community, Harvard University Press, Cambridge, Mass.
See also Clark, D. Ref.14.
26.See Ref.3 and every psychiatric textbook and official Ministry of Health publication.
27.Goffman, I. (1961) Stigma, Penguin, Harmondsworth.
Sontag, S. (1978) Illness as Metaphor, Farber, New York.
Comaroff, J., Maguire, P. (1979) Ambiguity and the Search for Meaning: Childhood Leukemia in the Clinical Context, Social Science and Medicine, 15, pp.115-123.
28.Hoenig, P. (1959) Psychiatric Inpatients in General Hospitals, Lancet, 2, p.122. Lancet (1959), 2, p.839, British Medical Journal (1959) 1, p.297.
29.Rapaport, R. (1960) Community as Doctor, Tavistock, London.
Shoenberg, E. (ed) (1966) A Hospital Looks at Itself, Tavistock, London.
30.Bion, W. R. (1961) Experiences in Groups, Tavistock, London.
Bales, R. F. et al. (1955) Small Groups Studies in Social Interaction, Knopf, New York.
31.Petrie, A. (1942) Types of Psychopathic Personality, Journal of Mental Sciences, 88, pp.491-3.
See also Ref.2.
32.See Ref.12 and: Stafford-Clark, D. (1959) The Foundation of Research in Psychiatry, British Medical Journal, 1, pp.1199-1204.
33.See Ref.16.
34.British Medical Journal (1945), 1, p.642; Lancet (1954), 1, pp.139-141; Lancet (1945), 2, p.591.
35.Lancet (1954), 1, pp.139-141.
36.Nursing Mirror (1954), pp.1055-6, p.1193.
37.Ibid.
38.Ibid.
39.Lancet (1959), 2, p.117.
40.Ibid and also: Norris, V. (1959) Mental Illness in London, Maudsley Monographs 6, London.
41.Lancet (1959), 2, p.117, Jones, K., Sidebottom, A. (1962) The Mental Hospital at Work, Routledge and Kegan Paul, London.
42.British Medical Journal (1954), 1, p.214, Bickford, D. (1954) Treatment of the Chronic Mental Patient, Lancet, 1, pp.924-927, British Medical

Journal (1959), 1, pp.293-296.
Editorial: Mental Care: A different pattern?
Lancet (1954), 1, p.1117.
43.Brown, G. (1959) Social Factors Influencing
Length of Hospital Stay of Schizophrenic Patients,
British Medical Journal, 2, pp.1300-1302.
44.See Ref.42.
45.British Medical Journal (1959), 1, p.945.
46.See Refs.14, 29, 11, 13.
47.Rees, T. P. (1957) Back to Moral Treatment and
Community Care, Journal of Mental Science,
pp.303-313.
48.Tredgold, R. F. (1958) Bridging the Gap,
Johnson, London.
49.British Medical Journal (1957), 2, p.1006.
50.Lancet (1954), 1, p.964, (1959) 2, pp. 282-4.
51.British Medical Journal (1954), 1, pp.1042-141,
(1959) 1, p.359.
52.British Medical Journal (1954), 1, p.1298.
53.See Ref.50 and Lancet (1959), 1, p.668.
54.British Medical Journal (1959), 1, p.99.
Lancet (1959), 2, pp.224, 1237.
55.Eysenck, H. K. (1957) Drugs and Personality: 1.
Theory and Methodology, Journal of Mental Science,
103, pp.119-31.
56.Lancet (1959), 2, pp.1256, 131, 575, British
Medical Journal (1959), 1, pp.293, 396.
57.British Medical Journal (1959), 1, p.361.
58.Lancet (1959), 1, p.135.
59.British Medical Journal (1959), 1, pp.293-296.
60.Lancet (1959), 1, pp.308, 411, 576, 577, 681,
736.
61.Lancet (1959), 1, p.472.
62.Lancet (1959), 1, p.13, British Medical Journal
(1959), p.361.
63.Lancet (1959), 2, p.347.
64.Lancet (1959), 1, pp.1005, 1129.
65.Lancet (1959) 2, pp.193-5.
66.Ibid, pp.347-8.
67.British Medical Journal (1954), 1, p.763.
68.Ibid and p.1206, British Medical Journal (1959),
1, pp.293-296.
69.British Medical Journal (1959), 2, p.234.
70.Colwell, C., Post, F. (1959) Community Needs of
Elderly Psychiatric Patients, British Medical
Journal, 2, pp.131, 214.
71.Nursing Mirror (1954), p.1055.
72.Nursing Mirror (1954), pp.1055-1193.
73.Nursing Mirror (1954), pp.1538, 1544, 1194.
74.Nursing Mirror (1957), pp.36, 1663-4.
75.Nursing Mirror (1957), pp.xiii-xi.

76.Nursing Mirror (1957), p.43.
77.Nursing Mirror (1957), p.180.
78.Nursing Mirror (1957), p.965; (1954), p.1193.
79.Nursing Mirror (1957), pp.xiii-xv.
80.McGhie, A. (1957), The Nursing Attitude, Nursing Mirror, pp.9-13.
81.Nursing Mirror (1954), pp.890, 1020.
82.Nursing Mirror (1954), pp.629-30, 761-2, (1957), pp.1189-90.
83.Nursing Mirror (1957), pp.vi-v.
84.Nursing Mirror (1957), p.1357.
85.Nursing Mirror (1957), pp.1497-9.
86.Nursing Mirror (1957), p.772.
87.Nursing Mirror (1954), p.769; (1957), p.965.
88.Nursing Mirror (1954), p.890; (1957), p.1438.
89.Nursing Mirror (1957), pp.xiii-xii.
90.Mittler, P.(ed) (1970) Psychological Assessment of Mental and Physical Handicaps, Methuen, Longon.
91.Sundberg, N., Tyler, L. (1962) Clinical Psychology, Appleton-Century Croft, New York.
Eysenck, H. J. (1960) (ed) Handbook of Abnormal Psychology, Pitman, London.
92.Guntrip, H. (1971) Psychoanalytic Theory, Therapy and the Self, The Hogarth Press, London.
93.Fairbairn, W. R. (1952) Psychoanalytic Studies of the Personality, Tavistock, London.
94.Klein, M. (1955) New Directions in Psychoanalysis, Tavistock, London.
Klein, M. (1963) Our Adult World and other Essays, Heinemann, London.
95.Winnicott, D. (1957) The Child, the Family and the Outside World, Tavistock, London.
Robertson, J. (1952) A Two-Years Old Goes to Hospital (film and guidebook), Tavistock Child Development Research Unit, London.
96.Freud, A. (1936) The Ego and the Mechanisms of Defence, The Hogarth Press, London.
97.Burlingham, D., Freud, A. (1942) Young Children in Wartime, Allen and Unwin.
98.Klein, M. (1957) Envy and Gratitude: A Study of Unconscious Resources, Tavistock, London.
99.Winnicott, D. (1978) The Piggle, Penguin, Harmondsworth.
100.See Ref.30.
101.Eysenck, H. J. (1958) Learning Theory and Behaviour Therapy, Journal of Mental Science, 105, pp.61-75.
102.Ibid, p.12.
103.Eysenck, H. J. (1957) The Dynamics of Anxiety and Hysteria, Routledge and Kegan Paul, London, p.200.

104.Ibid, p.38.
105.Eysenck, H. J. (1960) (ed) Behaviour Therapy
and the Neuroses, Pergamon, Oxford, p.466, and
Ref.103, p.249.
106.See Ref.103, p.4.
107.Ibid, p.233.
108.Ibid, p.203.
109.Ibid, pp.279-80.
110.Eysenck, H. J. (1952) The Scientific Study of
the Personality, Routledge and Kegan Paul, London.
Eysenck, H. J. (1955) Cortical Inhibition, Figural
After-Effect and the Theory of Personality, Journal
of Abnormal and Social Psychology, 51, pp.96-106.
Eysenck, H. J. (1956) The Inheritance of
Extraversion and Intraversion, Acta Psychologica,
12, pp.95-110.
Eysenck, H. J. (1971) Race, Intelligence and
Education, Temple Smith, Philadelphia.
Rose, S. (1972) Environmental Effects on Brain and
Behaviour. In: Richardson, K. et al(ed) Race,
Culture and Behaviour, Penguin, Harmondsworth,
pp.128-146.
111.Meyer, V. (1957) The Treatment of two Phobic
Patients on the Basis of Learning Principles,
Journal of Abnormal and Social Psychology, 55,
pp.261-266.
Bevan, J. R. (1960) Learning Theory applied to the
Treatment of a Patient with Obsessional
Ruminations. See Ref.105, pp.165-169.
112.See Ref. 103, p.223.
113.Ibid, p.232.
114.Ibid, p.262.
115.Ibid, pp.203,240.
116.See Ref.111.
117.See Ref.103, p.10.
118.Wolpe, J. (1958) Psychotherapy by Reciprocal
Inhibition, Oxford University Press, London.
119.See, for example, Ref.111.
120.Walton, D. (1960) The Relevance of Learning
Theory to the Treatment of an Obsessive Compulsive
State. Ref.105, pp.153-164.
121.See Ref.105.
122.See Ref.112, pp.20, 281.
123.Ibid, p.264.
124.Ibid, p.281.
125.See Ref.101 and: Eysenck, H. J. (1952) The
Effects of Psychotherapy: An Evaluation, Journal of
Consulting Psychology, 16, pp.319-324.
Eysenck, H. J. (1961) Psychoanalysis: Myth or
Science, Inquiry, 4, pp.1-36.
Glover, E. (1958) The Uses of Freudian Treatment in

Psychiatry, British Journal of Medical Psychology, 31, pp.3-4.
126.Eysenck, H. J., Wilson, G. D. (1973) The Experimental Study of Freudian Theories, Methuen, London.
Fisher, S. (1977) The Scientific Credibility of Freud's Theories and Therapy, Harvester Press, London.
127.Skinner, B. F. (1972) Beyond Freedom and Dignity, Pelican, Harmondsworth.
128.See Ref.90.
129.Goldberg, E. M. (1957) The Psychiatric Social Worker in the Community, British Journal of Psychiatric Social Work, iv, 2, pp.4-15.
130.See Ref.1.
131.Ibid, p.51.
132.Thomas, E. (1958) Social care of the Mentally Ill: Hospital and Local Authority, British Journal of Psychiatric Social Work, iv, 4, pp.5-11.
133.See Ref.1, pp.92.
134.See Ref.132.
135.Editorial, British Journal of Psychiatric Social Work, 1948.
136.French, C. W. (1958) Legal Aspects and Implications for Local Health Services, British Journal of Psychiatric Social Work, iv, 4, pp.17-23.
137.Le Mesurier, A. (1949) The Duly Authorized Officer, British Journal of Social Work, Vol.1, pp.49-51.
138.See Ref.129.
139.Yelloly, M. A. (1980) Social Work Theory and Psychoanalysis, Van Nostrand Reinhold, New York.
140.Perlman, H. (1957) Casework: a Problem-Solving Process, University of Chicago Press, Chicago.
141.See Ref.1, p.157.
142.Wootton, B. (1959) Daddy Knows Best. In: Social Science and Social Pathology, Allen Lane, Ch.ix and: (1960) The Image of Social Work, British Journal of Sociology.
143.Armstrong, P. (1947) Aspects of Psychiatric Social Work in a Mental Hospital, British Journal of Psychiatric Social Work, pp.36-44, and Ref.132.
144.Walderon, F. E. (1949) The Meaning of the word "Social" in Psychiatric Social Work, British Journal of Psychiatric Social Work, 3, pp.7-18.
145.Goldberg, E. M. (1949) Comment I, British Journal of Psychiatric Social Work, 3, pp.8-21.
146.Hunnybun, N. K. (1949) Comment II, British Journal of Psychiatric Social Work, 3, pp.21-23.
147.See Ref.1, pp.30-31.

148.Editorial, British Journal of Psychiatric Social Work, Vol.1, 1, 1947, pp.3-7.

149.Timms, N. (1960) Theorizing about Social Casework, British Journal of Psychiatric Social Work, pp.70-74,137-141.

150.Goldberg, E. M. (1960) Parents of Psychotic Sons, British Journal of Psychiatric Social Work, 4, pp.184-194.

151.Crump, M. (1959) Social Aspects of Physical Treatment in Mental Illness, British Journal of Psychiatric Social Work, pp.19-25.

152.British Journal of Psychiatric Social Work, 1958, Vol.iv, 4.

153.Heap, J. S. (1958) Community Care, British Journal of Psychiatric Social Work, iv, 4, pp.12-16.

154.See Ref.132.

155.Myers, E. S. (1958) The Royal Commission and the Psychopath, British Journal of Psychiatric Social Work, iv, 4, pp.27-33.

156.See Ref.136.

157.See Ref.145.

7 Politicians' Concerns and Attitudes in the Fifties

7.a.The Involved MPs

As in the 20s only a small number of MPs participated actively in the major debates on mental distress. The first debate took place in 1954, leading to the establishment of the Royal Commission on the law related to mental illness in 1954. Following the publication of its report (Cmnd.169) the second discussion took place in 1957. Sixteen MPs contributed to this debate (H.605, 35-105). Twenty-three MPs participated actively in the third and more crucial debate on the 1959 Mental Health Act (H.605, 232-351, 403-483). Twenty-four of these MPs represented the Labour Party. All of the remaining fifteen were Conservatives. When it came to voting about 120 MPs were there to answer "aye" or "nay". Within the participating group of Labour MPs it is difficult to indicate a specific ideological common denominator: some came from the background of the trade union movement, some others from academic or professional life. Several were old hands in the parliamentary game, while others were new to it. None of them identified himself/herself as socialist in the context of the debates. The biographies of several MPs reflect a life long interest in health matters.

In contrast to the 20s, there were two psychiatrists in the House of Commons (Dr. Bennett and Dr. Broughton). Three more medically qualified MPs were present (Dr. E. Summerskill, Dr. D. Johnson and Dr. S. Hastings, who was an MP in the 1930 debate too). A number of MPs were members of hospital boards. The then president and vice-president of MIND (Mr. Butler and Mr.

Robinson) and a future president (Mr. Mayhew) were
among the active participants.
As a group, these MPs give the impression of
commanding a greater degree of professional
knowledge about psychiatry than the MPs of the
twenties. Four MPs showed a particular interest in
regard to mental distress: Mr. N. Dodds, Dr. D.
Johnson, Mr. C. Mayhew and Mr. K. Robinson. The two
MPs-psychiatrists contributed less to the debates
than these four MPs. The entries in Who's Who
(1959) provide us with some background information
about them.
Dodds, Norman Noel: MP (Lab and Co-op). Erith and
Crayford since 1955, Dartford 1945-55; member of
central advisory committee to Minster of Pensions
1950-1951; Parliamentary Private Secretary to
Minister of Labour May-Oct 1951; Director, People's
Entertainment Society, since 1945; Hon. Secretary
Homeworkers Products Society, b.25 Dec 1903. Educ:
Dunston-on-Tyne Council School; served with RAF.
Johnson, Dr. Donald McIntosh, MA, MB, BCh(Camb);
MRCS, LRCP(Lond); MP(C) Carlisle since 1955;
Chairman and Managing Director, Christopher
Johnson, publishers, b.17 Feb 1903. Educ:
Cheltenham College; Caius College, Camb. St.
Bartholomew's Hospital; qualified as a doctor 1926;
barrister in law, 1930. Medical Officer Cambridge
University. East Greenland expedition 1926;
Casualty Officer Metropolitan Hospital, 1926;
Medical Officer to Harringron Harbour Hospital,
internat. Grenfell Assoc, Labrador, 1928-29,
general practitioner, Thornton Heath, Croydon,
1930-37; a demonstrator of anatomy, Oxford Univ.
1937-39. Served war in RAMC (Capt. TA) 1939-54.
Member Croydon medical ed. Min. of Labour and
National Service 1951-55. Publications: A Doctor
Regrets, 1948; Bars and Barricades, 1952; Indian
Hemp: A Social Menace, 1952; A Doctor Returns,
1956; A Doctor in Parliament, 1958. Recreations:
golf, photography. Clubs: Oxford and Cambridge.
Mayhew, Christopher Paget; MP(Lab) Woolwich East
since June 1951; broadcaster and journalist; b.12
June 1915. Educ: Hailsbury Coll.(Scholar); Christ
Church, Oxford (open exhibitioner, MA). Junior
George Webb-Medley Scholar (Economics) 1937;
president Union Society, 1937. Gunner Surrey
Yeomanry RA, March 1939; BEF Sept. 1939-May 1940;
commissioned Intelligence Corps, Sept. 1940, served
with BNAF and CMF; Capt. 1943; joined special
forces BLA (1944)(despatches), major 1944. MP Lab.
South Norfolk, 1945-50; Parliamentary Private

Secretary to Lord. priv. of the council, 1945-46;
Parliamentary Under-Secretary of State for Foreign
Affairs, 1946-50. Chm. Soviet Relations Cttee.
British Council, 1955-. Publications: Planned
Investment - The case for a National Investment
Board, 1939; Socialist Economic Policy, 1946;
"Those in Favour..." (television play), 1951; Dear
Viewer..., 1955; Men seeking God, 1955, Commercial
television: What is to be done? 1959. Recreations:
music, tennis, golf.

Robinson, Kenneth; MP(Lab) St. Pancras N. since
1949; member: Exec.Cttee of the National Trust,
1951; NW Metropolitan Regional Hospital Board,
1951, Vice-President National Association for
Mental Health since 1958; b.Warrington, 1911.
Educ: Oundle School. Insurance broker at Lloyds,
1927-40. Served war of 1939-45, RN 1941-46;
ordinary seaman, 1941, commissioned 1942.
Lieut.Cmdr. RNVR; 1944 served Home Fleet as company
secretary 1946-49. Asst. Whip(unpaid), 1950-51, an
Opposition Whip, 1951-54. Publications: Wilkie
Collins, a biography, 1951; Policy for Mental
Health, 1958. Recreations: going abroad, reading,
listening to music.

Dr. Johnson merits extra attention on several
grounds. A doctor, a barrister, a publisher, he was
the only self-confessed ex mental patient in
Parliament at the time (H.605, 345). Termed often
"sensational" and "irresponsible" by other MPs he
reached newspaper headlines in 1950 with the report
of a bizarre psychotic episode and a short
hospitalization period which followed. As Dr.
Johnson has recounted the tale in his books(1)
there is no need to retell the story. Dr. Johnson
was convinced that his psychotic episode resulted
from a deliberate poisoning. He felt that his
hospitalization was unnecessary, and that he had
been unjustly denied contact with his wife and
solicitor. The last point was undisputed. The
possibility of poisoning has been emphatically
denied by the NHS psychiatrists but accepted by
Canadian psychiatrists retrospectively. The NHS did
not bother at the time to test Dr. Johnson's
food/environment. The fact that his wife displayed
very similar symptoms on the same occasion but was
not hospitalized adds doubts as to the validity of
the reasons for his involuntary detention.

Subsequently Dr. Johnson became one of the
main campaigners for patients' civil rights. With
Mr. Dodds, he campaigned for the legislation of the
Royal Commission's report. This campaign was the

first and so far the only one initiated by MPs in the attempt to make mental illness into a public issue.

At the same time Dr. Johnson did not ask what were the reasons for the unsatisfactory state of the psychiatric system. He shared the belief of the majority of MPs in the superiority of psychiatric judgement on mental illness, the value of professionalism and medicine. Therefore for him the way to secure patients' rights for a dignified treatment was to protect them from personal idiosyncrasy by providing more than one professional opinion and by advocating community care. His contributions during the debates illustrate his beliefs (H.560, 463-71, 573, 81-87).

Mr. Dodds represented a very different style of life but not in approach to mental distress. Coming from the co-operative and trade unions movements he was definitely for a fully fledged welfare state. Mr. Dodds distrusted bureaucratic organisations such as the Board of Control and did not trust fully professionals. He saw the patients as human beings caught in the web of the system. His enduring efforts were aimed at rescuing them from the impersonal machinery, fighting on their behalf even when it implied inconvenience or insults laid at Mr. Dodds' door in the process (e.g. the Board of Control refused him entry to visit patients from his constituency (H.568, 11-15, 14-39). While being a Labour MP he gives the impression of going his own way rather than toeing the Party line. Dr. Johnson commented that "No Question Time is complete without the intervention of Mr. Dodds on some matter of human and political interest in contrast to the ideological basis which underlies the questions of so many of his colleagues on the Socialist bench"(2). We do not know whether Mr. Dodds would accept this pen-portrait. Yet his contributions to the debates would confirm lack of interest in conceptualization and intervention coupled with a high degree of respect towards the mentally ill as people. Despite being an outspoken critic of the existing psychiatric system Mr. Dodds never outlined the types of replacement he would like to see established.

Despite his gallant attempt to reverse the harm created by the psychiatric system, Mr. Dodds, like Dr. Johnson, did not ask himself what might have led the Board to act in the way it did or what caused the professionals to reach decisions he disagreed with.

Mr. C. Mayhew was involved in radio and television programmes on mental illness. His interest in mental distress seems to be focused not so much on the plight of individuals as on securing their civil rights as a matter of principle. Ensuring that the Ministry and the professionals do actually carry out the policies they set out explicitly to implement was his other main emphasis. Accordingly, Mr. Mayhew's questions related to the sum of money available for research on schizophrenia; overcrowding and resources. (£11,000 were spent on this type of research on the 54,179 patients diagnosed as suffering from schizophrenia - see H.573, 63). His critical comments did not however lead to questioning the policies themselves or the strategies for accomplishing them.

Mr. Robinson was MIND's vice-president in 1959 and later Minister of Health (1966-70). One of the initiators of the 1954 Royal Commission investigation, he was one of the very few MPs who throughout their parliamentary career showed a consistent interest in mental illness. Mr. Robinson was disappointed at not becoming the Opposition spokesperson in the debate(3). Mr. Robinson's interest in mental distress was more akin to that of Mr. Mayhew than to Dr. Johnson's and Mr. Dodds, namely in achieving a more efficient and just system of services, rather than in the critique of the existing framework. He did not see any fault in the way professionals operated in principle. To the contrary, he was full of praise to them (H.580, 9-12). Instead Mr. Robinson was preoccupied with the global aspects of the system - i.e. the Board and the Ministry. With Mr. Mayhew he shared also the interest in the implementation of community care policies (H.600, 30). Not accidentally these two MPs focused on allocation of resources more than anybody else.

This lengthy description of the four self-appointed MPs is necessary for the understanding of the issues they were concerned with and the methods used in the attempt to achieve desirable outcomes. Despite sharing an interest in mental distress coupled with a dignified approach towards the mentally ill, the four did not work together as a lobby, a point to be taken up in the coming section.

7.b.Tactics

Several of the tactical measures employed in the twenties were used in the fifties. They include:

1.Requests for statistical information, used as a method to initiate a debate on an issue (e.g. request for information on the number of married couples within the inpatients population, or the number of inpatients who died during the first week of admission (H.642, 20, 574, 1055).

2.Repetition of a question on the same topic (e.g. questions on hospital farms, date of publication of the Commission's report, nurses' wages and working conditions (H.574, 855-6, 1960-1).

3.Use of amendments as pressure for last minute changes in legislation. Often amendments were withdrawn if reconsideration was offered (e.g. the demand that mental welfare officers will be trained social workers (H.548, 1342-3, 549, 821-4, 828, 550, 1770-72).

The reluctance to press for voting on an amendment stemmed from the fact that the government had an overall majority and therefore would easily defeat the Opposition's suggestions at any point if it wished to do so. It is interesting to note that despite the fact that the bill was introduced as bi-partisan it could so easily revert into a Government/Opposition division.

4.Checking on the implementation of agreed upon policy. For example:

a.Requesting the number of local authorities which have submitted plans for the implementation of community care and the number of plans already approved by the government (H.623, 3-4).

b.Whether guidelines on cash payments for patients' work have been issued as promised (H.601, 12-13, 605, 482).

c.Progress in recruitment of student nurses (H.567, 797, 551, 2458).

5.Attracting attention to the injustice done to specific patients, either in the attempt to change their circumstances or as a means to draw attention to a more general point. For example:

a.The case of a man who over-stayed in Rampton for 18 months after it was recommended that he should leave because a more suitable place was not found for him (H.609, 859).

b.The case of a patient who murdered someone while on a trial discharge was brought up as an

example of the risks inherent in an
over-permissive release policy (H.592, 173-4).
On the whole the debates in the 50s were a
model of courtesy, mutual praise and especially
full of compliments expressed toward the Minister
of Health, Mr. D. Walker-Smith (H.605, 270, 279,
282). This explicit congratulatory tone implies not
only a basic agreement between all of the
participants but also satisfaction with the
position reflected in the debates. Given this
background there was no need for the Minister to
treat differences and criticisms seriously. The
Ministry was provided with an implicit permission
to do as it pleased with a very wide margin. The
implications of this stand will be taken up in the
discussion on community care.
In addition to these tactics several others
appeared only during the 50s.
1.Mass media was not mentioned in the 1930
discussion. In contrast the BBC and quality
newspapers (The Times, The Guardian, The News
Chronicle) were commented upon more than once in
the 50s (H.573, 71, 605, 418, 435, 454). The use
of the media varied depending on the
agreement/disagreement with the message (H.573,
45, 76, 609, 805).
The greater importance given to the media was
a reflection of its recently acquired central
place in everyday life. By 1959 the media was a
powerful pressure factor and its influence was
echoed by the MPs who used it in the debate.
Non-quality dailies were not mentioned. MPs
either did not read these papers or were not
interested in the opinions of the "man on the
street" or both.
2.Despite presenting the Royal Commission report
and the Act as bi-partisan activities, the 1957
debate took place in opposition time (H.573,
158). The government did not consider the issue
as sufficiently important to deserve its own
time.
3.Frequent requests were made by MPs for the
provision of written guidelines and for
ministerial pressure on health and local
authorities (H.574, 854, 615, 1039-40, 620, 78).
Such requests were not expressed in 1930.
The pressure could be an indication of the
greater degree of knowledge of the field. Yet there
is no evidence of an organized lobby on mental
illness and health matters in both periods. The
lack of collective action was likely to be related

to:
1.The belief in the positive value of consensus in politics.
2.The lack of worked-out alternative paradigm in regard to conceptualization and intervention.
3.Differences in regard to the use of publicity. MPs agreed that the media should be used as a means of public education for greater tolerance and understanding of mental distress. Yet no debate and agreement on the ways of employing the media followed. The majority of MPs objected to any so-called "sensationalist" mode of presentation on the ground that it vulgarized the issue and focused too much attention on misdeeds of individual professionals (H.560, 468, 573, 78). The minority did not mind exposing the wrongs of the system in a way that would attract public attention, even if it implied a blemished professional or institutional reputation. Such a difference could have prevented the possibility of a shared activity.

Thus means and ends, form and content of the debates were interrelated.

7.c.Issues of Concern

The most frequent concern expressed in the 50s debates pertains to criticism of the existing psychiatric system.
a.A major bone of contention was the claim that about 25% of the inpatients population should not have been in a mental hospital (H.574, 1055, 560, 470, 573, 154-157). Several categories of patients were included within this group:
1.The elderly who were either severely physically ill and/or demented, who tended to die shortly after being hospitalized (H.571, 820; 597, 329).
2.Special hospitals inpatients who have not been found guilty of criminal offences (e.g. about 50% of Rampton's population). Particular attention was drawn to patients considered by the special hospital authorities as rehabilitated enough to be moved to an ordinary hospital but for whom suitable places could not be found (H.618, 801-3, 206-7). (e.g. a case of a patient waiting for a year and a half for such a place has been quoted, H.567, 797.)
3.Certified patients who have been institutionalized for a long period and who were judged as capable of living in sheltered

accommodation but for whom such accommodation could not be found. An example was provided by Mr. Dodds who recounted the escape from the Littlemore hospital in Oxford of three elderly ladies. The patients have been in the hospital for about twenty years. They returned after a fortnight due to lack of suitable accommodation in the community (H.558, 1062-3; 562, 1692-1703; 563, 651; 560, 451).
4.People who have been hospitalized as a result of professional misapplication of psychiatric diagnosis. Examples of this type include detention because of reported non-conforming behaviour by lay people to the mental welfare officer, the GP or the psychiatrist. No aggressive activity has been recounted in these examples, implying a relatively high degree of interpretation of potential a-social behaviour. Two possible sources for this major concern could be identified: a.Lack of possible accommodation inside and outside the hospital. b.Professional misjudgement. While the first was not denied the second was strongly disputed by the majority of MPs, yet upheld by the minority (H.597, 323-7, 1702-3; 549, 324; 573, 76).

The acceptance of the first claim meant acknowledging the system's shortages rather than admitting to the possibility of wrong principles.

For example, in the famous Thornton case (see section 7.d.) the first psychiatrist suggested to Mrs. T. to seek legal advice on domestic issues rather than psychiatric intervention. The second psychiatrist hospitalized her. Following an independent examination by a third psychiatrist, she was discharged from the hospital despite the opinion of the hospital authorities (H.553, 592, 556, 361-70, 557, 914, 560, 464-71). In another example, a young woman was diagnosed as mentally retarded. It later transpired that she needed psychiatric help and definitely was not retarded (H.563, 650-1).

Dr. Johnson and Mr. Dodds informed the House of allegations of professional misjudgement and misconduct which patients have submitted in writing to them. Several of these submissions refer to the activity of the Duly Authorized Officer (H.605, 932). Convincing as they were, these cases did not provide conclusive evidence that the majority of professionals embarked knowingly on unethical behaviour. But the MPs who exposed this material did not proceed to examine whether there existed a generalized component for concern in the tendency to dismiss the would-be patient's version in favour of accepting everybody else's interpretation as a principle of practice.

The assertion that a quarter of the hospitals' population needed not - and therefore should not - have stayed there was generally accepted in Parliament.

As already mentioned the majority rejected the possibility that this state of affairs reflected on professional practice, especially that of psychiatrists. Even the likelihood of a mistaken assessment was dismissed a priori, especially by MPs who sat on hospital boards (H.573, 89, 76). Thus Mr. Robinson agreed wholeheartedly with the criticisms on the lack of resources and accommodation. But these short-comings were seen as belonging outside the realm of professional activity and inside that of the Board of Control. Thus the Board became the target for blame (H.573, 82, 557, 85-6, 556, 361-70, 579, 878).

The notion of a complete separation between professional, administrative and policy functions presupposed by the majority of MPs does not reflect on the reality of the social context of psychiatric policies described in chapter 1. The belief in it and the assumption of full professional autonomy reflected on the one hand the prevailing myth on professionalism. On the other hand this value preference helped to give more autonomy to professionals and to continue to disregard the consequences of the interrelationships between professionals and administrative activities.

b.Critical comments on other types of shortages in the existing system were made:
   1.Overcrowding.
   2.Staff shortages.
   3.Inadequate level of staff training.

Compared with similar comments made during the 1930s debate the majority of those uttered in the fifties were less angry and less frequent. The difference in urgency could well be the reflection of the expansion of the services that took place between 1946 and 1959. At the same time the statistics and case descriptions indicate serious shortages resulting in unmet needs. Alternatively therefore the quieter tone of complaints could be related to the assumption of goodwill on behalf of the Ministry and looking forward to the implementation of shared plans for the future.

c.Similarly, while criticisms were directed at the

Board of Control they were fewer in number than in
1930 and the majority of those comments were more
subdued in tone. The minority remarks were far from
muted. The Board was described by Mr. Dodds as
"callous", "indifferent to patients", "interested
in the exploitation of patients" and "preventing
justice from being done" (H.556, 361-70; 562,
1692-705, 579, 378). By 1959 the evaluation of the
Board's activities took place in the knowledge of
its incorporation into the Ministry of Health in
the near future, as part of the Royal Commission
recommendations which were accepted by the
government. Therefore MPs were likely to feel that
it might be futile to concentrate on an obsolete
body.
d.It was pointed out by MPs that the high rate of
discharge did not signify cure for the majority of
patients. Instead it was implied that this state of
affairs reflected upon a basic failure of the care
system (H.573, 57, 605, 45). This sophisticated
argument was not taken up any further. One wonders
if the majority of the politicans shared this
disbelief in the optimistic picture often portrayed
by the Minister, his aides and various MPs.
e.Following the same line of argument MPs attacked
the government for consistently allocating too
meagre resources to the psychiatric part of the
NHS. "Cinderella of the NHS" (H.573, 81) was the
term employed to describe the situation in which a
third of all hospital beds were allocated only 15%
of the budget(4). With the exception of new
building, in terms of top professional posts,
training opportunities, qualified personnel, even
less than 15% was spent. Mr. Mayhew in particular
was good at providing the House with the necessary
figures and in indicating the rather obvious
implications for the quality of the psychiatric
services.
     Yet no explanation of the possible motives
behind this preference was attempted by Mr. Mayhew
or by others, only a plea was made to correct the
allocation ratio.
     Insufficient investment in research - both in
personnal and in sums of money - was an aspect
singled out to exemplify the inappropriateness of
the allocation of resources and its dire
consequences. Mr. Robinson, Mr. Mayhew and Mr.
Elliot brought the matter before the House more
than once (H.573, 56-58, 63). They pointed to the
absurdity of the small sums given to this type of
research work and to cases of top researchers

leaving the country because of the unsatisfactory conditions (H.573, 63, 55). As before, no attempt was made to outline what was causing the Ministry and the Medical Research Council (MRC) to opt for this policy.
f.A minority of MPs repeatedly stressed the risk of early discharge of patients exhibiting aggressive behaviour. A recent case in Scotland was given as an illustration of the issue: a patient seen regularly at an out-patient clinic murdered someone two days after attending an appointment. The MP who described the incident called for less leniency and warned that the public might well refuse to co-operate in the implementation of community care policies if it felt that personal safety was at risk (H.649, 226-7, 651, 1560). Perhaps the more surprising fact is the relative lack of such stories throughout the debate and that this incident did not lead to a campaign against early discharges.

In Praise of the Existing System
Favourable comments on the prevailing services were made nearly as frequently as the critical ones. Several MPs expressed the two types of comments on different occasions without an indication of a sense of contradiction. Singled out for praise were the following areas:
a.Voluntary admission. The fact that by 1957 75% of the inpatients population was there on a voluntary basis was heralded as a major achievement of the system (H.573, 40, 642, 20). Voluntary patienthood seemed to imply that patients were in hospital out of their own volition rather than through coercion. As designed in the 1930 Act this status carried with it a greater measure of citizens' rights and hence of personal dignity. The defenders of the system interpreted this finding as implying that patients and relatives were less stigmatized (H.573, 85). It was also assumed that they came to appreciate the services offered (H.549, 1446).
      The less flattering view of voluntary admission emphasised that:
   1.People went into a hospital due to persuasion by significant others and professionals rather than out of their own wish.
   2.They went and stayed in hospitals due to lack of alternatives and the existence of a hostile environment outside rather than because of liking it inside.
   3.Staying in hospital fostered chronicity

regardless of a patient's formal status(5).
b.The "new look" of hospitals was often commented upon: open wards, occupational therapy and rehabilitation departments, new buildings or repainted in bright colours (H.573, 63).
c.Intervention achievements were specified:
1.The elimination of general paralysis (H.273, 45) which took place mainly during the 30s.
2.The "revolutionary" use of Electro Convulsive Therapy (ECT) (H.605, 432).
3.The use of psychotropic drugs (H.573, 79, 410).
4.The establishment of day hospitals (H.554, 979, 564, 140, 605, 475).
5.Observation units in general hospitals (H.549, 598, 560, 470).
6.The development of domiciliary services (H.571, 882, 690, 78).
7.The "open door" policy. As outlined in chapter 5, the latter was the least mentioned as a causal factor leading to discharge. But several projects in which this policy was a major feature were mentioned positively in Parliament (e.g. the Worthing experiment - H.573, 38, 92).
d.Praise of professional activities was often expressed in global terms but at times was more specified:
1.Child guidance was singled out as a mode of intervention where the focus was on preventive work (H.560, 469-70).
2.A system of domiciliary and residential care for the elderly developed in Oxford by Dr. Cosin was suggested as a model to be employed in the future (H.573, 38-39, 46-47, 91, 605, 419).
3.At times nurses, social workers and volunteers wre specified as worthy of praise. Usually positive comments were either generalized or aimed at doctors. The work of occupational therapists, psychologists, administrators and domestic workers was never acknowledged as worthy of a specific comment.

Alternative Modes of Intervention
The 1957 and 1959 debates on mental distress were full of references to "new modes of treatment" as well as to mental health. The catch phrase was "community care". As the only definition it got was "having the mentally ill in the community", the concept needs to be looked at through the specific alternatives which were mentioned in order to build up the image politicans had of community care.
    Halfway houses, hostels, day centres,

domiciliary services, psychiatric wards in general
hospitals were the services which MPs liked. They
were aware of general schemes such as the Amsterdam
and Worthing projects. Experiments in therapeutic
communities such as in Belmont were also known and
highly praised by the politicans (H.560, 47, 578,
82, 573, 430-44).

Whilst not being antagonistic to hospitals,
the impact of institutionalization was acknowledged
as an outcome to be avoided by the majority of the
politicians (H.573, 420). The emphasis was put on
alternatives to traditional hospitals, on
possibilities which would enable potential patients
to stay outside the hospital prior to the first
admission and/or afterwards.

MPs recognized that in many cases it was
neither feasible nor desirable to return a patient
home after discharge; hence the pressure they
attempted to put toward establishing day care and
domiciliary facilities. On one occasion an MP was
checking on the implementation of such policies.
He asked about the progress made in regard to
specific attempts to start a hostel that had been
thwarted by the inability to find the right
accommodation. After a whole year all the Minister
was able to say was that the efforts to find a
place will go on (H.591, 15-16).

Little thought was given to other than relief
needs of family members. While patients' needs for
occupational rehabilitation were considered
psychotherapy was not, with the exception of
mentioning therapeutic communities. Concerning the
latter it was left unclear whether the communities
which were praised were viewed as examples to be
followed and whether MPs considered the feasibility
aspect of intervention methods.

One MP - Dr. Johnson - raised the issue of
the possible harmful effects of ECT and
psychosurgery (H.549, 820). His query was not
treated seriously. On other occasions ECT was
mentioned as a revolutionary treatment in a
positive sense (H.605, 432).

To summarize, MPs' unsystematic ideas on
intervention focused on services in the community
over those in hospital. Their weakness in securing
the means for implementing these ideas in practice
adds a component of wishful thinking to their
comments on intervention.

The Place of Local Authorities in the system of
Psychiatric Services: Relations between Central and

Local Government

The 1930 Mental Treatment Act postulated that local authorities were permissively responsible for after care services. Following the 1930 Act a highly varied system of such services developed in which central government has little to offer. With the establishment of the NHS, hospitals became finally the main concern of central government (e.g. by being more directly financed by it). MPs were quite aware of the prevailing state of "laissez faire" in regard to community services. Those who were keen to secure such facilities made public their unhappiness with the overall unsatisfactory service system.

The Royal Commission (Cmnd.169) had recommended broadening the local authorities' duties by adding the responsibility for residential care as an integral part of after care services. The committee made it clear that it wished that these tasks would become mandatory and funded with a specific contribution from central government. The 1959 Mental Health Act in its various drafts and in the final version includes the added responsibility but excludes any reference to a mandatory nature and means of funding (The Mental Health Act, 1959, part II, pp.3-8).

Such a discrepancy between the Commission's report and the drafted Act could not have escaped MPs' attention. For those familiar with the 1930 debate (e.g. the two MPs in 1959 who were MPs in 1930) it must have had a strong component of a "deja vu" feeling about it. MPs were quick to indicate that unless financial help was provided by central government it was doubtful that the local authorities would be able and willing to implement community care policies. For example, Sir K. Joseph, who cannot be accused of wanting central government funding usually, raised the matter too (H.873, 71) (other MPs - H.873, 147-150, 582, 32, 383, 605, 410, 414, 314). Mr. Sorenson called attention to the fact that without funding these policies will be dead words with no more than lip service paid to them (H.605, 464).

Much less attention was given to the decision to let these duties stay permissive. MPs felt - perhaps understandably - that if the money would have become available for this specified aim then local authorities would be willing to use it for this purpose. They also were apprehensive of adding to the already heavy burden of local authorities without the financial support of central

241

government. It is interesting, however, that they did not consider the likelihood that by making the provision of community care mandatory, a pressure would be put on local authorities which would force them in turn to put direct pressure on central government. One wonders if this omission on behalf of MPs committed to community care was the outcome of the very courteous and congratulatory atmosphere commented upon in the section on tactics. The large number of comments and the strong feelings of frustration in respect to this issue did not tally either with MPs' praise of the Minister or of the Mental Health Act in its different stages. This manifest inconsistency is not easy to explain. It is not assumed here that MPs were insincere in their wish to see community care services implemented. As little was to be gained politically from the beginning by being involved in mental illness/health legislation there is no reason to suppose that such gains were a consideration which prevented MPs from being more consistent in pursuing this aspect of the 1959 Act.

MPs' reluctance and apprehension of their impotence to establish a powerful opposition to the government and its majority was likely to be a major factor in leading them to give up even the attempt to fight the Ministry for community care. The history of the House of Commons is full of examples of how MPs' initatives become abortive if a sizeable majority of MPs did not sway in the direction of an initiative. In the case of mental illness the indifference of the majority of the politicans, rather than actual opposition, would be the frustrating component that would lead MPs' attempts nowhere. On similar occasions MPs mounted public campaigns in the attempt to change government's and Parliament's positions. Recent examples include the debates on the death penalty and abortion. Given the basic agreement on mental illness/health policy in 1959 it would have been difficult for MPs to initiate a public campaign against a detail of a policy to which they subscribed wholeheartedly. The fact that this particular detail unmasked the lack of government's commitment to community care was a point that MPs did not acknowledge or wish to expose.

The inherent belief in incremental progress was likely to be another reason which comforted MPs who were unhappy about the lack of government's support for community psychiatric care.

Lastly, but perhaps of greatest importance,

the basic acceptance of psychiatry as a branch of
medicine put the possibilities of advancement of
knowledge in the hands of the professional group
whose position has been strengthened considerably
as the result of the 1959 Act. Thus MPs who
believed that the major obstacle to successful
intervention was the isolation of psychiatry from
medicine must have felt that they had done their
best to secure the end of this situation. The
specific meaning given to community care, outlined
in chapter 6 and in the section on the Ministry's
position, illustrates some of the implications of
this value preference.

Patients' Rights

a.Tribunals
The Royal Commission's suggestion to establish
tribunals for review and appeal purposes was
greeted enthusiastically by all politicians.
Previously appeals were part of the brief of the
Board of Control. With the dissolution of this body
in mind it became necessary to ensure the
continuation of the appeal possibility.

Mental Health Review Tribunals (MHRT) were
designed to hear reviews only in cases of
compulsory admission. It was proposed that
membership of a tribunal panel would consist of a
psychiatrist, a lawyer and a representative of the
public. The planned composition was not disputed
despite the fact that representation of the public
usually tends to be strongly biased toward members
of the middle class to the exclusion of working
class people, not to mention the unemployed or
physically disabled members of the community. It
was never suggested that members of MIND, similar
voluntary organizations, family members and
ex-patients would have a more significant
contribution to make than ordinary citizens and a
different one from that of the professional members
of the tribunal panel. Thus the ideas behind public
participation came as a replacement of the
magistrates' potential function in a board of
appeal. At no point were tribunals seen as having
to do with broader issues of mental illness and
health. A person dismissed from work on the grounds
of a mental illness history could apply to an
industrial tribunal but not to a MHRT. Likewise
clients in out-patient services were not going to
have access to the tribunal as a matter of right.
Some MPs, however, deplored the decision that

243

access to tribunals would be possible only after hospitalization took place and not before (H.605, 418).

The discussion centred on four main issues:
1. Frequency of the right to appeal of both compulsory and voluntary patients.
2. The hearing procedures tribunals would have to adopt.
3. The demand for periodical reviews of detained patients.
4. The degree of independence of tribunals.

Initially it was suggested that in-patients on order would be entitled to ask for a review once in every two years. A minority of MPs requested that this period should be reduced to once every year, on the grounds that a two-year period is much too long for enduring any serious grievance. The Minister reconsidered the matter and came up with the alternative that every detained patient would be entitled to appeal once in the first year of hospitalization and subsequently every second year. This amendment was greeted positively by Mr. Robinson, the MP who campaigned for the reduction of the waiting period. The Ministry feared that tribunals would be swamped by appeals. In effect the opposite proved to be the case. Between 1960 (when tribunals started to operate) and up to 1970 roughly the same annual number of review requests was made - 800 to 900(6). This figure represents a very small percentage of the in-patients population. Therefore the question to be asked is why indeed patients do not make much use of the tribunals, a point to which we shall return in the concluding chapter.

The draft of the 1959 Act suggested informal hearing procedures. When information was sought in regard to the hearing processes it transpired that informality implied: 1. Not having to adhere to the legal procedure of an ordinary court. 2. Yet a tribunal was required to provide representation for the patient at the latter's request. The representative could be a lawyer but did not have to be one. 3. Tribunals were to have the right to withhold information from the patient. 4. Tribunals were to have the right to prevent patients from attending the hearing if advised to do so by psychiatrists (H.605, 344, Standing committee 10/2/59).

These procedural instructions provide a curious mixture of accepting professional opinion as overriding personal rights yet attempting to create a flexible framework for the benefit of the patient who is also a citizen. In the guidelines patients are not treated as equal participants to the review. The fact that the client was the one who launched the complaint and did not occupy the status of a suspected person is significant only for setting up the review but not for any other stage of the process. While not all MPs were content with these procedures (H.605, 454), no counter attack was mounted or an alternative plan proposed. Though the issues mentioned above were not debated in Parliament it may be useful to attempt a tentative reconstruction of the logic behind the suggested procedure - a logic implicitly shared by many MPs. The reasoning can e summarized by paraphrasing G. Stern's famous phrase, "A patient is a patient is a patient". Being a patient implied to the politicans a special vulnerability as well as mistrust and a tendency to misinterpret the world, including the actions of professionals. Thus the procedures were aimed at offering a certain type of protection for both patients and professionals, though the latter was never mentioned in this context. This set of unspoken assumptions has an underlying layer to it which doubts a priori the validity of patients' complaints: if mistrust and misinterpretation are inherent features of being mentally ill then the likelihood of accepting the patient's version becomes slim before any investigation into the specific complaint has even begun.

It is important to remember that this line of thinking was not due to the psychiatrists' lobby but to the shared beliefs of a relatively progressively minded group of MPs. Thus the requests for patients' rights did not aim at treating patients as ordinary citizens as much as possible. The real dilemma of reconciling citizenship with patients' rights and duties has been highlighted in the case of the tribunals procedures. However, the denial of the need for differential treatment of the mentally ill patient versus other patients prevented politicians from becoming aware of such a dilemma, let alone resolving it.

A periodical review of detained patients had been suggested by Mr. Robinson (H.605, 307, 989-91). Such a review was to take place irrespective of whether patients were complaining or not about their treatment. Although Mr. Robinson was far from doubting professional competence, he nevertheless felt the need for reassurance that patients' hospitalization would not be unnecessarily prolonged. He expected the tribunal to undertake the functions of providing a second opinion to the first one given by the hospital's psychiatrist. In a sense, tribunals could then become the watchdogs of the hospital system. This plan was mentioned on several occasions, but was rejected outright by the Minister on the same pragmatic reasons as the suggestion to shorten the intervals between appeals. Interestingly, the rejection was not on the grounds that psychiatrists' opinion need not be rechecked.

The desirable degree of independence of tribunals was of major relevance in providing them with the authority required to carry out their primary function, namely that of investigating appeals and reviews. Appeal courts have to be outside and/or above the system they investigate in order to gain the power required for overriding previous decisions.

In this context it was agreed that tribunals had to be free of any specific hospital authority (H.605, 330). Yet this decision left unanswered several important questions:

1. Should tribunals be part of either/and/or a local authority, area health authority, the courts?
2. Where should tribunals be physically located, as a symbol of their position and relations?
3. How to secure through the membership of a tribunal its independence plus the necessary ties with the local community.

There was no model which could have been easily copied. The part performance of the Board of Control could not have been taken as a desirable precedent. The Board was an independent public body which acted in a highly centralized way. It did not inspire trust or confidence in it by patients or relatives: the number of complaints made annually was incredibly small - only two in 1958 (H.600, 30). The courts provided an alternative model but one based on somewhat different aims.

The MPs who were pressing for more patients' rights were also those asking for a greater degree of independence to be given to the tribunals (H.573, 67, 605, 454, 614, 977). In a manner typical of the 1959 debate this issue was left to be resolved by the Minister after consultation with local government and health authorities. Such consultations were a straightforward logical step but one which could have been performed between the publication of the Royal Commission report in 1957 and the debate on the Mental Health Act in 1959. Thus the strategy adopted by the Minister was one of delay.

The overall impression left from the discussion on the tribunals is one of great enthusiasm and satisfaction with the principles behind having them. At best the implementation of the principles was left in the air and at worst they were given up as "unrealistic demands" (e.g. hearing procedures).

b.The abolition of censorship of inpatients' mail

Full censorship was becoming rapidly an impractical task which therefore was not executed in any systematic way. Mr. Robinson asked for the abolition of censorship in regard to voluntary patients, leaving it in force for those detained (H.574, 354-5, 605, 436-7, 332-7). He argued that people who were free to enter and leave the hospital were unlikely to write inappropriate letters. To free this group of censorship would be in line with encouraging patients to retain as many of their citizens' rights as possible. Furthermore it was outlined that this unnecessary restriction of personal freedom would prevent people from applying for voluntary admission. This line of reasoning presented above was supported by several MPs. The Minister however opposed the amendment on the ground that censorship was anyhow applied only selectively by hospital staff. Therefore he saw no need to abolish it formally. He went on to point out that in reality the differentiation between voluntary and compulsory admitted patients was minimal. The two groups shared the same wards and facilities. Therefore it might have become advisable to read a voluntary patient's mail for the same reasons which applied to reading the writings of detained residents (H.605, 437). While factually correct, the Minister's position reveals the tendency to view all mentally ill patients en masse, an approach which contradicted the explicit beliefs of the Ministry.

The Minister need not have worried that the discrepancy between the official and the implicit bias against patients' rights be exposed: not even one MP spotted it. The proposer of the amendment did not deny the necessity of censorship in regard to detained patients. Therefore the argument for abolition only for voluntary patients became

247

considerably weakened. The symbolic meaning of abolishing censorship did not seem to capture the imagination of MPs and certainly not that of the Ministry. The fact that enforcing censorship provided a leeway for exploitation of professional privilege and symbolised coercive control was not acknowledged. Like many other amendments this one too was withdrawn before voting. Officially, censorship was reinforced for all categories of patients, despite the common knowledge of the impossibility to implement it in practice.

c.Positive Rights of Patients
The right to retain control over one's financial affairs was mentioned as one of the Mental Health Act aims. As many as 30,000 patients were under financial guardianship (H.605, 413). The importance of self-control over a major aspect of power and prestige in our society and the fear of being exploited did not have to be stressed for MPs. Yet apart from emphasizing that only the court should gain access (and not family members) little was said by the government in regard to meeting this stated factor of the new legislation. Equally the politicians said virtually nothing about this topic, despite the fact that it came up in some of the case descriptions presented before the House (H.564, 15-16; e.g. the case of Mrs. T., see section 7.d). It could be assumed that both the Ministry and MPs were satisfied that the courts would provide justice and prevent exploitation and arbitrariness. But the courts were to be acting only on the recommendations of psychiatrists as to the patient's ability to exercise rational judgement. Therefore all of the doubts concerning the validity of clinical judgement should have been echoed here by the MPs who expressed them before in regard to patients who should not have been in a psychiatric hospital. Yet the same politicians abstained from taking part in the discussion on the right to control one's property and finance.

d.The Request for written information pertaining to patients' and relatives' rights
The reader may remember that this issue came up in the House already in 1930. From MPs' comments it appears that little has been done about it between 1930 and 1959. It was a matter of chance for patients and relatives whether they were informed on their rights or not (H.605, 226, 413). The attempt to reopen the issue and to secure its

resolution seemed to achieve only modest results. The Minister was ready to provide hospitals with leaflets on consumers' rights but not to reinforce their distribution (H.605, 483). The objection to the active reinforcement of this demand was related to the wish to abstain from any pressure deemed as unnecessary on the hospitals. This issue will be looked at again in the context of the government's position.

e.The Right to be paid for work in cash
This request differs from the rest insofar as it does not call for abolition, restriction or the maintenance of minimal standards. Instead the focus is on providing patients with the same benefits that ordinary people receive as a matter of right. The first claim illustrates clearly this point. Mr. Dodds asked on several occasions why patients were not paid in money for their work but instead were paid in kind (H.605: 405, 1312-13). He went further to suggest that the cash would be kept for patients until discharge to enable them to use it when they go back to the community.

Mr. Dodds wanted the change from payment in kind by cash on ground of dignity. He seemed to be unaware that by stipulating that the money should be kept he became self-contradictory in regard to patients' rights for self-determination. If patients were to be paid in cash then it should be up to them to decide what to do with the money. The first ministerial reaction was that types of payment were used as therapeutic measures and therefore best left to the direction of professionals.

As Mr. Dodds persisted the Ministry became ready to permit payment in cash yet leaving the decision up to each hospital, and lastly to sending official guidelines which promoted the cash payment preference (H.605, 481, 601, 12-13). Whether the change in the Ministry's stand was due to the wish to appease Mr. Dodds or to becoming convinced by his argument is unknown. It remains also unknown whether hospitals' management committees and the professionals saw the Ministry's final directives as interference or as a welcomed suggestion. As always, nobody bothered to learn about patients' wishes or reactions.

f.The Right to refuse hospitalization
It was pointed out in Parliament that with the exception of contagious diseases no one is detained

for refusing treatment in the case of physical illness (H.560, 465). In contrast, a large section of the 1959 Act was devoted to various measures of compulsory admission and detention in hospital. Thus for once MPs admitted that mental illness was perceived and treated unlike physical illness by Parliament and the professionals. Those who put forward this argument were against an increase in compulsory admission possibilities, though full abolition of it was not suggested by anyone. The analogy of physical illness was used to suggest that the mentally ill should be treated in a similar form and not as a special case - i.e. mental illness was not acknowledged by the protagonists of patients' rights as an entity on its own (H.573, 91). Linking mental illness to physical disease as much as possible was seen as taking a progressive stance. Following this line of argument, the mentally ill should be seen as people capable of taking the responsibility for their present and future, able to request professional help when necessary and to use it appropriately when given. In 1959, however, we can observe a firm belief in the goodness of compulsory intervention (H.605, 426). This belief was expressed in particular in regard to psychopaths as we will see below. The underlying acceptance of the then current psychiatric practice as helpful was very strong, despite the endless criticisms made about it by MPs. Given this belief, anyone who refused to concur with professional opinion would be seen as a person incapable of self-management. With this background, any attempt to ease compulsion was not likely to get an unbiased hearing. The lack of even a discussion on the right to refuse treatment; the valid and invalid links between mental distress and physical illness; the degree of inevitability of compulsory admission and hospitalization - can be understood in the light of this value judgement.

Psychopathy
This category was put up as the third main category of mental disorder - and the only new one - in the Royal Commission's report (the two others were mental disorder and mental deficiency). As an innovation it was bound to be discussed in the general debate of 1957 and 1959.
    The issues involved in the conceptualization of this new classification and in working with it in practice were multiple and complex: 1.Its definition. 2.The reliability and validity of the

professional assessment. 3.The criteria by which socially undesirable behaviour becomes designated as a mental illness/as a crime/or remains unlabelled. 4.The conceptual justification of perceiving psychopathy as a category equal to mental disorder and mental deficiency. 5.Weighing the potential of social risk a psychopath may prove to be vs. the potential of harmful labelling of socially unacceptable behaviour as mental illness to the individual. 6.The type of intervention seen as useful, its availability and effectiveness.

Out of this variety of aspects the parliamentary debates focused on the following: 1.The definition. 2.Compulsory detention of psychopaths. 3.Available methods of intervention and their effectiveness. 4.The possibility of prediction of future behaviour of a psychopath.

There is no evidence to allow us to assume an increase in the number of people exhibiting psychopathic behaviour during the 40s and the 50s. The likely reasons for singling out psychopathy seem to be linked in several factors which operated simultaneously during the post war period:

1.The Poor Law was completely phased out and many of those who could be defined in terms of these laws were now without a social definition.

2.Reactions to the Second World War and the Cold War that followed indicate the wish for stability and the fear of aggressive non-conformity. Seen in this light, psychopathic behaviour was likely to attract more attention than before.

3.Many would-be psychopaths were either involved in petty crime or just led socially undesirable lives (e.g. frequent change of employment, address, partners, doing as they pleased, drinking heavily, failing in school). They were unlikely to be sent to prison but nevertheless constituted a social problem for the conforming members of society.

4.The increasing dissatisfaction with the way insane offenders were treated from the perspective of those involved - e.g. the prisoners, relatives, prison officers, other prisoners (H.571, 890, 597, 229-301). The prisons and special hospitals were more and more overcrowded and detention in a psychiatric hospital could offer a temporary relief to the whole prison system. The psychiatrically disturbed offender, as a marginal case in both the prisons and the hospitals attracted to himself the worst aspects of the two systems.

251

5.Detention in an ordinary psychiatric hospital
could be continued on a nearly unlimited basis in
contrast to a perison sentence. From the
perspective of protecting society against
dangerous elements, such a possibility is
attractive.
6.As other diagnostic categories were receding at
the time (e.g. hysteria) (7) psychopathy became a
more noticeable category in its own right.
Interestingly, female psychopaths were/are often
described as exhibiting hysterical features. Thus
psychopathy was needed as a residual category.
7.The move towards encouraging people to seek
psychiatric intervention voluntarily and the
growth of out-patients clinics stressed the
"residual" character of those who were not
overtly psychotic, neurotic or ordinary but who
would not seek treatment.
8.The use of the psychotropic drugs at the very
end of the fifties made it easier to contain
aggressive behaviour within a psychiatric
hospital or a psychiatric ward of a general
hospital(8). Nevertheless the reluctance of most
hospitals to have psychopaths remains as firm
today as it was in the fifties.

The definition of psychopathy
The role of definitions of mental distress meets
the functions of: 1.Crystallization of meaning, or
covering up for the lack of clarity. 2.Providing a
yardstick for social, administrative, legal, and
clinical action. 3.A means of linking new category
to existing approaches. 4.Relating the phenomenon
to a more specified social role.
     The price paid for having a definition is
mainly related to the negative outcome of
labelling, rigidity of conceptualization, research
and policies.
     The interest in securing a definition for
psychopathy should be looked at from the
perspective of the lack of definition in any bill
for mental disorder and the fact that in 1959 - as
before - the legislators seemed content with this
omission (this issue was discussed in chapter 4).
Hence one of the questions we should ask ourselves
is why there was such a greater felt need to define
psychopathy. The question is inseparable from that
of why/how did psychopathy become prominent after
the Second World War. After deliberating the issue
of definition, the Commission decided that "we have
considered

considered whether the law should attempt to define or describe psychopathic personality more precisely as a guide to the doctors who are called on to make the diagnosis. In our opinion it should do much more harm than good to try to include in the law a definition of psychopathic personality on the analogy of the present legal definition of mental defectiveness"(9).

These are strong words for flexibility to be found in a Royal Commission report. It implied that legislators, judges, administrators, patients and relatives would have to trust doctors' judgement even more than before while acting upon this professional assessment. Yet it rightly indicates that psychiatrists lacked even a good enough working definition of psychopathy. Perhaps the Commission wanted to encourage doctors to continue to experiment with definitions and diagnostic indicators as a way of arriving at a more precise description. At the same time the Commission did not doubt at all the correctness of the intuitive diagnosis.

However, the Commission did not show hesitation in calling "it" psychopathic personality - a global term which has never been used in regard to mental disorder and deficiency. The professional literature too wrote about psychopathic personality and inadequate personality but not about a mentally ill personality despite the fact that mental disorder too was left undefined by the Commission.

Thus the Commission gave us an example of the process of labelling a la Goffman and Garfinkel (10), namely moving easily from an identifying detail of deviant behaviour to a reconstruction of the whole personality. Dr. Summerskill, shadow speaker on mental distress, gave an apt example of the implications of such an approach: the suffragettes would have been seen as abnormal because of acting at considerable variance with the majority's expectations at the time (H.573, 49). While accepting that definitions of psychopathy were subjective, she was nevertheless happy to endorse Professor Henderson's definition of psychopathy(11). The components of this definition, discussed in chapter 6, are three: 1.Intact intellect. 2.Demonstrated anti-social or a-social behaviour - i.e. non-conforming behaviour. 3.Lack of change of this pattern despite social and medical effort.

Presumably the last feature clinches the description into one of a disturbance, though equally it could have been put down to obstinacy or dogmatism. Despite the harm entailed by the application of a wrong diagnosis she did believe in the existence of "moral insanity", the term used by Maudsley to describe psychopathic behaviour (H.573, 50). Moreover she saw the acceptance of this category as a mental disturbance as a progressive step: to view a person as "ill" and not as a "criminal" implied for her and for others a more emphatic and caring approach toward him. Dr. Summerskill summarized her position by saying that "it is the new approach to the psychopath - indeed the official recognition of his condition - which I attach the greatest importance and which will come to be regarded as another step forward in the evolution of our civilization" (H.573, 50-51).

A lot of rhetoric, you may feel like saying. Yet a very accurate description of what the majority of MPs felt and thought in regard to the inclusion of this category within the Mental Health Act. Thus the firm belief in the goodness of psychiatry and a charged emotive dimension attached to psychopathy were in evidence.

The message of Dr. Summerskill's position seemed to be highly contradictory. Yet the inconsistency was never acknowledged. In the discussion which followed Dr. Summerskill's opening speech, Mr. Robinson sided with her regarding the need to have a definition, against the Commission's stand (H.573, 70). While unhappy with Professor Henderson's definition, he did not come up with another one instead. Dr. Bennett, one of the two psychiatrists in the House who specialized in working with psychopaths in the Maudsley Hospital stressed: "It has been one of the most unsatisfactory fields in which to work because of this very difficulty about definition ..almost every psychiatrist will probably think that he will be prepared to diagnose a psychopathic personality when he meets it, but I doubt if he would define the condition to anybody else" (H.573, 73). Thus the mystery surrounding psychopathy became more profound than before. Therefore the listing of indicators for diagnosis became urgently required. However, Dr. Bennett did not describe the characteristics, dimensions or qualities on which the classification of psychopathy was based. Instead he was happy to conclude that "the attitude of the Royal Commission to the psychopathic personality is somewhat ahead of its time, in that it leaves the diagnosis to the medical profession, which has got very far in ten years toward reaching some sort of definition" (H.573, 73). Yet we are left in the dark as to what this "sort" of statement may include. Dr. Broughton, the other psychiatrist in the House and the only then in practice, did not voice his opinion on psychopathy apart from basically agreeing with Dr. Bennett (H.573, 77).

Mr. Sorenson saw the term "psychopath" as less offensive than that of an "idiot" (H.573, 90), hinting that the two are synonymous, an analogy which contrasts with Professor Henderson's assumption on intact intellect. Mr. Butler rose to answer Dr. Summerskill on behalf of the government. He too saw the introduction of psychopathy as a major achievement of the Commission. In terms of the description he emphasized that "the minds of this group have developed unevenly, so that although they may be capable of normal or near normal performance in intelligence their powers of reasoning or of emotional control may sometimes be dangerously immature" (H.573, 102). While this implicit definition concurred with Professor Henderson's to an extent, it introduced "emotional control" and "dangerously immature" as substitutes for "anti-social and a-social behaviour", perhaps implying that the latter was the outcome of the first.

In 1957, Mr. Butler stated that the government would study further the issue of definitions before drafting the Bill. The definition offered and endorsed in the 1959 Mental Health Act reads as follows: "Persistent disorder or disability of the mind (whether or not including subnormality of intelligence) which results in abnormally aggressive or seriously irresponsible conduct and requires or is susceptible to mental treatment"(12).

The salient components of this definition are: 1.The persistence of the disorder. 2.The assumption that it is in the mind. 3.The appearance of irresponsible behaviour 4.The link to medical intervention which confirmed the category as a psychiatric one.

Compared with Professor Henderson's definition, "anti-social behaviour" was modified to "seriously irresponsible and aggressive behaviour", a characteristic which sounds more objective and less to do with conformity. While other-directed aggression is relatively easy to observe and diagnose, "irresponsibility" is a much more questionable concept. As psychiatrists were to make the diagnosis it would be up to them to decide what would be the boundaries of "seriously irresponsible behaviour". The definition allowed the omission of all of the acceptable clinical indicators of mental disorder from the diagnostic process. In contrast with the 1957 debate, not much was said in 1959 about the definition issue. Dr. Bennett rightly concluded that "It (the Bill) has laid down a social definition of the psychopath. Hitherto, the psychopath was been defying all sorts of attempts at appraisal. The fact that the definition had come unscathed through all the critical discussions of the Bill undoubtedly shows that not merely Hon. Members but those outside who wished to be heard, and were by way of being experts were unable seriously to suggest any better form of definition" (H.605, 423).

If we had any doubt, then Mr. Ironmonger went on to spell out for us the social message of the definition: "It is that of the changeling and the waif. They are not so different from those who, in these days, pathetically and fantastically refer to themselves as the 'beat generation' and 'rebels' and all that sort of thing. There seems to be one thing which all these people have in common, they are incapable of forming real, lasting and valid relationships with the rest of society" (H.605, 430). Here the definition received not only an immediate translation of irresponsible behaviour into non-conformity but a touch of psychological theorization of an assumed defect too. This interpretation of the research into maternal deprivation gives us the flavour of the use of psychologization for clear-cut ideological preferences.

Dr. Summerskill's warning concerning the danger of identifying non-conformity with psychopathy made only in 1957 materialized fully already in 1959. Yet no one in the House protested at Mr. Ironmonger's version or offered a different interpretation of this social definition. In the meantime Baroness Wootton was criticizing the concept and the definition in "that other place"; the House of Lords (H.217 Lords, 393-395). She - and others in the Lords - pointed out the danger to basic citizens' rights by confounding non-conformity with either mental illness or with the possible psychological motivation behind it. Baroness Wootton preferred psychopaths to be defined as offenders if they were found guilty of a

256

crime and to be free of any other connotation if
they have not commited an offence. She strongly
objected to the over-generalization embedded in the
term "psychopathic personality". However, the
majority in the Lords did not concur with her
views. In both Houses the majority was not only
content with the inclusion of the category but saw
it as a positive step in a more humane direction.
This conclusion was based on the above mentioned
assumption that psychiatric care and allowing a
person to adopt the sick role constituted a more
benevolent approach than to see the same person as
a criminal or as a responsible but non-conforming
member of society. Thus we are back to the
recurring belief in the goodness of psychiatric
understanding and practice.

Intervention in regard to Psychopathy.

a.Compulsory intervention. The Royal Commission
report suggested that if a psychopath refused
psychiatric treatment he/she should be detained for
intervention purposes (H.573, 25-27, 59-60). The
proposal did not differ in essence from any other
compulsory admission of people suffering from
mental distress. In the drafted Bill the
recommendation was that psychopaths should be
detained until aged 21 or 25 if admitted between
the ages of 21 and 25 (H.605, 410). This suggestion
is of particular significance if we remember that
Professor Henderson and other psychiatrists did not
see hospitalization as a promising avenue of
treating psychopaths (see chapter 6, section
6.a.i). Furthermore why did the legislators find it
necessary to stipulate a specific and restrictive
clause only about psychopaths? Why did the age of
25 become the limit for incarceration? Why should
age be considered as the main criterion for
clinical intervention? In part the formal reason
for the specification lies in the recognition that
"the disposal of the psychopath may present
difficulties until the new attitude towards this
problem is generally accepted" (H.605, 493). In
part it relates to the wish to impose this category
of patients on hospitals: "The psychopath will not
be acceptable to the neighbours in the ward"
(H.605, 426). By stipulating a specific regulation
it becomes somewhat more difficult for hospitals to
refuse to admit a psychopath than otherwise, even
under the regulation of the hospitals'
de-designation.

Some MPs were concerned that the age limit weakened to some extent the authority which could be exercised over people of 25 years and above (H.573, 59-60, 605, 433). They would have liked to have psychopaths detained without an age limit. Yet other MPs were concerned with the notion of such a hazy classification in which the probability of success of intervention was admittedly small (H.573, 75). The age limit is of little value by way of intervention that might be offered to a psychopath who is 25 (H.605, 423). The observation that these two presuppositions contradicted each other was not made during the debate. MPs treated the regulations pertaining to psychopathy as experimental and therefore in need of review in the near future. The fact that people might pay dearly for the sake of such experimentation was hardly mentioned.

b.Content and effectiveness of intervention
On the one hand it was stated that very little could be done for the psychopath by an authority in the field who happened to be MP, Dr. Bennett (H.605, 432). On the other hand Dr. M. Jones' work with psychopaths was praised (H.605, 417, 424-5). Likewise MPs had no hesitation in congratulating themselves on being progressive and benevolent toward the psychopath by virtue of including him under the umbrella of mental illness rather than being seen as an offender. Thus, while it was not clear what psychopathy was or what may lead to it, MPs did not doubt the basically beneficial effects of compulsory psychiatric intervention for this category.
With the de-designation of hospitals in the offing and the encouragement of establishing psychiatric wards in general hospitals the likelihood of refusals to admit psychopaths was increased. However, these difficulties were hardly mentioned.
Facing the meagre results of psychiatric intervention the consolation came from the assumption that psychopaths after the age of 25 show a high rate of "spontaneous recovery". This supposition was put forward by Dr. Bennett as a professional statement, though the evidence to support it was neither referred to nor presented. In a sense this argument added to the mystery about the origins and development in which psychopathy was shrouded from the beginning of the parliamentary debate about it.

The two psychiatrist MPs gave the distinct impression that it was with trepidation - rather than with professional confidence - that they approached the diagnosis and intervention of these clients (H.452, 2450, 548, 1342-3). As indicated in chapter 6, this attitude was shared implicitly by other psychiatrists in practice.

Thus psychiatrists entered the offical classification of mental illness as a major category, becoming a classical example of the use of psychiatry in the service of social control. It seems that the frontiers of the psychiatric realm were extended not so much because of the desire of psychiatrists for empire building but as a means to allow others to get rid of psychopaths. An added dimension was the social satisfaction that this potentially threatening group was to be taken care of clinically and administratively, despite the failure to give it a clear meaning.

Attitudes to Professional Groups
Nurses.
As in 1930, nurses were the professional group most frequently mentioned. MPs expressed concern over the acute shortage of nurses, recruitment programmes, low wages and unsatisfactory negotiation machinary (H.551, 1450-1). several MPs kept the issue alive by coming back to it from time to time. The bulk of the questiona and comments were made in 1956-7 - i.e. before the debate on the Royal Commission's report and the 1959 Act. The politicians were sympathetic to nurses and criticized the Ministry for lack of attention to the nurses' needs.

Despite the successful experiences of women's work during the Second World War, the Ministry actively discouraged mature women from becoming student nurses. Grants regulations during training discriminated against this group (H.564, 16-17). It is difficult to figure out the reasons behind this policy apart from it being a relic of a more distant past.

Only on few occasions were nurses described in a negative light. For example, Dr. Johnson asked for clarification in a case where a senior male nurse was found guilty of maltreatment. He was re-employed soon after his trial in a similar responsible position. Dr. Johnson's comments were therefore not less a rebuke to the authorities than to the guilty man himself.

Nurses' training, their move to community

based services, relations with other professional groups were mentioned only once: Mr. Robinson requested clarficiation of their tasks in the community and inter-professional relations in 1961 (H.605, 317, 412).

Psychiatrists

Psychiatrists were the second most frequently mentioned group. The majority of comments were favourable - e.g. praising their work, innovations, siding with them against the press and courts (H.553, 980, 557, 1062-3). Remarks related to specific cases often cited neglect, indifference and misjudgement for which the psychiatrist in charge was seen as the responsible figure. Names of doctors were never mentioned, while names of patients were disclosed (H.573, 42, 605, 317-20, 419).

The critique laid down at the existing system could have become an indirect critique of psychiatric practice. However there is no evidence to indicate that this view was adopted by MPs. To the contrary; the politicans stressed their faith in psychiatry as a positive healing force (H.560, 471, 571, 882, 573, 4302). This discrepancy between the explicit and implicit meaning of the critical moments on psychiatry is linked to two major beliefs shared by most MPs: 1.An unquestioning acceptance of the clinical-somatic view of mental illness. 2.Perceiving professional autonomy not only as a desirable feature but as a realistically dominant characteristic of the NHS in the 50s.

Given these two premises it is logically possible to see psychiatrists' activities in a positive light. Thus institutionalism could be seen as a negative development but one which was not created by psychiatry. In the wording of the 1959 Act consultant psychiatrists were given pride of place (H.605, 427, 441 and the Act itself). By the application of all of the 1948 NHS Act to the psychiatric services from 1959, consultants became the embodiment of clinical judgement, main receivers of research money and were given independence as against the superintendents. This policy fitted with both MPs and government's preferences.

Social Workers-Mental Welfare Officers (MWO)

This group was given major responsibilities under the new Act(13). The new duties (clauses 25-31) focus on compulsory admission, giving the MWO the duty and authority to evaluate a person's mental

260

state as well as to initiate a hospital admission. In all of these cases the MWO's decision has to be ratified by one or two psychiatrists. Yet the authority given to the social worker was/is crucial for the first step in an admission procedure, or in the process of the moral career of the mentally ill, to use Goffman's phrase(see Ref.10).

In the guidelines that followed from the legislation, e.g. the 1963 Community Care paper discussed below, social workers were given additional tasks in establishing community services for the mentally distressed. On the surface this move looked like the "coming of age" of British psychiatric social work. Indeed, if professional status is defined in terms of statutory obligations bestowed on a professional group and the readiness of other disciplines to accept the first as potentially able to fulfil those tasks then the psychiatric social worker "made it" into psychiatry.

A different slant is provided by the following facts:

1.According to the Ministry's publication only 50% of the required number of social workers in psychiatric services were in employment in 1961.

2.The majority of the social workers were unqualified and untrained ("the amount of formal training varied considerably and is often slight" - Cmnd 1973, p.25, 1963).

In the light of these facts the new responsibilities given to MWOs look more like an imposition of the Ministry on social workers, due to the weakness of the latter as a professional group. In chapter 6, section 6.d, it was indicated that psychiatric social workers were doubtful about these additions to their role from the viewpoint of client-worker relationships.

The discussion pertaining to MWOs' training highlights the points made above. Mr. Robinson tabled an amendment according to which MWOs should receive professional training in social work and would be employed only if qualified (H.605, 246-7). The supporters of the amendment (all of them Labour MPs) were aware of the shortage of MWOs and especially of qualified ones. Therefore a gradual move toward the required training and qualifications was proposed by the group. MWOs were often abused by the public and by other professionals for not being well prepared for the tasks they were performing. Even without taking a negative stand, their ability and authority were in

261

doubt. Formal training could only enhance their image and capabilities. However even the modified version concerning gradual introduction of qualified MWOs was unacceptable to the Ministry. The latter preferred to wait for the forthcoming Younghusband's report on social work education. The amendment was withdrawn without voting in the hope that the issue will be reconsidered, although no date was set up for such a discussion.

It is difficult to imagine any Ministry or government in Britain in the 20th century permitting unqualified doctors to carry on professional duties. Yet the Ministry had no such hesitation in regard to social workers.

On the whole, social workers' performance was viewed favourably (H.573, 39,47).

Other professional groups were not mentioned in the debate reflecting on their small number and lack of importance vis-a-vis the statutory aspects of the psychiatric system.

7.d. Description of Individual Cases

The most famous case to be repeatedly mentioned in Parliament in the 50s was that of Mrs. Thornton. Thanks to Mr. Dodds MPs were often reminded of her (H.506, 18-19, 849-50, 858, 1056, 553, 702, 562, 106-7, 1699-703, 564, 15-16, 560, 488-9). He narrated the happenings in regard to her hospitalisation; the offshots of the case; the way Mr. Dodds himself was treated by the Board of Control and the general issues that arose of the particular case.

Mrs. Thornton was first mentioned by Mr. Dodds in 1956, ending with the question "When will Mrs. T. get her freedom as well as independent medical examination?". She got both a few months later. From Mr. Dodds' description it transpired that Mrs. T. was a middle-aged woman with a history of marital difficulties and a keen believer in spiritualism. At one point she was referred by her GP for a psychiatric evaluation because of what seemed to be paranoid fears and complaints about her husband. The psychiatrist suggested that she was in need of a solicitor's advice in sorting out her marital problems. However, when Mrs. T. complained about a murder attempt by her husband she was compulsorily admitted to a psychiatric hospital and diagnosed as suffering from paranoid hallucinations.

Mr. Dodds came on to the scene three years later at the request of her relatives, who tried in vain to discharge her from the hospital. While attempting to secure an independent psychiatric opinion via the Board Mr. Dodds had interviewed Mrs. T.'s husband, son and other relatives at some length. According to him, most of her complaints were real - e.g. there was an attempt by her husband to push her over a bridge, which was stopped by the local policeman. The hallucinatory flavour of her communication was put down to the impact of her belief in spiritualism.

As Mr. Dodds did not receive an answer to his letters from the Board of Control, he wrote instead to the Minister of Health who replied in writing, as well as in the House. Mrs. T. was at last examined on 29 June, 1956 and the psychiatrist recommended her discharge. By that time she was discharged for a trial period and finally released on 25 October of the same year. Neither Mrs. T. and her son, nor Mr. Dodds were informed of the outcome of the psychiatric assessment by the hospital, the Board or the Ministry. Only as Mr. Dodds persisted in bringing up the matter during Question Time he got the details from the Minister's secretary plus an apology for the delay (H.562, 106-7).

Mr. Dodds did not pursue the issues of explanation, apology or compensation to the patient. Instead he used this case as an example for the many more people who were unnecessarily in hospital. One must admit that Mrs. T.'s history as a patient provided a rather convincing illustration of the different types of waste involved, be it financial, professional or of human potential. The uncalled for suffering and humiliation no doubt resulted in a hostile approach toward psychiatric services and their personnel by Mrs. T. and those associated with her. Members of the general public who happened to hear or read about the case would too be likely to become uneasy about psychiatric intervention. Surprisingly, however, Mr. Dodds did not have any suggestion to make on how or why was this state of affairs arrived at. Thus the reader is left with his/her own deductions from the case. My own speculations lead me in the direction of suspected neglect and indifference rather than toward any intentional maltreatment. The readiness to accept a priori relatives' and GPs' versions as against an out-of-hand rejection of the patient's is crucial in directing a psychiatrist toward a misleading assessment. The lack of knowledge of the patient's cultural background and system of beliefs is usually due to lack of time, interest and belief in the validity of the patient's account. Therefore the chances of misinterpretation of the intricacies of the client's relationships and perceptions increase significantly in those situations where the patient's experience differs from that of the psychiatrist. The assumption that hospitalization provides care and cure would tend to make psychiatrists hesitant towards early discharge without clear signs of change. While relatives' sanity is on the whole left undoubted their position is not perceived as reliable or as valid as that of another professional or an outsider of good public standing. Therefore the requests made by Mrs. T.'s relatives would tend to be ignored, genuinely forgotten or pushed aside by a busy psychiatrist.

The case illustrates that the chances of an ordinary person/family to initiate a change in psychiatric attitudes and opinions were very limited and the degree of social pressure required for any such change was high.

The long waiting period between the end of the independent examination and the final discharge give us a glimpse of the organizational aspects of the hospital. The independent psychiatrist's conclusion must have been viewed as a snub to the prestige of the hospital, its superintendent and the psychiatrist in charge of Mrs. T. In this particular case the Board of Control was told off too because of its insistent refusal to order an independent inquiry at Mr. Dodds' request. This inevitable facet of the recommendation to free Mrs. T. had probably led to internal and external wrangling (i.e. between the hospital, the Board and the Ministry) resulting in delays in reaching and implementing decisions. The Ministry's initial reaction was one of denial of Mr. Dodds' allegation. If Mr. Dodds had not persisted the matter would have rested there. Due to his insistence and position as MP, however, the Ministry too had to make its own inquiry. Once convinced of the truth of Mr. Dodds' claim the Ministry went to ensure that the necessary steps would be taken.

In terms of illustrating power relations among the hospital/Board/Ministry this case provides a good example of the overseeing position of the Ministry and not of the Board, whose official function it was. This state of affairs also demonstrates that the Board has become a branch of the Ministry rather than an independent public body.

The lack of concern over the harm done to Mrs. T. again typifies large bureaucratic organizations. This attitude stood in sharp contrast to the assumed values of psychiatric care. This point was never taken up in the House. With the exception of Dr. Johnson and Mr. Dodds no one referred to Mrs. T.'s case in the 1957 and 1959 debates. The isolation of these two MPs from the rest of those with manifest interest in mental distress politics was already mentioned in the section on tactics. Sadly this isolation went as far as not putting to good use relevant material brought up by them - thus demonstrating the impact of ideological and personal differences in the context of Parliament.

Another case highlighted by Mr. Dodds is worth our attention (H.651, 1560). A ten-year old girl was assessed as in need of being placed in a school for maladjusted children. Due to lack of a suitable place she was put in a 1,200 bed ordinary psychiatric hospital on an adult ward. Under the parents' and Mr. Dodds' pressure the Ministry found her a more suitable placement. In the course of exchanges between Mr. Dodds and the Parliamentary Secretary for Health the latter accused the parents of aborting attempts to find her a place by refusing to let her go to some of the possible institutions. It is unknown whether the parents were/were not justified in their decision not to accept a specific placement. But the fact remains that for a period as long as seven months the little girl was in an adult ward, a policy that met with everybody's disapproval.

This case pinpoints certain aspects which differ from those prevailing in Mrs. T.'s: the scarcity of specialized units, the felt inability to look after this girl in her family or elsewhere in the community, the use of hospitals as dumping grounds. We do not know what was the position adopted by the professionals involved in the care of the child. But we do know that as a professional group they publicly kept quiet about the affair and did not attempt to use it for bearing pressure towards the improvement of suitable placement of children.

Dr. Broughton described briefly several cases (H.563, 80) in his attempt to convince the House of the need to look at physical causes behind the

265

appearance of mental illness. The vignettes vary in terms of age, sex, severity of disturbance and consequences but in all of them the primary cause was defined as somatic. Dr. Broughton did not elaborate on any other relevant connection and therefore it is impossible to contextualize his judgement. His plea for the traditional psychiatric explanation was symptomatic of the convictions of the majority of British psychiatrists who were moving towards community care without any basic change in their adherence to the clinical-somatic model.

On the whole, the frequency of reference to individual cases has diminished in comparison with the references made in 1930.

Reactions to Public Attitudes
Fewer references have been made in regard to the public in the 50s than in the 20s. The main thrust of the comments was that the public exhibited an enlightened approach but one which needs to be even more so. The public was praised for its tolerance, understanding and readiness to have the mentally ill in its midst (H.573, 37, 605, 435, 452, 465). Not a single example was provided to substantiate this claim. At the same time it was argued that the public should be educated toward the full acceptance of mental illness as physical disease. It was hoped that psychiatric wards in hospitals would help to demonstrate this belief and to reduce further the stigma still believed to be attached to the mentally ill (H.605, 475, 564, 21). Open days in hospitals and schools' programmes on leading "a happy life" were some of the other educational means mentioned (H.573, 38, 51). No references were made as to what led the public to change its negative attitude towards the mentally ill or why traces of it were still lingering on. Several MPs were prominent members of MIND, as already mentioned. Voluntary organizations were commented upon positively on a number of occasions (H.573, 32, 42). Only once did an MP warn against stretching public tolerance too far by "releasing dangerous criminal lunatics" (H.561, 1560).

The BBC's approach was cited as a positive example of attempts to change attitudes by providing a balanced view (H.605, 670). The only clear indication of the desirable balance was given by the Minister when he snubbed the BBC for being biased in favour of ex-patients (H.605, 805).

7.e.The Ministry's and the Government's Position

The 1951-1964 Conservative government was in a very
different position from the 1930 Labour one:
firstly, it had a secure majority in both Houses.
Secondly, the world economy was in a relatively
good state and the cabinet was engaged in an
attempt to convince the people that the British
economy was prospering too.
     In particular, Harold Macmillan's team (i.e.
from 1957 onward) could be described as one of the
most progressive Conservative governments during
this century. Yet health matters were seen as
relatively insignificant when compared to the state
of the economy or foreign affairs. For example,
Macmillan's memoirs of the 1956-1959 period contain
two references to the NHS, both directly on its
budgeting though indirectly related to its
underlying social values(12). No reference was made
to any other topic within the health field.
     Between 1957 and the election on 9 October,
1959 the Government tried hard to woo the
voters(13). The introduction of the Mental Health
Act was one of the steps taken in this directon.
     Mr. Walker-Smith was one of the "young
generation" ministers appointed by Macmillan in
1957 in an attempt to rejuvenate the image of his
cabinet, only to be dismissed in 1960 with six
other ministers. His pull in the cabinet was that
of a junior minister and it is known that he was
frustrated by not being appointed in 1957 or later
to a more senior post. There is little in Mr.
Walker-Smith's biography to suggest either interest
or knowledge of mental distress matters prior to
becoming Minister of Health.
     Despite these disadvantages, Mr.
Walker-Smith's speeches and comments during the
debates and at the standing committee stage
indicate his keenness on passing the mental health
legislation and on ensuring that the new Act will
be an improvement over the old legislation. The
impression gained is of a minister who worked hard
to satisfy the different groups and MPs involved in
the process. His attempts were aimed mainly at
securing consensus through compromises, but he did
not give in on any major bone of contention (H.605,
405, 407, 604). Thus Mr. Walker-Smith's strength
seems to lie in his negotiation skills as well as
his readiness to listen to other people's views. It
should be remembered that on the majority of issues

there was an agreement among the interested MPs and that a voting majority was available to Mr. Walker-Smith. Thus he was not going through a rough time in regard to this piece of legislation. His ability to listen and consider alternatives in a courteous manner won him the praises of all MPs - a rare sight in political life (H.605, 270, 271, 434, 412). Mr. E. Powell succeeded Mr. Walker-Smith as the Minister of Health in 1960 after the 1959 Act became law. Mr. Powell had a considerably more powerful personal position within the cabinet.

His style differed considerably from that of his predecessor. While being correct he was more decisive, less attempting to reach compromises, less listening to MPs, and/or reactions from the field (H.573, 96-103, 615, 403-408). Mr. Powell became Minister at a crucial period for the implementation of the 1959 Mental Health Act. The spirit of the Act had to be translated into action if it was not to become merely a dead word. The guidelines issued by Mr. Powell's civil servants seem to have remained mainly at a high level of generality and their suitability for the purposes mentioned above is doubtful.

The third Minister involved was Mr. R. Butler, in charge of the Home Office. Mr. Butler was a distinguished politician and a senior member of the cabinet. His brief appearance in the debate was more in courtesy to Dr. Summerskill than a necessity. His background as the president of MIND and his interest in offenders, coupled with the Home Office interest in transferring the main responsibility over psychopaths to the health service made him the most suitable cabinet minister to represent the government. His contribution was similar in content to that of Mr. Walker-Smith.

We lack knowledge of the specific relationships which existed between the Home Office and the Ministry of Health on matters of mutual interest and conflict, such as the handling of psychopaths. It would be of interest to know if the Ministry of Health was keen to accept psychopaths under its wings or not.

During the late 50s the Ministry was confronted with several salient problem areas in the mental illness/health field. References to these points were given in chapter 5 and in the section concerned with the critique of the existing system in this chapter. These include:

1.A steady increase in the rate of admissions, due mainly to readmissions.

2.The high rate of discharge pleased the hospital authorities, but must have been worrying for those in charge of community services.
3.A steady increase in out-patient appointments.
4.A continuous stream of criticism of the Board of Control and hospitals' mode of operation by professionals, lay people and the media.
5.Chronic shortage of nurses, social workers and consultant psychiatrists.
6.Lack of sufficient number of specialized units (e.g. for children, for psychopaths).
7.Lack of adequate accommodation facilities in the community.
8.Constant increase in the costs of any facility, especially of hospital beds.
9.Over-populated prisons with a component of prisoners considered to be mentally disordered.

The problems listed up to now were easily perceived as such. The following issues were perhaps less obvious and it is unknown whether the Ministry conceived of them as problematic.
10.Considering the alternatives to the existing system. Such an orientation has been termed as the "rationalist approach" by Hall(14), who contrasts it with the incremental approach. In the latter policy decisions were taken from the standpoint of accepting the existing system as basically valid but in need of improvement.
11.Any alternative would have to be considered in the light of the structural relationships between the different components of the psychiatric services.

After looking at the Ministry's approach to specific content areas the options selected by the Ministry will be summarized.

Tightening Up Loose Ends
As already pointed out the Ministry was putting on pressure to get a definition of psychopathy (H.639, 891, 640, 917, 641, 622). It went ahead to secure a definition despite the refusal of the Commission to do so and the expressed doubts on the validity of this category during the debates. Following the Royal Commission's suggestions, the Ministry proposed a set of new clauses concerning compulsory admissions (The Mental Health Act 1959, part IV, section 25-32, H.605, 321-284). In all 59 of the 150 clauses of the 1959 Act deal with compulsory incarceration, while only 20% of the total in-patient population was admitted by sectioning. These regulations are both more comprehensive and

tougher than before in the sense of including:
1.More options for detention than before. 2.An easy
transfer from voluntary status to a compulsory one
(but not vice versa). 3.Getting rid of magistrates'
involvement in admission procedure. 4.Giving MWOs
the authority to investigate and act upon requests
for admission.

Concerning the issue of magistrates'
involvement the Ministry simply omitted any
references to magistrates in the re-drafting of the
new regulations on compulsory admission. It was
left to individual MPs to express their Cabinet's
interest in mental health matters. The amount of
money spent (£49,824,776 in 1959-60; H.605, 480)
has to be looked at in terms of growing in-patients
and out-patients numbers, percentage of the total
NHS budget vs. percentage of the clients of
psychiatric services and the budget items to which
the money was allocated.

In more general terms the questions pertain
to direct and indirect (i.e. loss of production)
costs and "hidden" costs (e.g. the percentage of
GPs appointment which are caused by psychiatric
complaints(15)).

As already mentioned, the percentage of the
total NHS budget on hospitals allocated to mental
illness amounted to 15% (H.625, 480). The
psychiatric services did better on capital
expenditure where their share was up to 30% in
1959-60 and 27.6% for the period of 1948-50.

A look at staffing ratios(16) shows the
psychiatric services to be much below the ratios of
teaching, acute and chronic wards for the
physically ill in terms of medical staff, nurses
and catering personnel. At the same time the number
of psychiatric beds was a third of all NHS beds
(138,176 beds out of a total of 450,629)(17). In
contrast to the high cost of a bed in a hospital
the cost of a place in a day hospital was
considerably lower, including the investment which
amounted to about £300 per place as calculated by
Farndale(18). The government knew that community
facilities were likely to reduce the overall cost
of the psychiatric services.

Direct grants were given only to regional
health authorities (RHA), i.e. primarily to the
hospital system. As the total turnover of
inpatients figure was increasing during the 50s the
bulk of the budget was spent on meeting standards
already defined in the past rather than towards
innovation.

Hospitals were in need of more money, to judge by the urgent request to provide vitamins to Claybury Hospital in April 1957 (H.552, 815, 554, 1048). This request was met soon after by the Ministry, but the very fact that such a matter was not handled prior to being brought before the House sounds ominous: if a showpiece like Claybury was unable to finance a reasonable level of nutrition, the likelihood of much worse conditions in less well known places must have been greater. If even nutrition standards were not met it indeed implied the unlikelihood of providing adequate standards in so-called less basic areas - e.g. psychotherapy, occupational therapy and rehabilitation - within the hospital system.

The government left the services outside the hospital in the hands of local and health authorities. It was made clear that financing community mental health ventures was the responsibility of local authorities. It was the latter's decision how to use the central government block grant which was reintroduced in 1959 (exactly 30 years after views on the matter). The majority concurred with the Ministry's position (H.573, 69, 605, 315, 459, 467). A minority was sorry to see them go on the ground of lost civil control over admissions (H.605, 455).

The wish for maximum clarity of legislation and administrative instructions manifested here is easy to understand. For the sake of this clarity, however, the Ministry was ready to allow a measure of erosion of patients' and relatives' rights. An increase in psychiatrists' and social workers' power followed instead.

The final definition of psychopathy has already been analysed. The Ministry did not share the doubts and fears of lumping together mentally disturbed people with non-conformists. Likewise, it did not hesitate to endorse long periods of detention for psychopaths despite the knowledge that in most cases hospitalization did not amount to much more than a replacement for imprisonment.

The 1959 Act abolished all previous legislation on mental illness. As the number of its clauses came up to 150 considerable skill was required to prevent the new legislation from not becoming as cumbersome as the old one.

Living with the Existing System
As before, the Minister and his secretaries tended to defend the activities of the Board of Control

and of any other official involved (H.573, 75, 605, 417). Despite the decision to abolish the Board - to which the Ministry was a partner - any criticism uttered against it was firstly dismissed as untrue. Secondly, if the critics persisted, the Ministry would concur with the accusation yet would continue to see the Board's action as positive in principle and as mistaken on that particular occasion.

When the shortages in the provision of services were exposed the Ministry refused to accept it as such; even a chronic condition such as the insufficient number of nurses and new recruits into nursing was described by Parliamentary secretary in optimistic terms. She would neither accept that lower pay was one of the reasons for the shortage, nor that the figures of new students were far from reaching the target set up by the Ministry itself (H.569, 1447, 1700-1703). When lack of hospital places for children was revealed the parents of the little girl concerned were blamed for being too choosy (H.561, 1560). Thus the delicate balance between admitting some shortcomings yet not accepting that wrong policies were involved was maintained.

Intervention: the Ministry's preferences and activities.

Community care vs. hospitals

The government emphasized that it was putting more money than ever before into the psychiatric services (H.552, 2570). This fact was proclaimed as proof of the Ministry's interest in this sector.

The lack of active cabinet and ministerial commitment to community care has been discussed above. The government did not exhibit an interest in exploring the possibilities of community mental health or in encouraging actively local authorities to do so. One can only speculate as to the reasons behind this lack. An obvious line of reasoning was the wish to maintain financing standards and therefore not to deviate from the block grant principle under any circumstances. This decision followed a good administrative logic, but was (and still is) also a hindrance to any innovative move. Several ways for a token financial encouragement to local authorities were open before the Ministry. For example, it could finance new programmes for a specific period (e.g. the American Federal government's method) or earmark a sum from the amount given to health authorities for psychiatric community care.

The fact that none of these means were even considered in public implied that the government's commitment to community care was far from being a serious one, as the Minister would have liked us to believe ("I yield to none in my desire for the steady progress and gathering acceleration of the local authority mental health services")(19).

Like its critics, the Ministry too knew well that without mandatory legislation little was going to change in an uninterested local authority. Therefore the question begs itself: why did the government decide not to provide active inducement for a programme that could have been helpful in a number of directions, i.e: 1.In easing the pressure off the hospitals. 2.In reducing the overall level of expenses. 3.In satisfying explicit value preferences for a greater degree of integration of the mentally ill into the community.

As is indicated above, the resources at the disposal of the 1959 government were far greater than those available to the 1930 one. Yet the decision in regard to community care was the exact replication of the one taken in 1930.

According to Hall et al.(20) a new policy direction stands a better chance of being adopted by a government if it meets the criteria of legitimation, feasibility and support. On the surface the community care approach was accredited a high degree of legitimation and support by all professional groups involved, the media, MPs and the Ministry.

The feasibility aspect was never discussed in Parliament (see the comment at the end of paragraph on intervention). An indirect reference to the Ministry's doubts was by Mr. Vaughan-Morgan in 1957 (H.573,35). He spoke enthusiastically about improvements in the hospital sector but said "when it comes to the local authority services for the mentally ill, it is not easy to point to any obvious developments" (H.573,39). Shortages of manpower in regard to MWOs and social workers in general were mentioned as the reasons for the slow progress.

The possibility of a lower overall cost in the long term and the relatively low price of establishing new community care facilities as against hospitals' expenses, which were accepted by the Ministry at the time, were never acknowledged.

Yet the lesson learnt from the case of the 1970 Local Authorities Social Services Bill is that

the financing aspect was put aside to ease the path
for mandatory legislation of the Seebohm
Committee's recommendations (see Ref.14).

Two main differences seem to emerge between
the community care and the Seebohm Committee cases:
1.The Royal Commission did not come up with a
specified set on the organizational aspects of
community care, while the Seebohm Committee
offered such a set.
2.Apart from the attempts by Dr. Johnson and Mr.
Dodds, no public campaign was mounted to secure
that the Commission's report would be implemented
in full. Neither the committee members nor the
professional groups involved attempted to alert
the public and Parliament to the fact that the
main constructive policy thrust of the Commission
was to be thwarted: to the contrary, as has been
demonstrated in this chapter, MPs and Ministers
congratulated each other on legislating the Royal
Commission's recommendations. As indicated in
chapter 6 the professional groups too were not
seeking change.

The main reasons for these differences are
looked at below and in the summary of this chapter.

Indirectly the Ministry had made up its mind
throughout the fifties: the unpublicized decision
to import the psychotropic drugs on a massive scale
was the key decision in regard to the future of the
psychiatric services. It reaffirmed the belief in
chemotherapy over and above other modes of
intervention. While this belief did not imply a
rejection of other methods, in a situation of
scarce resources the consequences amounted to the
same outcome: namely of putting more money and
faith in the drugs and much less money and faith in
all other means put together. The advantages of the
drugs' effects from the Ministry's viewpoint were
quite clear: 1.Mental distress could become more
controllable at any stage - i.e. prior to
hospitalization, during the stay in hospital and
upon discharge. 2.Drug prescription and use did not
entail intensive use of manpower, either
professional or semi-professional. 3.It could lead
to shorter periods of hospitalization and longer
periods outside.

Thus the hoped for effects of the drugs were
expected to meet two out of the three objectives
which community care could satisfy. By 1959 however
sufficient evidence was available on the rate of
admissions, re-admissions, discharge and length of
hospitalization (see table 2, appendix 1). These

statistics show that while hospitalization periods
were shortened all other indicators continued to
increase simultaneously. One self-evident
conclusion to be reached was that the bottleneck of
the system lay in the periods in which patients
stayed in the community. As patients' chemical
make-up was assumed to be under control (via the
drugs) it was only logical to presume that the yet
unresolved difficulties related to the
psychological and social factors of mental
distress. The Ministry however showed very little
interest in this approach. It tolerated
experimentation in intervention methods which
included psychosocial components but did little
else.

Equally the Ministry was disinterested in
learning about the disadvantages of the
psychotropic drugs. The sums allocated for research
in psychiatry in general (£55,000 for 1957-8,
H.573, 25) can be described only as ridiculous in
proportion to percentages of patients, beds, or in
comparison with the resources given to research on
physical illness. The sums invested in importing
the drugs were becoming larger and larger but were
never questioned as they carried with them the halo
of medication and cure.

The belief in the psychotropic drugs was of
course closely related to the basic adherence to
the clinical-somatic understanding of mental
illness and modes of intervention. The government
was committed to this approach. Its concept of
community care was one of extending the practice
from the hospital into the community. To the extent
that psychiatrists did not object to the
involvement of other professions and other than
clinical-somatic means of intervention, the
Ministry too was ready to follow suit. In
discriminating positively consultants against
superintendents and against any other professional
group in the psychiatric services (especially
against nurses) the Ministry was manifesting its
preference for medical expertise as the most useful
type of knowledge. Thus committing itself
wholeheartedly to the drug policy, the Ministry
must have felt that it had done its best for the
population served by the psychiatric services.

Seen from the perspective described above,
any development in community care would be
beneficial within the available system as trimmings
and not as essentials. It was pointed out in
chapter 5 that community mental health cannot in

principle be introduced as trimmings to the clinical-somatic model, as the two are incompatible. Yet the Ministry's position is an attempt not to change the essence of this model: while claiming to be for community care, it would neither make this policy mandatory nor contribute actively in any way toward the implementation of such an alternative.

The pressure mounted by MPs toward mandatory legislation and central government funding for community care could not have been really effective in view of the basic ideological agreement between MPs, the Ministry and mainstream British psychiatry. This shared understanding and alliance clearly favoured the clinical-somatic approach, over and above all other approaches.

Thus the Ministry was acting in a logically consistent way in its lack of commitment toward community care, even if this preference led to an uneconomical solution.

By adopting a pro-community care policy the Ministry was giving in to requests from the media, MPs, from within the psy complex and the voluntary sector.

The Ministry was ready to provide some guidance to local authorities on how to plan their community care programmes. It was also ready to look at submitted plans which had to be approved by the Ministry. The Community Care paper (Cmnd. 1973) provides a summary of the Ministry's conceptualization and proposed activities and inactivities in regard to the subject matter. Nowhere is there a definition of community care or an attempt to clarify what was meant by it, nor were any thoughts given as to its boundaries. Community care came to stand for services and facilities that could be offered to the mentally distressed by local authorities. At no point was it suggested that central government had any role to play in creating such a system. Terms such as research, psychiatrists, nurses, psychologists, occupational therapists or vocational training for the mentally ill are never mentioned. Instead social workers assume in the document the overall responsibility for community care. While the paper acknowledged that only 50% of the necessary social work force is available and that its overall training level is "slight" it did not refer to how these two gaps were going to be bridged or how social workers were going to work together with the professional groups mentioned above. The absence of research, psychiatrists, etc. is not accidental. These key areas belong to medicine and the hospital system in the eyes of the authors of the paper and their contribution to the care of the mentally ill was not expected to be modified as the result of the community care policy. When asked the Minister referred to the establishment of the Central Council for Social Work Training (CCSWT) in November 1962 and the establishment of some of the "Younghusband courses" - i.e. generic and non-university training courses (H.641, 628). However, it was not envisaged even by the Ministry itself that these courses would meet the demand for social workers in general (i.e. not only in psychiatry) in less than twenty years, while officially MWOs and social workers were to establish community care then and there. The basic ideology behind community care was stated in this document, namely that it is for the individual's benefit - as well as for his primary group and community - to stay in the community and outside a psychiatric hospital a much as possible. Therefore social workers' efforts and local facilities should be mobilized in this direction. The public should be educated toward a greater degree of tolerance of the mentally ill in its midst. But the only method of education suggested was the creation of community care facilities as an example for the public. A successful community care centre would be likely to have a persuasive quality, but for it to be successful a measure of community support is required as a starting point.

The command paper on community care should be looked at in conjunction with the previous paper by the same Minister on the future of the mental hospitals (Cmnd. 1604, 1962). The paper projected a cut of 20,000 psychiatric beds in the period up to 1970. Therefore the hidden assumption in regard to community care must have been that the resources in the community could cater for the equivalent in number of patients to 20,000 beds (which is much more than 20,000 people, as many patients stay in hospital for short periods but remain in the community for a longer duration).

The money saved from the closure of beds was to be circulated back into the hospital system and not to the community sector. The wide gap between the means allocated to community care and the expectations from it leave one with a distinct impression of ill consideration on behalf of the Ministry.

Overseeing the Hospitals: Tightening organizational control and extending psychiatrists' professional autonomy

The emphasis on community care implied an inevitable component of disillusion with the therapeutic impact of hospitals. The Ministry carefully avoided blaming hospitals for institutionalization or neglect. Instead its representatives took the line of praising the "good" hospitals and curbing hospitals' independence. The latter's independent position was eroded considerably by the introduction of the NHS and its organizational structure.

The limitations were more felt in small and medium sized hospitals than in the large ones. As the Ministry's policy to do away with mental hospitals' farms (H.548,718; 599,500,1317-24) was aimed primarily at the big hospitals which controlled large arable agricultural areas. The policy was to sell these farms to private hands, either for building development or for agricultural purposes. Being a Conservative government it refused to hand over the land to the RHA or the local authority. The decision to sell the farms was coated with therapeutic meaning as the Ministry's official reason was put down to the lack of use by patients while those who opposed the policy praised its therapeutic benefits. The MPs who opposed the government's intention represented the interest of the hospitals. The latter naturally objected to a cut in their property, a restriction on staff's perks (e.g. recreation grounds, free vegetables, free plots) and an end to another outlet for the patients. The resistance put on the hospitals' behalf in Parliament took the form of repeated questions and protesting comments (H.548,718; 599, 1317-24). However these efforts did not help to alter the Ministry's decision. Were the farms a profitable revenue? It is impossible to say without checking on specific transactions and their long term ramifications. Yet the Ministry's firm stand in favour of the de-designation of hospitals (H.605,477,573,37) and of consultants' status implied a preference for the professional independence of the institutions, rather than their administrative independence. The distinction between organizational and professional autonomy is not a simple one to make as in practice they tend to overlap to a considerable extent. Yet tightening the administrative control over hospitals by the health authorities and central government did go side by side with strengthening the position of clinical expertise, even if these two facets were not acknowledged as co-existing. This point reaffirms the Ministry's preference of betting on the professionals, especially those medically qualified. The Ministry's refusal to discuss specific methods of psychiatric intervention in the House is another indication of the firm belief in the clinical judgement and authority of psychiatrists. Similarly the rejection of the suggestion to distribute in writing patients' and relatives' rights and to stop censorship of voluntary patients' mail provide two more examples of the wish to extend the realm of professional responsibility and judgement.

The decision on psychopathy, however, marked the limits of the degree of autonomy the government was ready to grant. Despite the reluctance of several psychiatrists to be responsible for this group and to have a legal definition attached to it the Ministry went ahead with both directives.

Attitudes towards professional groups

The Ministry's position toward psychiatrists was already outlined. They were seen as the top of the psy complex pyramid. This attitude was translated into the greater measure of professional autonomy given to this group.

Nurses were at times recognised as carrying the main burden of the hospital services (H.573, 41). Yet this acknowledgement was not transmitted into improved level of pay or even pay negotiations. The government was adamant that negotiations should go through the established channels as already mentioned. The obvious administrative logic and fear of precedence were probably the reasons behind the Ministry's stand. While the acute shortage of nursing staff was recognized and a campaign for new recruits was mounted, the rigidity of regulations in respect of mature students prevented the use of a major resource for new students (H.567, 797, 551, 2458). In short, the unimaginative bureaucratic approach prevented any significant change in either work conditions or role and training openings (the omission of nurses from the 1963 document on community care is one further example of this direction).

As described above, social workers were given more power, greater responsibility and more tasks

279

than before. The necessary support for this expansion was not provided by the Ministry. Its opposition to ascertaining the training of MWOs bears evidence for the lack of such support (H.605, 249-257).

The assumption that an untrained, unqualified and small group such as the MWOs, or even all of the social workers in the psychiatric services put together, would be able to carry out the main thrust of community care sounds incredible. It is difficult to believe that anybody in the Ministry accepted this supposition. Therefore the Ministry was acting under the naive assumption of gradual growth that will eventually lead to the desirable results. The figures provided by Jones (see Ref.8, p.364, table 14) show an increase of less than 600 social workers in the mental health services between 1962-1970. They illustrate how unrealistic was the belief that the gradual growth will meet the needs. Alternatively the Ministry's attitude demonstrates indifference toward both the social workers and their clients.

While professional autonomy was granted nearly fully only to psychiatrists, the Ministry normally preferred not to interfere in any inter-professional conflict. For example, in 1961 - nearly two years after the Act became law - MPs were informed about unclarity and anxiety among superintendents and nurses, the two groups which were afraid of being out-setted by the implications of the Mental Health Act. Mr. Robinson asked the Minister (Mr. Powell) to provide clarification (H.639, 819). Apparently the Minister was both unaware of the tensions and unwilling to intervene. The lack of awareness may be due to indifference and/or blocked communications. The unwillingness had probably more to do with the wish not to interfere with the inter-professional relationships.

Voluntary organizations were praised by the government and by MPs (H.573, 96-101). Their existence suited Conservative ideology. Yet no systematic thinking on the potential use of para-professionals and volunteers in community care had been attempted by the Ministry.

View of the public's role

The Ministry shared with the MPs the position that public tolerance has increased but needed to move further in the same direction - i.e. of accepting mental illness as physical illness (H.564, 21). No

specific plans were offered. The only direct
intervention in regard to a segment of the general
public was made when the Minister personally
rebuked the BBC for a programme on treatment of
mentally ill patients (H.600:805). The allegations
were made by ex-patients and the Minister felt that
the programme was biased against the hospitals and
professionals. The Minister never found programmes
to be biased in the opposite direction (e.g.
over-favouring professionals).

Stand taken towards patients and relatives
On several occasions the Minister opted against
extending patients' rights. In regard to
censorship, publication of leaflets on patients'
and relatives' rights, tightening up the
regulations on compulsory admission and introducing
it as a basic condition for psychopaths. At the
same time the establishment of tribunals, the
reinforcement of voluntary patienthood and the
belief in the possibility of community care for the
mentally ill point to steps taken in an attempt to
preserve certain basic rights.
    The Ministry shared with the professionals in
the field and with the majority of MPs the
assumption that patients' experiences and self
reports were less valid than those of professionals
and/or anybody else who was not suspected of being
mentally ill. Thus the government too was an
accomplice to the maintenance of labelling and
stigma. So long as this assumption was taken for
granted patients' citizens' rights were going to
have a low priority on the Ministry's agenda.
    To summarize, while acting under very
difference circumstances from those which prevailed
in 1930, the 1959 positions show striking
similarities to those taken in 1930:
1.Defending the existing system.
2.Attempting to get an unambiguous legislation
and one which is easy to operate and administer.
3.Readiness to pay lip service to community care
but lack of readiness to substantiate the
commitment by deeds.
4.Local authorities were expected to carry more
of the burden of community services than in 1930.
Yet the permissive basis and lack of direct
financial support from central government were to
remain.
5.Mental illness continued to be perceived as a
medical domain. A clear preference for
psychiatrists as heads of the professional

281

pyramid followed logically from this ideology.
The emphasis on the common features in the
two periods of study should not disguise the
differences which existed.
1.Social workers emerged as the professional
group in whom the government was ready to invest
social control authority in the psychiatric field
between the 1930 and 1959 Acts. They were given
power and authority in the 1959 legislation but
not manpower and financial resources.
The place given to this group concludes in a
nutshell the core of one of the two major
directions that evolved between 1930 and 1959.
Social work symbolized the emphasis on
psychological and social factors as well as on
providing a personalised service. Yet its task
was constructed in a way which ensured the
maintenance of social control. Moreover, the
exercise of this control secured the hegemony of
the clinical-somatic approach and a secondary
place to psychological approaches, leaving social
models as a poor third.
2.The readiness to include psychopathy as a major
mental illness category, signified a major change
in conceptualization and intervention in regard
to the mentally disturbed. a.Mental illness
categorization was used to solve difficulties in
social control and social definition of deviant
behaviour. b.Readiness to apply compulsory
detention for any one diagnosed as such and is
under 21. This decision implies a deviation from
the rule that detention in hospital is a matter
to be decided ad hoc in each case depending on
needs, rather than on a diagnostic tag. c.A
belief that hospital care for the mentally ill
offender was more humane than the one provided in
prison.
In terms of the problems with which the
government was confronted in the field of
psychiatry certain directions of resolution can be
detected.
1.Opting for chemotherapy as the main solution
for the problem of growing numbers of in and out
patients.
2.Opting for professionalism, with the consultant
psychiatrist heading the hierarchy.
3.Opting to change the existing system as little
as possible, yet allowing for experimentation
with alternatives.
4.Opting for using mental illness classification
and services as a coercive social control device.

5.Opting for tightening organizational control
and having more clearly defined bureaucratic
structure and relationships.
6.Minimizing central government's responsibility
for community psychiatric services.

7.f.The Missing Issues

1.The lack of resistance to the government's
position on community care
1.a.The government's questionable commitment to
community care has been pointed out above. MPs
who opposed the Ministry's position were aware of
it too. No MP, however, did query this mixture of
explicit endorsement and little readiness to
follow it in terms of the reasons for this
curious stand. Without understanding the
government's line of reasoning, the effectiveness
of fighting against it was seriously weakened.
1.b.At times MPs described the Ministry's
position as paying merely lip service to
community care. However no attempt was made to
expose the full scale of the hypocrisy
incorporated into the Ministry's attitude, or the
harm it entailed to the mentally distressed and
the community.
1.c.At no point did MPs appear to be considering
the obstruction of the parliamentary game as a
protest against the government's decisions. To
the contrary, they had no hesitation in endorsing
the Ministry's drafted Act and the Minister's
role in it in particular as beneficial for the
mentally ill and the future of the psychiatric
services.
Given these beliefs there was no need to
obstruct the process of debate and legislation.
Giving in over the major policy issues of the Act
was not perceived as such at all. Thus the
missing issues have to do with the specific
ideological preferences of MPs.
2.Investigating the reasons for the poor quality
of the existing psychiatric services
2.a.Surely MPs knew that within the given limits
on financial resources every Ministry enjoyed a
degree of freedom to earmark money in specific
directions. Even if the government's version on
the lack of sufficient resources was accepted the
question of priorities, cost and effectiveness of
the Ministry's decisions still stood. For
example, why would a third of the total number of

hospital beds in the NHS be allocated only 15% of
the total budget or only 10% of the Medical
Research Council money? (See Ref.16) Was an
investment in medical technology more justified
than in community centres? On what grounds? MPs
did not ask these questions, despite having
deplored publicly the facts.
2.b.Individual case descriptions and general
reading into the hospital system revealed that
the poor quality of care could not be put down
only to lack of resources. Indifference, neglect
and in some cases misjudgement and maltreatment
were in evidence. MPs did not question at all the
possible background on which such features have
developed, which is astonishing in view of the
volume of critical comments they unearthed
themselves.
3.The boundaries, definitions, content and
structure of community mental health services
have not been thought through or discussed. MPs
and the Minister never stopped to proclaim their
belief in community care. But despite mentioning
specific programmes from time to time they did
not work out a comprehensive plan of what shape
it should take in the UK.
   Community care was promoted as an alternative
to the hospital-based system. By skipping over
the stages of conceptualization and overall
planning into experiments and pragmatic
solutions, the chance of building it up as a
viable alternative was seriously curtailed.
4.No references were made to the structure of the
psychiatric services system. The NHS framework,
interdisciplinary power relations, hospitals and
local authority links, professionals in the local
authority vs. the area health authorities are
some of the components of that structural facet.
Without an attempt to look at the structure and
understand its effects any attempt to modify the
system was likely to be doomed to fail. For
example, little thought was given to the desired
degree of biting power of tribunals and the
effect of lack of such power on their position
vis-a-vis psychiatric hospitals.
5.Explanations of what leads to or causes mental
distress rarely featured in the debates. With the
exception of a few references to the aetiology of
psychopathy no other explanation has been
ventured. While more investment in research was
called for the desired content of research
initiatives was never explored.

In view of the explicit emphasis on community care the lack of any references to social factors is especially noticeable. Social variables could be seen as of either causal, precipitating or accompanying importance, but to ignore them totally stood in sharp contrast to the stated belief in community care.

6.The right for treatment. Although intervention was more frequently mentioned in the 50s debate than before. But at no point was it stated that the right for adequate psychiatric care should become part and parcel of any citizen's rights. According to the law people were receivers of intervention and certain bodies had to provide services (usually at a permissive level). Yet they were not entitled to a good quality service. In this respect the UK legislation was within the mainstream of Western world mental health legislation in the 50s. Nevertheless it is disappointing that the matter was never raised in a parliament that praised itself for being concerned with the rights of the mentally ill.

It is suggested here that a common denominator did exist behind the different missing issues listed above:

Mental illness was perceived as an integral part of the medical domain. The implications of this view were/are:

1.Medically trained people and clinical-somatic forms of intervention are the most relevant means of tackling mental distress.

2.The individual and in particular the biological component become the predominant aspects of understanding and intervention.

Such a focus excludes the different groups of which the person is a member and their impact on him/her from becoming an equally important focus of understanding and intervention.

By locating the problem in the individual the issues are defined in a specific manner. We no longer question whether a problem exists concerning the focus of attention, but move to ask what to do about it(21).

3.The missing issues listed above become of minor significance within the medical framework, while they would have been of major importance within a multi-factorial paradigm of mental distress.

This line of reasoning relates in a straightforward manner to the absence of explanations and lack of place for social factors. However it may seem rather far fetched in regard to other missing issues. In effect this argument continues to be quite central. For example, the above mentioned basic contrast on extending patients' rights was put down to the view of the insane as less responsible than the sane members of our society. Likewise patients' own accounts were seen as less valid than those of others. Any psychiatric textbook exemplifies this perspective(22).

Given the adherence to a clinical-somatic model shortages and shortcomings of existing psychiatric systems could be acknowledged as due to lack of resources. The possibility of faults in the principles or the structures of the system could not have been perceived by MPs who accepted the supremacy of this view. There was no point in creating a row with a Minister with whom one agreed in principle and when no alternative was in the offing. As mentioned above community care was permitted to emerge only as an appendix to the already existing system, seen as it was as part of the clinical-somatic approach and not as an incompatible alternative.

Two types of pragmatism met in 1959: that of British politicians and that of British psychiatry. The result of this matching was the 1959 Act and the community care policy with its advantages and disadvantages that are still with us today.

References
1.Johnson,D.M. Dodds, N. (ed)(1957) A Plea for the Slient, C. Johnson, London.
2.Johnson,D.M. (1958) Doctor in Parliament, C. Johnson, London, p.143.
3.Personal communication.
4.Accounts 1959-60, NHS 124, summarised accounts of RHA, DHSS, London, table 6, p.13.
5.Barton,R. (1959) Institutional Neurosis, Wright, Bristol.
6.Jones,K. (1972) The History of the Mental Health Services, Routledge and Kegan Paul, London, p.360, table 5.
7.Baruch,J. Treacher,A. (1978) Psychiatry Observed, Macmillan, London.
8.Ibid.
9.Royal Commission on the Law in relation to Mental Illness and Mental Deficiency, 1954-57, par.357.
10.Goffman,I. (1968) The Moral Career of the Mentally Ill. In: Asylums, Penguin, Harmondsworth, pp.117-155.
11.Henderson,D.K. (1939) Psychopathic States,

Norton, New York.
12.Macmillan,H. (1967) Riding the Storm, Macmillan, London. pp.344,366.
13.Sked,A. Cook,C. (1979) Post War Britain: A Political History, Harvester Press, London.
14.Hall,P. (1976) Reforming the Welfare, Heinemann, Lodon. pp.40-41.
15.Fein,R. (1950) Economics of Mental Illness, Basic Books, New York.
16.See ref. 4, table F, p.15.
17.Ibid, table 6, p.13.
18.Farndale,W. (1964) The Day Hospital Movement in Britain, Pergamon Press, Oxford. pp.112-3, 116-7, table F1 and F2.
19.Standing Committeee on Mental health, 1958-9, p.145.
20.Hall,P. Land,H. Parker,R. Webb,A. (1975) Change, Choice and Conflict in Social Policy, Heinemann, London.
21.Zola,I. (1972) Medicine as an Institution of Social Control, Sociological Review, 20, pp.487-504.
22.Sim,M. (1968) Guide to Psychiatry, Churchill Livingstone, Edinburgh.

8 Implications of this Study

8.a.Introduction.

The figures presented in the introduction(1)
demonstrated the current prevalence of identified
mental distress and illness. The magnitude of the
numbers involved justifies approaching mental
distress and psychiatry as public issues and not
only as a personal concern.

The Changing Political Climate.
From the end of 1973 the Western world has been
aware of an economic crisis. This awareness
contrasts with the impression of affluence
prevalent in the fifties. The eighties have
inherited a deepening economic recession which so
far shows no substantive signs of improvement.
Concurrently, the British people moved further to
the right ideologically(2). These changes,
exemplified best by the current Conservative
government, have implications for welfare policies
of which the psychiatric service is one section.
    Parton(3) has correctly identified that we
are faced with the end of the consensus of having a
welfare state and of taking for granted the duty of
our society and government to protect its
vulnerable sectors in the way we have been used to
since the Second World War. We will come back to
the specific implications of this change in section
d.i., which will look at the relationships between
the government, the politicians and the
professionals.

8.b.The Inter-relations between Politicians and
Professionals in the Twenties and the Fifties.

Bearing in mind the change in the political climate mentioned above only implications of a general nature will be looked at. The following text is based on chapters 4 and 7.

In the two periods under discussion the interaction between these two groups took basically the same form. Politicians looked up to the professionals for an overall directive as well as for detailed proposals. At the same time they saw themselves as the ultimate decision makers, who use professional knowledge as background information.

From the debates it is possible to distinguish between issues coming out of the professional fold and those initiated by the politicians. The latter were more keenly interested in the physical conditions of inpatients and in basic civil rights for this group.

In the twenties politicians were preoccupied with the risk to the sane of being certified as insane, a concern not shared by the professionals. In the fifties this interest largely disappeared, probably because of the increased public confidence in psychiatry.

The direction of restoring civil rights to in-patients, in evidence in the twenties, was strengthened in the fifties and continues to be a major issue today. Yet again it is a subject of great concern for politicians than for professionals in psychiatry. Politicians viewed themselves as guiding the public and elevating it to their level of understanding of mental distress. The inferiority of public opinion was assumed, even when an improvement in it was spoken about. Professionals' views and attitudes were seen in a different light. Their goodness and soundness were never doubted. With the acceptance of the value of expert knowledge, politicians could hardly discuss comfortably the content and methods of psychiatry. Only the legal framework of such a practice and some touches of a humanitarian approach continued to be the speciality of politicians.

Vis-a-vis the public, politicians perceived themselves as allies and equals to the professionals. In their relationships with the professionals the inferiority of the politicians was accepted as a given.

MPs and Ministers appointed themselves to the role of the intermediary between the public and the professionals, but not between the latter and their clientele.

Only once in the two periods under discussion did MPs attempt to make mental illness and psychiatry into a public issue. In 1957 Mr. Dodds and Dr. Johnson published a collection of patients' writings, A Plea for the Silent(see chapter 5). They followed it by a campaign to legislate the Royal Commission report of the same year. Although the report was largely written into the 1959 Mental Health Act, mental distress did not become a public issue.

It would seem that the two MPs failed in their task because they were branded as anti-professionals and as sensationalists. Other MPs and professionals claimed that: 1.Their allegations could not be treated seriously. 2.The material was damaging the cause the MPs were fighting for. In fact, both MPs were pro-professionals, in particular Dr. Johnson, but this belief did not blind them to faults in the psychiatric system.

The episode demonstrates how far politicians can go when they opt to rebuke some principles of a professional system, even when they are far from opposing it in general. At stake in this affair were: 1.A disagreement about the adequacy of the prevailing psychiatric model which invalidates people's understanding of their own experiences from the beginning. 2.The right of non-professionals, yet influential public figures, to challenge professional conduct. Interestingly only the second point enraged professionals and self-appointed "responsible" MPs. Perhaps the first point was left unacknowledged because of being so far removed from a context which accepts fully the right of professionals to interpret patients' experiences.

The case illustrates also the type of sanctions meted on those who appear to oppose the professional framework. The sanctions included: 1.Refusal to take the critique seriously. 2.Labelling it as underhanded and overgeneralizing. 3.Refusal by other MPs to collaborate with the culprits.

The overall attitude of accepting the superiority of professionals in psychiatry was not distributed equally towards the four professional groups. Psychiatrists were held in high esteem, nurses in sympathy without much esteem. Social workers were seen as auxiliaries to psychiatrists and psychologists were left out of consideration.

The attitude towards psychologists could be due to the small numbers involved and because their contribution was attributed to psychiatrists.

The psychologization of everyday life referred to in chapter 6, was mentioned in Parliament with due respect. It was perceived as part of psychiatry and not as coming from a distinctly different conceptual framework.

In fact, the idea the politicians adhered to was that of mental illness perceived as a physical illness - i.e. a clear preference for the disease model. The politicians' slogan got in a nutshell the message which mainstream psychiatry was providing. Accordingly, the changes in the field of mental distress were interpreted by the politicians in the light of the clinical-somatic approach.

The Government's Position.
During the two periods the government reacted as could be expected: It defended the status quo, it agreed to the not-so-drastic changes put forward by professionals and enforced regulations which secured the social control aspect of psychiatry. Both governments believed in professional autonomy as long as it went along with the social control function and therefore both legislated measures to enhance it. Equally the governments refrained from investigating the forms of approaching and intervening with recipients of the services.

As community care was largely sloganized, the government in 1959 easily got away with rejecting the Royal Commission recommendation on financing community care and making it mandatory for local authorities. This fact signified the existence of an underlying consensus among the government, the politicians and the professionals that community care needed not be taken seriously, while reaffirming the belief in the soundness of the existing psychiatric system.

In the two periods the professional literature had very little to say about politicians or the government. It is as if the last two categories did not matter for the purpose of professional activities. Legislation was covered to various degrees in professional journals and internal correspondence on its significance was published. But these contributions too did not refer directly to either MPs or the Ministry.

Perhaps the unevenness of the relationships and the cultural construction of professional activity as independent of the state and its political apparatus ware the reasons for this state of affairs.

At the same time we should not lose sight of the fact that the majority of MPs were uninterested in mental illness or health during the two periods. Usually MPs feel the need to participate under at least one of three conditions: 1.The theme relates directly to their constituency and there is pressure from below upon them to do something about the matter. 2.When they are the experts or appointed spokespersons on the specific area. 3.When an issue looks like becoming, or has already become, worthy of a public debate in the media.

With growing specialization and the general ambiguity towards mental distress the last two conditions are only rarely met. Thus only the first condition and personal interest remain as reasons for participation, i.e. reasons which are unlikely to lead to participation by the majority of MPs.

8.c.The Legacy of the Past.

8.c.i.Conceptual Approaches.
Behaviourism.
In the period that elapsed since the 1959 Act was legislated, behaviourism has consolidated its hold in academic psychology and as a respectable method of intervention. Its principles did not change from those outlined in chapter 6, though additional and more sophisticated techniques became part of its repertoire(4). Its research aspects and the theoretical work are carried out primarily by psychologists and psychiatrists.

The psychodynamic approach.
The impact of orthodox psychoanalysis has declined, but the influence of psychodynamic approaches based on specific techinques has been on the upturn, as the interest in family therapy and groupwork demonstrates. Not accidentally both examples highlight a move from a highly individualistic model to a system framework(5). Psychotherapists of different initial disciplinary background are those who develop its conceputal base.

The clinical-somatic approach
The disease model for understanding and intervening in regard to mental distress has re-emerged in full strength since the late sixties. It comprises of

two main variations; one without any social dimension and the other with a particular brand of it. In both the psychological dimension has been incorporated into the biological component and is not recognized as an independent criterion. The first version, exemplified by Hunter, Siegler and Osmond's work(6), simply does not consider the possibility of a social dimension and suggests that adherence to a medical-somatic perspective on its own is sufficient for psychiatry. In fact it relies on a sociological explanation for this source of medical authority in the eyes of lay people. It prefers however to treat this assumed authority in the same mythical fashion which it attributes to laypersons' understanding.

The second version, exemplified by the work of Wing in this country(7), is considerably more knowledgeable and sophisticated. It endorses the disease model as the basic principle for understanding and intervention in psychiatry. Yet the impairments caused by the disease are assumed to be important because of their social significance. Therefore the best way to tackle the impairments is at the level of social interaction rather than at the level of pure medical intervention. The difficulties which confront a person who suffers a mental disturbance are perceived as due to his/her vulnerability and not due to social factors, such as the reactions of the environment. The possibility of the social dimension as an independent variable is thus never confronted, because the "social" is no more than trimmings to a basic disease model. Despite the research carried out by Wing himself on the negative impact of institutionalization, at the end of the day institutionalism is viewed as a personal quality of vulnerable people and not of the institutions in which they live. Processes of self and social identity are not considered, as the following quotation demonstrates: "S. Mann and W. Cree found that only after two or three years in hospital the "new" long stay patients already wanted to stay where they were"(8). From the perspective of either psychology or sociology two or three years in a total institution for a person in a personal and social crisis are more than sufficient to secure the fear of getting out and the inability to do so on his/her own, in terms of changes in self identity and social role.

The really intriguing question is why it was found necessary to add any social component to this

version, since its conceptual use is so
insignificant within this approach. The
significance may lie in legitimizing the practice
- which is richer than any dogma - and the
dominance of psychiatrists within the field of
mental distress.

Therapeutic communities.
The model of the therapeutic community continued to
have its minority followers and in some cases has
been recreated outside hospital settings and
outside the NHS (e.g. the Richmond Fellowship).
Influenced by the anti-psychiatry approach to an
extent and even more by the US model of CMH this
type of therapeutic community is led by social
therapists with a social science background rather
than by psychiatrists. No new theoretical
innovations have emerged since the 60s.

Community mental health.
At the conceptual level the CMH approach was
refined rather than developed in new directions in
Britain since the 50s. For example, the research
into types of family interaction which may enhance
the likelihood of relapse for a person suffering
from schizophrenia(9) is valuable in terms of the
implications for practice and the understanding of
schizophrenia.
        Likewise, the research on the life of
ex-patients in the community(10) has been useful in
alerting us to the qualitative and quantitative
poverty of their life.
        The more sophisticated research on the social
origins of depression in women set out to
investigate the conceptual assumptions on the
interaction of socio-economic and psychological
factors, already looked at during the 50s in the US
in another context. This research has added
considerably to our understanding of the
specificity of such an interaction(11).

Anti-Psychiatry.
The anti-psychiatry framework is the only large
scale conceptual innovation in psychiatry which has
appeared in Britain since the 50s(12).
Anti-psychiatry was critical of the clinical
approach to people and of the assumed somatic
aetiology of mental distress. Instead it saw mental
distress as a reflection of psychological distress
rooted in family relationships, leading to an
untenable position of one family member. The

294

relationships mirror the society in which we live, its violence and contradictions. Traditional psychiatrists were seen as primarily agents of social control albeit unwittingly. Thus anti-psychiatry has produced a far reaching critique of the professionals and the society they serve. It proposed to remedy the situation by: 1.De-labelling and doing away with the classical psychiatric diagnostic system. 2.Providing psychotherapy to individuals. 3.Encouraging regression in crucial stages of distress under support. 4.Prevention of the use of physical means of intervention and hospitalization. 5.Breaking down the barrier between the severely mentally distressed and the rest of us by living toegether in a communal form.

At the more global and conceptual level it wanted to see the family reconstructed and for madness to be accepted as intelligible. Some of the pressures on members of our society were perceived as the outcome of a capitalist system of production and relationships.

The language used by the originators of this approach was geared towards preserving and presenting the subjective and intersubjective experiential component.

For its critique and proposed remedies it attracted considerable public attention during the late 60s and early 70s. Some of the non-professional attention was supportive and even enthusiastic, linking anti-psychiatry to the events of 1968 in Europe and the US. Others have criticized it for formulating a logically and philosophically unsound approach(13).

Most of the professional reactions were openly hostile, as was the Ministry's(14). Professional followers of anti-psychiatry were not allowed to practise their methods of intervention inside the NHS. It was claimed that these methods were unprofessional, unethical and damaging. The conceptual framework was attacked as promoting anarchy, subversive and as simply misunderstanding what mental distress is about.

The viciousness of the reactions stood in direct proportion to the publicity the approach received in its heyday from the media. The latter was attracted not only to the newsworthy element of anti-psychiatry but to its appeal to the subjective and inter-subjective levels of reality.

Only the issue of diagnosis led to a reasonable debate on the advantages and disadvantage of having a diagnostic system. Though no less important, the other issues raised by the anti-psychiatry approach failed to get a discussion going. Instead of re-evaluating psychiatry from within, came a defensive reaction of closing the ranks. This attitude is understandable in terms of the group's monopoly. However, it stands in contrast to the eclectic approach on which mainstream British psychiatry prides itself(15).

While anti-psychiatry had a dimension of sociological critique, it had neither a worked-out dimension of a social structure analysis nor an alternative programme for a national service system. Its retreat from the social perspective into psychodynamic and existentialist psychotherapy in the mid 70s was indicative of these shortcomings.

Although the popularity of anti-psychiatry has declined considerably since its peak it is still perceived as a threat today. Thus Mr. Fowler, Minister of Health in 1982 felt the need to declare that "First of all, the commitment in this country to community care for mentally ill people has nothing to do with the anti-psychiatry lobby"(16). Indeed, such a comment almost suggests that the fear of the impact of anti-psychiatry might have had the effect of promoting community care in Britain.

To summarize, very little has changed at the conceptual level of mainstream psychiatry since the 50s. The only far reaching critique of it was fended off, without leading to internal rethinking. Other approaches which view mental distress differently from mainstream psychiatry have been allowed to exist in the margins of the psychiatric system, perhaps because in essence they do not threaten the hegemony of mainstream thinking.

Epidemiology.
Instead of further conceptual development, considerable effort has gone into epidemiological research by mainstream psychiatry. Epidemiology is attractive for several reasons: 1.It provides a set of quantified, assumed to be scientific and objective measures and predictions. 2.It has been used successfully in public health and was related to progressive measures in that field. 3.It lends itself to further statistical analysis, especially factorial analysis. The latter had been championed already in the 50s as the royal method to sort out our conceptual problems by behaviourists (see

296

chapter 6, section 6.c.).

Epidemiology is a research tool which can be useful and powerful. Its value rests on the type of conceptual framework within which it operates, the beliefs which inform such a framework, the specific questions put and the set of information given in response. In short, a research method cannot operate without a theoretical model, no more than a computer can be constructed without a programmer.

The collection of papers "Evaluating a community psychiatric service"(17) merits our attention in considering how epidemiology has been used by the leading figures of British psychiatry. In the introduction we are told that evaluators have to ask themselves: 1.What are the needs of people who come to the services? 2.Are those needs met? 3.How do their needs compare with the needs of people with similar problems who have not come to the services?

Needs are then defined as "illness or disability for which there is effective and acceptable treatment"(18). With the exception of three pages on theory, the rest of the book is devoted to describing needs in terms of psychiatric symptoms and disabilities which are seen as the outcome of the symptoms and/or their social significance.

The logical fallacy of equating needs with symptoms or an illness for which there is treatment, thus confounding needs with both a diagnostic system and its methods of intervention a-priori, is not spotted. Moreover it does not even feel uncomfortable to the distinguished group of researchers, perhaps because they are more preoccupied with measuring than with considering what are they measuring.

In the small section on theory the senior author laments the lack of relevant sociological theory necessary for the evaluation of psychiatric services. Published in 1972, the book contains some reference to sociological studies on psychiatry, though no use is made of them. The theoretical and empirical work on small and large groups, professionalism, hospitals as organizations, deviance, conflict theories, phenomenology and hermeneutics (which concern themselves with subjective and intersubjective experiences) is not referred to, perhaps because it was all dismissed as merely literary rather than scientific work.

8.c.ii.Practice patterns.

As in the fifties the variations in the actual
practice of psychiatry in different parts of
Britain remain considerable.
Continued patterns.
1.Specialization by type of psychiatric
symptomatology, age and objective (such as
adolescent units, work with the elderly,
psychopaths, rehabilitation wards).
2.Ordinary wards in psychiatric hospital still
remain places which foster passivity and lack of
even rudimentary autonomy.
3.Psychiatric units in general hospitals(DGH).
Their share of inpatients has increased since the
50s, in particular for first admissions (see ref.
1, tables A9, A11). The preponderance of first
admissions implies that the units continue to
prefer not to have the new or old long stay
groups. The philosophy of the DGH had not changed
too.
4.Many more hostels and group homes exist now
than in the fifties, though the number of
residential, non-hospital type, placements for
the mentally ill has gone down since 1975(19).
Both types of accommodation vary from those which
follow the therapeutic community model to those
which merely offer a place to stay.
5.Social workers' attachment to GPs' practices
was innovated in the fifties, but was expanded
considerably during the seventies. Although
viewed as successful by both clients and workers
it is still up to the specific GP firm to decide
whether to have such an attachment or not(20).
6.The prescription of minor tranquillizers for
the bulk of patients who come to their GPs with
personal, social and psychiatric problems started
in the fifties but took off in a big way during
the sixties. Though no somatic aetiology is
postulated for the majority of these complaints,
chemical means of intervention are used on a
massive scale. Moreover, an adequate warning on
side-effects, likelihood of addiction and waning
effects is not provided(21).
7.Family therapy started in the fifties but has
changed considerably in content and scope since
then(22). Today it is more likely to incorporate
a system view of the family unit and focus on
bringing concrete changes to the family's life.
It is still practised almost exclusively in

out-patient clinics, primarily when the index
client is a child and where the psychiatric
symptoms fall within the category of neurosis.

New patterns.
1.Community psychiatric nursing has been provided
from the early 70s. This change is primarily one
of mode of delivery of nursing than a change in
its content. As with the introduction of the
therapeutic community (see chapter 6, section
6.c.) this move has been utilized by some nurses
to promote counselling(23). However the majority
of psychiatric nurses are still employed inside
the hospital.
2.Crisis intervention services have emerged in
the 70s(24). These services operate on a 24 hour
basis, with a multi-discplinary team. They aim
primarily at the prevention of hospitalization.
Intervention takes place where the clients are,
though the latter still have to be referred by
another professional. Despite the demonstrated
success in preventing admission only very few
such services exist throughout the country.
3.Walk-in centres operate in some cities, where
they are run mainly by voluntary
organizations(25). Centres offer an alternative
social network and at times counselling.
4.Likewise emergency consultation on the
telephone is available via voluntary agencies.
5.Attention to the different cultural frameworks,
the implication of emigration and race relations
led to the consideration of the differentiated
needs of clients from ethnic minorities(26).
6.Mutual-help groups(27). This development,
together with feminist therapy, has been the most
radical innovation to emerge since the fifties.
It is radical because it marks a departure from
the majority of professional models of practice
and understanding of mental distress. It affirms
the value of subjective and intersubjective
experiences away from the clinical model. The
approach is based on the recognition of the
strength of this vulnerable sector of the
population, of the strength of group vs.
individualistic approaches to mental distress and
on the tacit acceptance that "The Community" does
not exist. Therefore alternative social networks
have to be created to support the mentally
distressed. How far it could/should replace
professional intervention is open to debate, but
it has demonstrated its usefulness in conjunction

with such an intervention and without it. Mutual-help is open to abuse either by providing a very authoritarian structure, by being "colonized" by professionals and local government, or by being used ideologically as a means to privatize psychiatric care.

7.Feminist therapy(28) has often been located in mutual-help groups, but also outside this method. It has been the outcome of a change in consciousness, theoretical work and the recognition of the limits of existing paradigms of practice. It clearly incorporates a social structure dimension and recognizes basic social conflicts. At the same time it does not neglect the subjective facet or the place of individuals within relevant groupings.

Those services which exclude men from receiving support perpetuate the ideology and practice of exclusion of the mentally distressed, even if unintentionally.

8.Regional secure units. One outcome of the de-designation of the mental hospitals, legislated in the 1959 Act, was the refusal of many hospitals to have patients with a record of aggressive behaviour. The special hospitals could not sort out this problem given the limited number of places they have. Moreover, patients stayed longer than required in these institutions because of the refusal of the ordinary hospitals to have them.

Thus the idea of a range of secure units was born. In contrast to the treatment of community care policies the necessary sum of money was earmarked for this purpose in 1974. However, up to now (1984) not many authorities have taken up the offer and established such units(29). Cases of misuse of the funds have been documented too. The main resistance to this idea comes from the nursing staff who feel that they will have to carry the brunt of the work with an undesirable group of clients.

The policy and its fate provide an intriguing case for investigating the relationships between central government, health regions, local government and the professionals. It also touches on the delicate relationships beteen social control vs. care in the role definitions of professionals and the balance of power among the different professional groups.

In a field as wide as mental distress different types of practice patterns are required.

A crucial issue is whether the most frequently practised methods are the most useful for the problems at hand.

Frequency.
Practice forms based on the disease model lead the league. The more innovative models are in a tiny minority, more likely to be practised by non-psychiatrists, outside the NHS than inside it. In addition the more innovative forms tend to be more available to middle-class than to working-class consumers.

Despite the variability of practice patterns, in terms of establishing community psychiatric services we see primarily the application of the clinical-somatic approach outside the hospital grounds. The massive use of minor tranquillizers signifies the use of psychiatric knowledge to contain the possible threat of psychologization to socially acceptable answers for individual unhappiness. At the same time this type of intervention widens the brief of psychiatry and reaffirms one of its major social functions, albeit one which the profession refuses to acknowledge (i.e. social control).

The non-professional voluntary sector.
This sector is an original British contribution, unparalleled elsewhere in the Western world. It does not constitute one form of practice, but is singled out here as a form of organization.

Voluntary organizations proliferated in the 60s and the 70s. Some are based on relatives' involvement and some are not. Those with a strong component of relatives in them come across as the more conservative associations and as the most ardent believers in the disease model. The other type of organization is more critical of the established professional wisdom and more innovative in its intervention. All of them offer valuable support to a group in dire need of it. In the current structure of the psychiatric services the contribution of the voluntary organizations covers a relatively small part.

Delicate and ambiguous relationships exist between the government - the provider of the bulk of financial resources - and these organizations. The incident in 1979 in which MIND was threatened with the withdrawal of its grant unless it toed the line on patients' rights offers one pertinent example.

The current government would like to see an increase in the activities of the voluntary sector, as part of its attempts to privatize the health system. This issue will be discussed further in section d.i.

To summarize, the practice is considerably richer than the theoretical perspective of mainstream psychiatry. So far, in contrast to the direction of developments in the US, a proliferation of practices aimed at positive valorization of mental health has not taken place in Britain.

8.c.iii.Legislation since the 50s.

The lack of definition of directives for practice of community care which typified the 1963 paper "Community Care" has been mentioned already in chapter 7.

Between 1963 and 1975 there were no ministerial official papers on psychiatry. This lull in attention was shared by Labour and Conservative governments alike.

Even the appointment of Mr. K. Robinson, usually active in Parliament in this field, to the post of Minister of Health in 1966, did not lead to any significant change. Mr. Robinson himself felt quite frustrated at the rough treatment meted on the budjet for health by the rest of the cabinet (personal communication). However, as many issues in psychiatry are not so dependent on additional resources but on direction and reallocation, the scope for change without additional sums of money was left untapped. The impetus for such a move had to come from mainstream psychiatry for it to be taken up by the Minister, a faithful supporter of it. Such an initiative did not surface.

The 1975 White Paper "Better Services for the Mentally Ill" (Cmnd.6233) came out as part of the intention to restructure the NHS and in the wake of the restructuring of the personal social services. Its content distills the British experience in the various parts of the country into one framework, which is centred on the needs of the mentally ill. The paper focuses on the organizational aspect and pays attention to the coordination of the available services. The district service - divided into health and social services - becomes the key service of the future.

The document treats the needs of the clientele not so much by symptoms and diagnostic categorization as by degree of impairment and needs which arise out of it.

Although professional roles are discussed, the content of intervention is not. Thus the aspect of the quality of the service is left out of the paper. As to quantity, the writers admit to the severe lack of resources for community services, but do not provide any explanation for it.

Positive developments in psychiatry are still interpreted in the paper as primarily the result of the "drug revolution". It is assumed that the public is not ready to have the mentally ill in its midst, but the issue of whether "The Community" is a viable entity is not mentioned. Attitudes of professionals towards community care are left out too. Until now (1984) this paper is the only one of two to concern itself with the rationale and organization of community-based services. Significiantly it was not seen as a basis for legislation.

The other paper pertaining to community services is the 1981 Green paper "Care in the Community", which proposes flexible joint funding between health and social services. However, it still envisages that ultimately social service funding will become responsible for projects started by joint funding. This principle brings to the open the underlying motive of the exercise, namely the transfer of financial responsibility from central to local government.

The Review of the 1959 Act, published in 1978 (Cmnd 7320) was based on consultations with the different professional and voluntary bodies. It was clearly influenced by the work of MIND's legal department. The most radical measure to be suggested in the review was the one concerned with procedures for consent and consultation on irreversible treatment.

The acceptance of the notion of an irreversible physical intervention marks an abrupt change from the enthusiasm expressed in the 50s for the same methods.

It introduces a note of caution about the value of such methods and the soundness of psychiatrists' judgement. The review proposed to set up local committees composed of professionals and lay people who would re-assess the need for such an intervention, even if the patient has given his consent to it.

The paper suggested also an increase in the frequency of appeals to review tribunals and to make it mandatory for tribunals to review detained patients' circumstances periodically without their requests. These proposals follow closely admendments tabled by Labour MPs in the 1959 debate.

The statistics relating to the activities of the tribunals between 1961-1976(30) demonstrate that they were underused systematically by eligible patients. The majority of the decisions taken by the review body followed largely professionals' views and not those of patients. Moreover, in cases which demand a Home Office decision the latter took a long time to deliberate and often decide against the panel's recommendations. On the whole patients were not given adequate support and advice concerning their future plans and therefore hardly stood a chance in the appeal against the reasoned argumentation put forward by professionals. It is therefore intriguing to consider what led the authors of the 1978 review paper to suggest an imposed increase in the use of tribunals. Was it the wish for justice to be seen to be carried out? Was it the hope that if enforced, tribunals would have a sufficient impetus to become less one sided?

The accreditation of social workers was put forward in the review. Thus the 1959 failure to ensure that social workers in psychiatry would be qualified was taken a step further on the ladder of defined professionalism.

Concerning community care the 1978 paper took a conservative line. It reaffirmed the lip service commitment to it but stopped short of introducing measures to ensure that community care would indeed be implemented. It rejected the proposal by the British Association of Social Workers (BASW) for community care orders(31), but did not come up with any other suggestion instead.

The 1978 paper did not follow the 1975 proposals, including those which did not require more money even though both were the products of Labour governments. Was it because it was assumed that we have already a good community care policy? Was it the lack of belief in the value of legislation to bring about policy changes? Was it fear of imposing policies on professionals who have not shown signs of wanting to promote them? These hypotheses attest to the general apathy among politicians, civil servants and the professionals in regard to this issue.

The 1983 Mental Health Amendments Act accepted the majority of proposals set up in the 1978 paper. Significantly the new Act does not replace the 1959 one in toto, because the latter is still considered to be a reasonable and relevant law to today's issues.

The 1983 amendments put the only innovative proposal of the 1978 review safely back into the fold of doctors. No lay members or members of other professions can sit on the committee which will deal with irreversible treatment. Nevertheless psychiatrists have expressed recently anxiety concerning possible limits put on their autonomy as the result of the legislation in toto(32).

The expansion of the tribunals' work is closely linked to the creation of the Mental Health Commission. The commission will be a public body of inspection in special hospitals and for detained patients elsewhere. The work will be executed mainly by professionals who will carry out their duties on a paid part-time basis.

The government has proposed to spend four millions pounds per year on the commission, or on 5% of the total inpatient population. As for the remaining 95% of this group and the many more who are known to be mentally distressed outside the hospital sector, the amendments and the government have little to offer.

We should be asking ourselves why should a government so keen to trim public expenditure especially for the non-productive part of the population - be ready to part with four millions annually for a body which will serve a very small number of people. The Home Office social service - the probation service - has been traditionally allocated more generous resources than the personal social services, relative to the size of the clientele it serves. Traditionally legislation on mental distress preoccupied itself primarily with those seen as a threat to the social order. The 1983 Act follows most loyally this tradition.

The more pressing reason was provided by the exposed scandals concerning the way detained patients were treated in Rampton recently(33). Similar incidents, but on a smaller scale, have been reported about the other special hospitals, sufficiently to put across the message that something is basically wrong with the special hospitals system. Instead of investigating the system and its structure, instead of attempting to change it - the government has opted for an inspectorate which will not have the power to enforce change but will have the duty to act as a watchdog.

While the Mental Health Commission may be carrying out its functions admirably it has been designed as a means to allow the existing system to continue without a proper reappraisal.

The 1983 Act legislates that social workers participating in certification have to pass a professional examination leading to their approval as capable of carrying out this task. Little doubt is left as to the social control function of this specific job. The examining body (CCETSW) is keen to use the process in order to broaden the knowledge base of social workers beyond certification. Whether this aim will be met is too early to assess. The fact that the DHSS has refused to allocate resources for this training component casts doubts on the wish of the Ministry to further the education of social workers in this direction.

The status of guardianship has been strengthened in the new legislation to include the use of services in the community. Consent for treatment, however, has been specifically excluded from the guardian's rights and duties.

Via the regulations on guardianship local authorities may have to provide community facilities for those who were under compulsory hospitalization but who are judged as fit to live in the community under close supervision. It is too early to know what this regulation would mean when implemented and if a local authority will be penalized for not complying with it.

To summarize the 1983 legislation strengthens the formal civil rights of detained patients and attempts to ensure reasonable standards of physical care and respect towards them.

As in 1959, the 1983 legislation reflects on problem areas within the psychiatric system for the government and the politicians.

Community care remained a low priority area: the legislation offers virtually nothing on community care and standards of professional practice for the 95% of the clientele of the psychiatric services.

The Ministry of Health has claimed on several occasions that there is no need to make local authorities' duties for mentally distressed people mandatory as they are already in this category by virtue of the Ministry's regulations. The variations and shortages of basic aftercare and residential services throughout the country cast considerable doubt on the validity of this assertion. Legally speaking, a lawsuit filed

306

against a local authority for breach of its
obligations to a mentally ill person will be thrown
out of court because the authority has no statutory
duty to provide such services. Thus the fine
distinction between "mandatory" and "statutory"
seems to be the crucial one.

8.c.iv.Professional roles and power.
The most radical shift in professional roles has
occurred in nursing. For the first time nurses have
started to work in the community with mentally
distressed adults. Some of them act as social
therapists while others are content with
administering doctors' orders. Yet - as already
mentioned - the majority of nurses still work
solely inside the hospitals. No attempt to
encourage a dual role - i.e. inside and outside the
hospital simultaneously - has been made so far.
        Psychologists can opt to be more involved in
psychotherapy and less in testing, as many of the
new generation of clincial psychologists prefer.
They tend to work more independently of
psychiatrists than in the 50s, especially those of
them who are involved in planning community support
services.
        The majority of social workers in psychiatric
settings are qualified by now. Nearly all of them
are employed by the local authority rather than by
the respective health authority, following the
reorganization of the personal social services in
the early 70s. Social workers in social services
departments are considerably more autonomous than
they used to be. However, working with the mentally
distressed has a low priority on the scale based on
attending first to statutory duties. (For a
critical description and evaluation of recent
mental health social work in social services
department see Fisher et al.(34).) Thus psychiatric
social workers (psw) in specialized settings (e.g.
child guidance) are engaged more than before in
psychotherapeutic work, while their colleagues in
the social services are carrying out less work of
this type.
        Specialized work in psychiatry has remained a
prestigious occupation in social work. Psw engage
now more in crisis intervention and problem-solving
work is taking place, side by side with family
therapy and groupwork.
        As a whole social work has been more
influenced by sociological models during the 60s
and 70s than have the three other groups. However,

this influence is less prevalent in its psychiatric sector than in other areas of social work: psw remained mainly psychotherapeutically orientated.

The accreditation of social workers under the 1983 legislation mentioned above may lead to a considerable change in the current place of mental health work within the structure of social services and to a change in its direction. Many psw would like to see a specialized service for the mentally distressed emerging inside social services. Such a service raises considerable conceptual and ethical issues vis-a-vis the rest of social work, the notion of generic social work, the risk of segregating the mentally distressed by having a specialized service and the relationships with the health services. The conceptual and practice contributions of social work will have to be re-evaluated prior to introducing such a drastic change. If this move does take place a shift in power relations between social workers and the three other groups will occur too.

Pertaining to psychiatrists, it is difficult to pinpoint any major change in direction. Some psychiatrists have moved into psychotherapy, either the psychodynamic type, behaviour modification or family therapy. The role of the psychiatrist as a psychotherapist has become more reputable within mainstream psychiatry than it was in the fifties.

The majority, however, remain where it was in the fifties: i.e. eclectic in regard to different types of physical intervention, ready to refer people for psychotherapy for delineated problems or when chemical intervention has failed to bring change. The adherence to the disease model has remained too, side by side with the scepticism towards other approaches, in particular towards social strategies. For example, Brown and Harris' research into the social origins of depression (see ref.11) has been acclaimed as a good study by eminent psychiatrists. Yet its implications for the practice of psychiatry with working-class mothers have not been taken account of in the discussion of their work. The inherent pragmatism has been useful in preventing a high degree of dogmatism, but equally it arrested any real change in the role definition.

Psychiatrists continue to head all of the services within the NHS. The fact that many of them now work outside a hospital setting has not led to a reappraisal of their role and philosophy.

Thus all four professional groups have gained

in power and autonomy, but some gained more than
others - i.e. consultant psychiatrists and social
workers. Despite the greater autonomy of the other
professions they have not challenged the dominant
position of psychiatrists but largely continued to
accept it(35).
Several issues need to be taken up in
conjunction with this development.
1.To what extent was the increase in professional
power and autonomy accompanied by a growth in
conceptual knowledge, skills and refinement of
the value preferences system?
2.As the analysis of professional literature
demonstrated only social workers were aware of
their role as intermediaries between the clients
and the broader social system. What was the
effect of further upgrading of formal
professionalism on the awareness and performance
of this role?
3.Is a higher degree of formal professionalism an
advantage or a disadvantage to the quality of
services offered and the relationships between
professionals and their clients?
Considerable doubt on the benefit of an ever
increasing professionalism has been expressed by
sociologists in the last decade concerning
general medicine. Similar criticism came from
consumers' associations, promoters of the
mutual-help orientation and from Marxist-oriented
critiques of social work(36).
4.In particular, the value of formal
professionalism and the clinical approach to
clients in psychiatry should be questioned in
connection with the attempt to establish
community based psychiatric services. Both formal
professionalism and the clinical approach
accentuate the inherent inequality in power
between a service provider and a client. The
vulnerability of the latter is thus increased
rather than decreased, contrary to the
professional aims. If such services are to
encourage self-referral and to be used as an
intermediary for the benefit of consumers and
their society then such a consequence is
self-defeating.

8.d.The Challenge.

8.d.i.Background:

a.Relationships among central government, politicians and professionals in psychiatry.

The change in the political climate and its implications for welfare policies was the starting point of this chapter. It closely ties with the formal preference of the current government to transfer its obligations towards the mentally distressed to local authorities, voluntary organizations and the female members of the nuclear family. Given the cracks in the consensus on welfare policies, the government's interpretation of community care as a method of establishing cheap and privatized care as much as possible is being put forward, despite the knowledge of the damaging effects of such policies in the US (see ref. 44). Some of the implications for the unpaid carers have been discussed in a recent publication by Finch(37).

More than in the 50s the current government does not shy away from imposing its wishes if they are not met otherwise. Therefore at one level it listens less to MPs, local politicians, civil servants and professionals. Yet because of its belief in capitalism and technology the government is bound to rely on experts who follow its value preferences. In fact we have seen recently several cases in which experts were brought from the outside and promoted above the heads of the civil service experts. Thus far from not depending on professionals, this government depends on them to carry out the massive changes from the recent past that it wants to achieve. Not least, professionals are needed to provide legitimation for this move.

While wanting to transfer the continuous care for the mentally distressed outside the NHS, the Ministry realizes that psychiatrists are the dominant professional group with whom the government has to come to an agreement rather than with social workers. The belief in the supremacy of medicine and the natural sciences creates a lasting bond between mainstream psychiatry and most governments, making the alliance desirable for both sides.

Thus for tactical and ideological reasons the direction of the Ministry's policy on mental distress is bound to be less straight-forward than it looks at the moment.

Up to now the government's economic policy has not led to redundancies of established personnel in psychiatry. This may happen in the near future to psychiatric nurses, as will be indicated in the next section. One of the issues is whether the realistic possibility of being made redundant would lead to a shift in the relationships with central government and to a re-evaluation of the professional role.

The place of local government in the changing welfare scene.
This study focused on central government, leaving local authorities out of the discussion for reasons stated in the introduction. Recently the power of local government has been eroded further by central government. At the same time the latter declared its wish to transfer the responsibility for community psychiatric services to the local level. There is no evidence to show that central government has considered the implications of such a move apart from the short-term financial aspect, though this policy fits well conservative ideology about the diffusion of power.

The Italian experience, referred to below, (see ref.42) demonstrates the possibility of using the local level of government to promote a radical change of the psychiatric system, provided it has real biting power over health, welfare and financial resources.

Such a move will necessitate the restructuring of the relationships between psychiatrists and nurses and the local authority as well as between health and local authorities. It will also imply strengthening the power of local government vis-a-vis central government in this field, an orientation which current central government activities have contradicted so far.

8.d.ii.Proposed policies for the future of the psychiatric services in Britain.
Recently, following the government's pressure, several policy documents on psychiatry have been published . Dr. Dick's paper, published in February 1983, ("The Components of a Comprehensive Psychiatric Service", DHSS advisory service) merits our attention because it represents both mainstream psychiatry and the DHSS professional thinking on the future of the psychiatric services.

Part I of the document outlines the desirable services for nine areas of psychiatry (e.g. general psychiatry, chronic mental illness, forensic psychiatry, childhood psychiatry). Under the heading of each such area the long list of services available in the country is mentioned.

311

Part II does the same for psychiatry in primary health care, in social services, housing, voluntary organizations and in self help and informal care. Part III suggests organizational arrangements.

Apart from the broad objective "to contain and eventually reduce the psychiatric morbidity" we are not provided with a rationale for what needs to be changed in psychiatry or why. No order of priorities for the services listed is porvided. Standards of quality or quantity are not mentioned.

The document does not discuss the possibility of hospitals' closure, though it states the desirability of intervention in the community. No reference is made to processes of closure or running down of existing institutions.

It may be therefore concluded that mainstream psychiatry sees no reason for change in the psychiatric services and it has not come up with a programme to do so. With few exceptions, this paper could have been written in the 50s.

The nurses' unions stand to lose by a systematic closure of mental hospitals, as their members are more likely to be made redundant than any other professional group. It became therefore essential that they should consider and state their views on the future of the psychiatric services.

So far neither COHSE nor the RCN have demanded a full redeployment policy. Instead COHSE(38) has proposed that all of the services for the mentally distressed be part of the NHS. It reasons this suggestion by what it sees as an unqualified success of the health services vs. the failure of social services in dealing with health matters. The paper does not pause to ask for the reasons for failure or to state criteria for either success or failure.

The document does not come up with a redefined role for all nurses in a system in which hospitals will not play a major role. Instead it reaffirms its belief in the medicalization of mental distress and hopes to spare its members' jobs by staying inside the health service. As in Dr. Dick's paper we are left in the dark as to why any change is necessary.

Community health councils and social services departments in various parts of the country have come up too with proposals for the restructuring of the psychiatric system(39).

Though the underlying assumptions of these documents are not made explicit, it is possible to

312

detect that they are adopting the view of mental distress as primarily a problem of living and not as a medical issue. These groups are very far from negating the value of mainstream psychiatric contributions, but the place of psychiatry in community services becomes limited once mental distress is viewed as a reflection of problems of living.

The proposals include use of local hospital facilities, walk-in centres run by social workers and volunteers, multidisciplinary crisis intervention teams, a backbone of community psychiatric nursing services, sheltered accommodation and day centres. In itself the list is not different from the one provided in Dr.Dick's document, only its rationale is made clearer.

None of the papers mentions redeployment, although some of them call for consultation with the staff, patients and local residents. Equally they do not suggest the gradual dismantling of the psychiatric hospital sector and processes of preparation for it.

Not even one of the papers acknowledges the non-existence of a vernacular community in most urban centres. Consequently they do not disucss the ramifications and implications of this act.

In 1982 the Ministry of Health sent a directive to all regional health authorities requiring them to attempt to close large psychiatric institutions. Several such authorities have recently decided to follow up this instruction, providing us with an indication of what is implied by a policy of closure of hospitals in present day Britain.

We will look at only one such available example. North East Thames has proposed the closure of two out of six psychiatric hospitals in the region and turning the rest into the headquarters of district services. In preparation for the consultation and decision making following the declaration of intent the region has:

1.Published its own criteria for the proposed closure, based on accessibility and financial considerations(40).
2.Asked for proposals from the involved districts on the system they would like to establish instead of the current one (but gave them a short period in which to do so).
3.Commissioned a study on patients' needs if closure occurs. In the study nurses and

psychiatrists' opinion on patients' needs were
asked for. Patients' own views were not
investigated, or those of their available
relatives and the rest of the staff inside and
outside the hospital.
4.Commissioned a financial feasibility study and
an evaluation of the feasibility stage.

At the end of these processes the region has
finally decided to close down one of the two
hospitals and to run down considerably the second
institution within a period of 5-8 years. Instead,
the inpatient population will go to other
hospitals, including DGH units or to various
housing schemes. Simultaneously it decided to cut
down by half the budget requested by the districts
for the development of community services. Yet its
chief medical officer claims that the region will
provide all of the services required for the
transfer of these patients and no additional input
would be expected from the local social services
departments(41). It is difficult to see in this
scheme, as it stands now, a major reprogramming of
the psychiatric system in the region.
Considerable opposition to this modest plan
of restructuring has emerged among the staff
groups. In one hospital the staff has enlisted the
support of the local MPs to prevent any change. One
of these two MPs happens to be the Prime Minister,
the other a left-of-centre Labour MP.

8.d.iii.Major developments in community mental
health outside Britain.
The study presented here has focused on Britain,
therefore only the lessons of major developments
outside this country will be referred to. The CMH
model has been developed further in particular in
the US and in Italy(42).
The US approach accepted the contribution of
labelling theory to understanding stigmatization
processes of the mentally ill. It did not agree
with these theorists on the lack of primary,
non-social, reasons for such deviancy. In certain
instances, however, social factors were accepted as
of aetiological importance(43).
The Americans have also realized that in a
highly industrialized society "the community" is a
rare bird. Therefore the creation of alternative
networks to support mentally distressed people was
given consideration as part of the CMH system.
The US approach called for the restructuring

of the psychiatric system by:

1.Running down and eventual closure of hospitals.
2.Creating CMH centres.
3.Establishing walk-in centres.
4.Using para-professionals and encouraging mutual-help groups.
5.Offering individual and group psychotherapy as the main method of intervention (though retaining physical means too).
6.Working with at-risk groups.
7.Attempting to educate the public towards greater tolerance of people under mental distress.

An implicit assumption was that a change in the psychiatric system is possible without a corresponding change in the attitude of the professionals. As well as working in the public sector, many of these professionals were working in the private one, where a very different set of preferences prevailed. In addition no upgrading of the welfare system was postulated as a necessary pre-condition for a radical change of the psychiatric sector. Thus the fact that many mentally distressed people are also poor people was ignored.

The 1963 federal legislation encouraged the beginning of innovative CMH schemes unevenly spread across the country. When federal financing was gradually coming to its end, it was largely left to each state to decide how to run its psychiatric services. Often local politicians used the CMH approach as a device to economize on state expenditure, by establishing third rate community services which became largely drug dispensaries. Moreover, many discharged patients went to live in private establishments where the wish for profit, rather than care, was the prime motive.

Instead of the provision of public-sponsored services people suffering from mental distress have been given the right to treatment and a limited form of right to refuse proposed interventions. To have the right to a non-existent or poor quality service makes a mockery of both civil and professional values.

The American experience shows that good community psychiatric services are not as cheap as was envisaged in the 50s, as well as demonstrating how harmful cheap care could be(44).

Today, the American system is highly

diversified. Its most recent development, unparalleled in Britain, is the focus on psychological intervention for the sake of promotion of mental health of people without any identified psychological or psychiatric problems. This development is taking place in the private sector and caters for the affluent component of the population. Castel, Castel and Lovell (see ref. 42) have recently described and analysed this trend, which they see primarily as an extension of the social control function of psychiatry.

The Italian approach started from an angle radically different from the American position, even though a number of similarities exist.

For the Italian professional pioneering group - Psichiatria Democratica - the place of the mentally ill in our society is the reflection of social contradictions and repression and not so much the outcome of individual pathology, even though the existence of mental distress is not denied. Hospitals are aimed more at containing madness than at curing it. The way out of the deadlock which hospitalization signifies includes:

1. Change of consciousness inside and outside the hospital. For this purpose patients are not only treated individually with respect but are also seen as part of a collective which has gradually the power to reach and implement decisions.
2. The change outside the hospital has to include policy changes by local health and social administration, local political parties and the general population. It is the professionals' task to initiate and participate in these processes.
3. Mental hospitals should be gradually dismantled in a process which enables residents to become more in control over their everyday life.
4. The process of closing down hospitals must be accompanied by the establishment of CMH centres run on an informal basis as walk-in centres.
5. It is the totality of the person's needs to which attention should be directed rather than to his/her psychiatric symptoms.
6. Professional activity is never value-free. It is always guided by value preferences. To assume otherwise is to engage in recreating the myth of the professional who is above society's concerns and conflicts.

These ideas were translated first into local programmes and later into a national mental health law in 1978. The law is unique in two aspects: 1.It states the aim of closure of psychiatric hospitals and legislates the steps towards this objective. 2.A policy of no redundancies due to the reform was legislated. Staff employed in the hospital sector had to be redeployed.

It is too early for a full evaluation of the Italian reform. So far it has demonstrated that on the whole it is possible to close down the hospitals without creating chaos and do so in a way which respects the clients, provided the alternative network of services is established simultaneously.

The process of the Italian reform offers insight into the processes of change in professional consciousness and roles. Such a change was facilitated by the lengthy collective work done in the hospital with inpatients and staff prior to dismantling them.

The ability of British professionals and the general public to learn from the experiences of other models and countries depends on the degree of openness and readiness for reappraisal of its own system. Learning should not imply imitating, but more a process of examining the relevance of other systems to the needs of the British population.

Summary.
Throughout this book I have not taken the position that psychiatry is merely an exercise in social control. I have viewed it as a combination of control and care, where the balance is modified in accordance to the social context and professional contributions. Consequently, the model on which a psychiatric system is structured matters to its impact on care and control. The summary is written in the light of this belief.

The message from the British, American and Italian contexts is that politicians follow the intitatives of professionals in psychiatry and not vice versa. Politicians can improve on or make worse the direction offered by the professionals, but in the society in which we live they cannot alter it radicaly without the overt and/or covert consensus of the latter.

Yet both professionals and politicians work within a specific social context. The Italian experience, the reaction of mainstream British psychiatry to the anti-psychiatry aproach; the reaction of the British government to the recent Rampton scandals - all point to the importance of making psychiatry into a public issue, beyond parliamentary debates. These instances demonstrate also that it is possible to do so under certain circumstances.

By now, despite the assumption of ignorance and hostility on behalf of the general public towards mentally distressed people the author believes that there is sufficient heterogeneity of views among the public. This quality could be put to positive use in a wide ranging public debate on psychiatric policies. Such a dialogue would also encourage internal reappraisal among the professionals.

Equally there is a place for the joint pressure by professionals and public on the government for an improvement of psychiatric policies and services.

But above all mental distress and the psychiatric service system should become a public issue because they are social policy issues with clear moral underpinnings. The proposed closure of the hospitals, the fate of the residents and the staff and the alternative service system have brought to the open the undeniable value preference implications of psychiatric policies.

Despite official declarations the British psychiatric system since the 50s has continued principally in the mould of the clinical-somatic approach, yet calling it community care when practised outside a hospital.

This study has documented how most professionals, in particular psychiatrists, and the politicians have not come to terms with the need for a real reconceptualization and restructuring of the psychiatric services if community care is to be established. To the contrary, considerable effort has gone into reaffirming and perpetuating the system as it is.

Superficially, the current system functions relatively smoothly in its controlling aspect. However, even within this dimension recent legislation was found to be necessary to wallpaper over the cracks (i.e. the 1983 Mental Health Amendments).

The system functions less well in its caring and rehabilitative aspects, despite having a caring group of staff.

The dismissive approach towards subjective and intersubjective meaning and social science knowledge are reflected in the invalidating attitude towards the clientele, in ignorance of and

318

lack of use of non-medical knowledge.

As in the 50s, professionals are claiming today that a large proportion of the long-stay and "new" long-stay patients could live outside the psychiatric hospital. But none of them has posed the question what has been done so far to prevent this group from becoming chronic in the first place. Similarly, nobody has been asking why ordinary hospital wards are still fostering physical dependence at such a detrimental cost to the patients and the staff.

The poor quality of life in the community of the bulk of those who have been inpatients is allowed to continue because it is not judged as a priority from a disease perspective. The failure to see the connection between the quality of life outside a total institution and the rate of readmission is astonishing, even from a "pure" administrative perspective.

The drugging of the majority of those who express unhappiness can be seen as a major exercise of social containment of dissatifaction. But let us not forget that it also represents a major deviation from the stated value preferences of every one of the involved professional group.

For its own reasons and in its own way the current government is forcing British psychiatry to reconsider its options. At this crucial period it is important to remember that the American, British and the Italian experiences demonstrate that in order to establish community based psychiatric services a well developed conceptual framework is not a luxury, but a necessity. The diversity of the CMH approaches and practice has come to mean by now that everything is possible under this umbrella. A rigorous reconceptualization is therefore called for which will take into account the lessons of the past.

For example, the absence of a vernacular community in the industrialized world must be taken into account in any future conceptualization, policy decision and implementation of community care. Some of the directions which can be utilized to compensate in part for the lack of this major component have been demonstrated in Italy and by the mutual-help and feminist movements elsewhere.

Perhaps an even more crucial component is the change in attitudes of professionals, the politicians and the general public towards mental distress and the objectives of the psychiatric system.

However, attitude change is a notoriously difficult task, especially when the interest of the dominant professional group is seen as vested in not changing the system.

Yet because psyciatry is an integral part of the social context in which it operates it cannot stay uninfluenced by changes in the cultural perceptions of and attitudes towards mental distress. Such a change may come via a minority professional group in a climate of social change.

References.
1.The statistics are taken from two sources:
a.DHSS, Personal and Health Statistics, 1982.
b.DHSS, Inpatients Statistics from the Mental Health Inquiry for England, 1980.
2.Bosanquet, N. (1983) After the New Right, Heinemann, London.
3.Parton, N. (1981) Rise and Fall of the Welfare Consensus, Social Work Today, 12, 34, pp.9-12.
4.Trower, P. et al. (1978) Social Skills and Mental Health, Methuen, London.
5.Minuchin, S. (1967) Families of the Slums, Basic Books, New York.
Pincus, L., Dare, C. (1982) Secrets in the Family, Tavistock, London.
6.Hunter, R. (1973) Psychiatry and Neurology: Psychosyndrome or Brain Disease, Proceedings of the Royal Society of Medicine, 66, pp.17-22.
Siegler, M., Osmond, H. (1974) Models of Madness, Models of Medicine, Macmillan, New York.
7.Wing. J. K. (1978) Reasoning about Madness, Oxford University Press, London.
8.Ibid, p.133.
9.Brown, G.W. et al. (1972) Influence of Family Life on the Course of Schizophrenic Disorders. A Replication, British Journal of Psychiatry, 121, pp.241-258.
Leff, J. (1976) Schizophrenia and Sensitivity to the Family Environment, Schizophrenia Bulletin, vol.2, pp.566-574.
10.Hughes, D. (1979) How Psychiatric Patients Manage out of Hospital, Disability Alliance and the Mental Health Foundation.
O'Callaghan, M. (1984) Rehabilitation and Community Care: Working Together. In: Reed, J., Lomas, G. (eds) Psychiatric Services in the Community, Croom Helm, London.
11.Brown, G., Harris, T. (1978) The Social Origin of Depression, Tavistock, London.
12.Laing, R. D. (1960) The Divided Self, Tavistock,

London.

Laing, R. D., Cooper, D. (1964) Reason and Violence, Tavistock, London.

Cooper, D. (1967) Anti-Psychiatry, Penguin, Harmondsworth.

Laing, R. D. (1971) The Politics of the Family, Tavistock, London.

13.See, for example, the article in the Sunday Times of 19.5.68 and the publication: Cooper, D. (ed) (1968) Dialectics of Liberation, Penguin, Harmondsworth.
For the critique of the anti-psychiatry approach from a sociological perspective see: Coulter, J. (1973) Approaches to Insanity, Robertson, London.

14.See ref. no.6.

15.See statement on eclecticism in: Clare, A. (1978) Psychiatry in Dissent, Tavistock, London, chapter 2.

16.Fowler, N. (1982) Working Together - an introduction, MIND annual conference, Mind Publications, Leeds. p.5.

17.Wing, J. K. et al. (1972) Evaluating a Community Psychiatric Service, Oxford University Press, London.

19.Ibid, p.15.

19.Hansard, vol. 951, p.437.

20.Corney, R. (1981) Clients' Perspectives in a General Practice Attachment, British Journal of Social Work, 11, 2, pp.159-170.

21.Lader, M. (1981) The Mind Benders - the Use of Drugs in Psychiatry, MIND Publications, Leeds.
Stimson, G. V. (1977) Do Drug Advertisments Provide Therapeutic Information? Journal of Medical Ethics, 3, pp.7-13.

22.Lieberman, S. (1981) Transgenerational Family Therapy, Croom Helm, London.

23.Carr, P. J., Butterworth, C. A., Hodges, B. E. (1980) Community Psychiatric Nursing, Churchill Livingstone, Edinburgh.

24.Hobbs, M. (1984) Crisis Intervention in Theory and Practice: A Selective Review, British Journal of Medical Psychology, 57, 1, pp.23-34.
Ratna, L. (1978) The Practice of Psychiatric Crisis Intervention, St. Albans: Napsbury Hospital League of Friends.

25.Cosgrove, J. (1983) Shelter in a Storm, Social Work Today, 14, 44, pp.13-15.
Ethrington, S. (1982) Housing and Mental Health, BASW Publications, London.

26.Lipsedge, M., Littlewood, R. (1982) Aliens and Alienists, Tavistock, London.

27.Ernst, S., Goodison, L. (1981) In Our Own Hands:
A Book of Self-Help Therapy, The Women's Press,
London.
Robinson, D., Henry, S. (1977) Self Help and
Health: Mutual Aid for Modern Problems, Robertson,
London.
28.Eichenbaum, L., Orbach, S. (1983) Outside In
Inside Out, Penguin, Harmondsworth.
29.Gostin, L. (1978) A Human Condition, MIND
Publications, Leeds, vol. 1, pp.137-46.
Lewis, P. A. (1982) The Regional Secure Unit Policy
as a Case of the Spread of Psychiatry in the 20th
Century. Paper read at the Conference on the
History of British Psychiatry, London School of
Economics, 15th May.
30.See ref. 29, pp.155-177.
31.British Association of Social Workers (1977)
Mental Health Crisis Services - A New Philosophy,
BASW Publications, London.
32.Higgins, S. (1983) The Psychiatrist's view of
the Mental Health Amendments, 1983, BASW conference
on the Mental Health Amendments, London.
33.See the Observer, November 1981.
34.Fisher, M., Newton, C., Sainsbury, E. (1983)
Mental Health Social Work Observed, National
Institute for Social Work, Social Services Library,
London, no. 45.
35.Goldie, N. (1976) Psychiatric Ideology and the
Medical Mandate. In: Wadsworth, D. (ed) Studies in
Everyday Medical Life, Robertson, London.
36.Freidson, E. (1970) Professional Dominance,
Atherton, New York.
Satyamorti, C. (1980) Occupational Survival: The
Case of Local Authority Social Workers, Blackwell,
Oxford.
37.Finch, J., Groves, D. (1983) (ed) A Labour of
Love, Routledge and Kegan Paul, London.
38.COHSE (1983) The Future of Psychiatric Services,
Draft Report, London.
39.See for example, Islington Community Health
Council working paper (August 1982) The Future
Provision of Services for the Mentally Ill.
40.North East Thames Regional Health Authority
(1982) The Future Provision of Services for the
Mentally Ill: A Consultative Document.
41.Walker, P. (1984) The Move to Community Care in
the North East Thames Region, BASW branch, Waltham
Forest, 9th January.
42.On the American scene see: Hirshowitz, R. G.
Levy, B. (1976) (ed) The Changing Mental Health
Scene, Wiley, New York.

Castel, R., Castel, F., Lovell, A. (1982) The Psychiatric Society, Columbia University Press, New York.
Braunm P., Kochansky, G. (1981) Overview: Deinstitutionalization of Psychiatric Patients: A Critical Review of Outcome Studies, American Journal of Psychiatry, 138, pp.736-749.
For Italy see:
Basaglia, F. (1980) Problems of Law and Psychiatry, International Journal of Psychiatry and Law, 3, 3, pp.17-37.
Mosher, L. (1982) Italy's Revolutionary Mental Health Act: An Assessment, American Journal of Psychiatry, 139, 2, pp.199-223.
Ramon, S. (1983) Psichiatria Democratica: A Case Study of an Italian Community Mental Health Service, International Journal of Health Services, 13, 2, pp.307-324.
43.Leighton, A. et. al. (1963) The Character of Danger, Basic Books, New York.
44.Shadich, W. R., Bootzin R. R. (1982) Nursing Homes and Chronic Mental Patients, Schizophrenia Bulletin, 7, pp.488-498.

Appendix

Table 1: Lunacy and Mental Deficiency. No. 70
Number of Registered Insane Persons*

Year	1**	2**	3**	4**	5**	6**
1920	86,632	857	16,039	5,856	4,380	116,764
1921	93,648	628	16,445	5,480	4,143	120,344
1922	97,360	640	16,606	5,071	4,037	123,714
1923	100,079	781	16,489	4,961	3,969	126,279
1924	103,892	785	16,589	5,107	3,961	130,334
1925	105,399	783	16,446	5,018	3,905	131,551
1926	107,836	781	16,446	4,925	3,895	133,883
1927	110,701	794	16,241	4,880	4,010	136,626
1928	112,726	817	16,021	4,786	3,943	138,293
1929	115,690	831	15,787	4,812	3,960	141,080
1930	117,249	827	15,557	4,826	3,928	142,387

* Reprinted from: Annual Report of the Ministry
  of Health, 1932-33, xxv, pp.82-84, HMSO, London.
  The statistics cover England and Wales.
**Category 1 - County and Borough institutions.
  Category 2 - State Criminal Lunatic asylums.
  Category 3 - Poor Law institutions.
  Category 4 - Other institutions.
  Category 5 - Private institutions.
  Category 6 - Total numbers of Registered Insane
               Persons.

Table 2: Trends in Hospital Population Statistics, 1951-1959, (a) Mental Hospitals*

| Year | Direct Admissions | | | |
| | Total | | First | |
	M	F	M	F
1951	24,412	34,876	16,193	22,496
1952	25,955	36,303	16,604	22,591
1953	28,278	39,144	18,234	24,556
1954	28,751	41,948	18,326	24,851
1955	32,369	46,217	19,400	26,502
1956	34,263	49,731	19,868	27,545
1957	36,830	52,113	20,664	27,602
1958	37,018	54,540	20,151	28,425
1958**	37,822	56,261	20,645	29,414
1959	41,878	63,864	22,414	32,633

| Year | Discharge | | Deaths | |
	M	F	M	F
1951	19,106	27,107	5,474	6,972
1952	20,343	28,908	5,100	6,561
1953	22,347	31,517	4,798	6,689
1954	24,459	34,390	4,991	7,003
1955	27,584	39,427	5,187	7,481
1956	29,462	42,910	5,400	7,471
1957	32,640	46,107	5,328	7,265
1958	33,129	49,439	5,212	7,722
1959	37,656	57,222	5,466	8,372

| Year | Patients on 31st Dec. | |
	M	F
1951	60,761	82,435
1952	61,296	83,287
1953	62,413	84,230
1954	62,954	85,126
1955	62,531	84,336
1956	61,531	83,637
1957	60,815	82,405
1958	60,442	81,724
1959	59,515	80,255

* Reprinted from: Table 1. The Registrar General's Statistical Review of England and Wales, 1959. Supplement on Mental Health, HMSO, London.
**From 1958 onward the figures include informal patients as well as voluntary, temporary and certified patients.

Index